BBC RADIO 4

GARDENERS' QUESTION TIME

All Your Gardening Problems Solved

BBC RADIO 4

GARDENERS' QUESTION TIME

All Your Gardening Problems Solved

JOHN CUSHNIE

BOB FLOWERDEW

PIPPA GREENWOOD

BUNNY GUINNESS

ANNE SWITHINBANK

Published in 2005 by
SILVERDALE BOOKS
An imprint of Bookmart Ltd
Blaby Road, Wigston
Leicestershire, LE18 4SE

Published by arrangement with the BBC and
based on the BBC Radio 4 Programme

First published in Great Britain in hardback in 2000 by Orion

First published in paperback in 2002 by Orion
An imprint of Orion Books Ltd
Orion House, 5 Upper St Martin's Lane, London WC2H 9EA

A CIP catalogue record for this book is available
from the British Library

ISBN 1-84509-189-2

Edited by Camilla Stoddart
Designed by Helen Ewing
Illustrated by Sue Aldridge at
Oxford Designers & Illustrators

Printed and bound in Singapore

CONTENTS

Subjects of Section Openers:

Trees, Shrubs & Herbaceous: Herbaceous peony
House Plants: *Phalaonopsis* moth orchid
Fruit & Vegetables: 'Cox's orange pippin' apples
Garden Design: Yew hedge in Lord Carrington's garden
Pests & Diseases: Whitefly on *Pelargonium* leaf

To Trevor Taylor who planted the seed, nurtured the leaves and made sure our book blossomed. Thank you.

INTRODUCTION

Bob Stead, a BBC producer in Leeds, did not know what he was starting when, in 1947, he devised the format for a programme called *How Does Your Garden Grow? – A Gardeners' Question Time*. It was originally scheduled for a six week run in response to the war time government's Dig for Victory campaign.

More than 50 years later it is still going strong and is now an established British institution. For more than a million people Sunday lunch would not be the same without *GQT*.

Over the years the teams have answered more than 30,000 questions and still the audience find new ones with which to challenge the panel of experts. However the core of questions, the ones which crop up week after week, remain the same. This book answers our most frequently asked questions, topics that we know will solve the vast majority of problems facing today's gardeners.

Listening to some of the early recordings of the programme makes one realise just how little has changed. Slugs and snails were just as big a problem in the '40s as they are today. Organic gardening, a hot topic today, was just as popular when the programme first started if for no other reason than chemicals were simply not available after the War. When I dug out the old 78 rpm discs of early *Gardeners' Question Time* recordings from the BBC archives and listened to Fred Loads, Bill Sowerbutts and Alan Gemmell argue about the best methods of ridding your garden of these pests, I could not help thinking how little has changed. Get Bob Flowerdew, Pippa Greenwood and John Cushnie in a huddle and you'll hear the same arguments today. Of course some of today's solutions are more sophisticated, but there is the same spread of opinions, the personal 'favourite' cures, the same heated, passionate quest for the perfect answer. But the problems are the same.

Assembled each week in a village hall somewhere in the UK are Britain's leading horticultural experts. It never ceases to amaze me what a vast wealth of experience and knowledge they have between them. In days gone by the team had several weeks prior notice of the questions – not any more. Today's team have no knowledge of what's coming. Chairman Eric Robson and I choose the questions and the first the panellists know about them is when the person in the audience asks the question. It's spontaneous; it's unrehearsed; it's unscripted and it's very impressive. They rely on their vast knowledge and substantial experience. It's even more impressive when you realise they are doing this in front of a microphone with a live audience of several hundred in the hall and more than a million listening at home. Of course they don't always agree – gardening is like that and in this book you will spot instances where opinions differ. However, on one thing they are all agreed: gardening is a passion, a consuming passion, which knows no equal and one which they share with Britain's millions of gardeners.

In this one book you'll find the answers to the nation's principal gardening problems. As you read it you'll 'hear' the voices of our well-known team of experts.

Sunday would just not be Sunday without *GQT* and now Britain's best-loved gardening programme can be your companion throughout the week.

TREVOR TAYLOR
Producer
July 2000

TREES, SHRUBS & HERBACEOUS

John Cushnie

I dislike vegetables. I am happy to grow them, but there is no way you will get me to eat greens, onions and many other forms of rabbit food. Bob Flowerdew loves them with a passion – so much so that he prefers them on their own, without chemicals.

I have other gardening love/hate relationships. I hate using pest and disease control chemicals and haven't used any for years, but love knowing that, when necessary, I have the chemical means to control pests such as gooseberry sawfly before they strip a plant. There is a lot of time wasted on weeding when a treatment of glyphosate weedkiller is quicker and the area remains clear of weeds for much longer.

I love mixing plants, incorporating shrubs, bulbs, perennials and even annuals in the same bed, but I am not a fan of mass planting of summer bedding schemes, as seen in parks. A good planting of heathers and dwarf conifers is hard to beat for interest, shape and year-round colour, and while they are out of favour at present, I think that I will start a movement to have them planted in every garden.

I garden on about 0.8 hectares (2 acres) in Co Down, in Northern Ireland, and in a 0.8-hectare (2-acre) walled demonstration garden at Delamont Country Park, just down the road, where courses on all aspects of gardening are held. My garden is not for public consumption and may not be to everyone's taste, but it is the way I like it.

It is great when your hobby is your work and, as a garden designer and contractor, I spend more time in other people's gardens than I do in my own. I write and lecture on gardening, and the best advice I can give you is to enjoy your gardening.

SPECIAL SITUATIONS/SOIL TYPES

Can you recommend a selection of tall shrubs that will grow in a limy soil? The chalk is a maximum of 30cm (12 in) below the soil surface.

Chalky soils tend to be free-draining and dry out in the summer, so digging in lots of compost will help the soil to hold moisture. Alkaline soils are ideal for a range of shrubs, and this selection will all grow to at least 2m (6ft) high.

Lilacs *(Syringa vulgaris)* are all sweetly scented and flower in early summer. Remove the dead flower heads immediately after flowering. The shrub rose *(Rosa rugosa)* variety 'Fru Dagmar Hastrup' has single pink flowers in summer and deep crimson hips in autumn.

Mock orange *(Philadelphus* 'Belle Etoile') produces large 5cm (2in) single white flowers with a maroon blotch in the centre and flowers in summer with a strong fragrance. *Osmanthus delavayi* likes an alkaline soil and has small dark evergreen leaves with clusters of small, fragrant white tubular flowers in spring. And there are many more, including *Berberis darwinii, Olearia macrodonta, Buddleia davidii* and *Forsythia* variety 'Lynwood'.

I have an alkaline soil and I would like to grow rhododendrons and heathers, but I am not sure if this is possible.

There are some heathers, such as *Erica vagans* and *E. terminalis*, that will tolerate a limy soil, but the majority of heathers and heaths do need an acid soil. The best way to get round the problem is to make raised beds by forming walls 20–30cm (8–12in) high, using second-hand railway sleepers or bricks, and filling the bed with imported soil that has been tested and is free of lime. Rhododendrons are shallow-rooting and dislike being planted deeply.

A simpler and cheaper method is to mound the imported soil without using side walls and then plant the heathers, which don't require deep soil, on the shallow lower part of the slope.

The soil in a raised bed is more likely to dry out, so dig in lots of compost at planting time and surface mulch to retain moisture. Analysis for acid or alkaline soil is shown as a pH reading where 7 is neutral, below 7 is acid and readings above that are alkaline or limy. A pH of 5–5.5 is ideal for rhododendrons.

What varieties of trees will grow in an acid soil that is well drained?

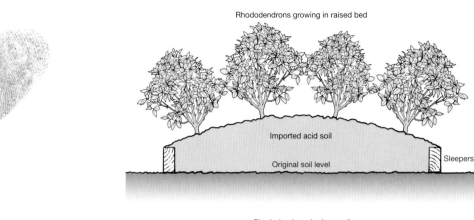

Rhododendrons growing in raised bed

Imported acid soil

Original soil level

Sleepers

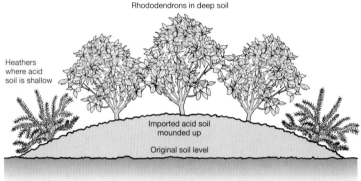

Rhododendrons in deep soil

Heathers where acid soil is shallow

Imported acid soil mounded up

Original soil level

Soil type can be changed by making raised beds of imported soil

There is a range of trees that are tolerant of both high alkalinity and high acidity, including beech *(Fagus)*, birch *(Betula)*, hawthorn *(Crataegus)* and Swedish whitebeam *(Sorbus)*. *Eucryphia* x *nymansensis* will grow to form a 12m (40ft) high columnar evergreen tree with clusters of pure-white flowers in late summer and early autumn. Another white flowering deciduous tree is the Pacific dogwood *(Cornus nuttallii)*, with tiny flowers in spring each surrounded by large white bracts, and good autumn leaf colour.

One of my favourite flowering trees is *Embothrium coccineum*, the Chilean fire bush, with dark evergreen leaves and masses of scarlet flowers in late spring and summer. It will grow to 10m (30ft) high and dislikes biting cold winds. Famous for its autumn leaf colour, the sweet gum *(Liquidambar styraciflua)* makes a big tree growing to 25m (80ft), but the variety 'Moonbeam' is slower-growing, with variegated foliage that turns deep red and yellow in autumn and grows to 10m (30ft). *Magnolia* 'Heaven Scent' is deciduous, with glossy green leaves, and flowers from mid-spring to early summer with goblet-shaped pink flowers that are white on the inside. The flowers and foliage may be damaged by late frosts. It grows to 10m (30ft) high.

Are there any trees that are suitable for a medium-sized garden with a clay soil?

Providing the soil is not waterlogged and the trees are planted in a prepared hole, with the base forked up and compost added to the soil, the following varieties will all do well.

Cotoneasterx 'Cornubia' makes a large shrub or small tree that is evergreen in sheltered gardens and is laden with bright red fruit in autumn. The birds love the fruit and will strip a tree in a very short time. It quickly grows to 5m (16ft) high. The Himalayan birch (*Betula utilis* var. *jacquemontii*) is deciduous with pure-white bark and will grow well in full sun. All the crab apple varieties (*Malus*) like a heavy soil, as do laburnum and the hollies. If you only have space for one holly, try *Ilex* 'J. C. van Tol', which has male and female flowers fruiting without a partner. *Magnolia* x *soulangiana* forms a spreading low tree with goblet-shaped white or purple-tinged fragrant flowers in spring followed by large dark-green leaves.

Choose the planting site for trees carefully, allowing plenty of space for them to spread to their full size without growing into the next tree and spoiling the shape of both. Bear in mind, tall trees will cast shade, and shade-hating plants will refuse to grow under the canopy of foliage.

What low-growing plants will succeed in a 2m (6ft) wide border with cold, wet soil that never sees the sun? There is a high fence at the back of the bed.

I have a bed in exactly the same position, with the addition of a lot of rain, and yet it looks good for most of the year. It is a site that would spell death to a lot of plants, but there are enough tough, interesting plants to allow you to choose. If you can dig in coarse grit, it will open up the soil and help the drainage. And remember that slugs and snails like these conditions and will be waiting to eat anything that is planted, so lay beer traps (see pp. 261-3).

Plant a mixture of shrubs and perennials, using the perennials to fill the gaps until the shrubs spread out and take over. Low-growing perennials, such as hostas, are ideal for this situation and are available in a choice of leaf and flower colour. The foam flower *(Tiarella cordifolia)* is a spreading perennial with pale-green leaves and spikes of creamy white flowers all summer, growing to 30cm (12in). Jerusalem sage *(Pulmonaria saccharata)* is a beautiful evergreen perennial with white-spotted foliage. From late winter to late spring it produces red, pink or white flowers, even in the worst of weather. It will grow to about 30cm (12in) high, with a spread of 60cm (24in).

I'm almost afraid to mention another perennial, the variegated ground elder (*Aegopodium podagraria* 'Variegatum'), with its deep-green leaves

splashed creamy white and its white flowers in early summer. It will spread, but not as badly as the weed with the plain green leaf. Perhaps it is best grown in a bucket plunged into the border.

You have asked for low-growing plants, but I would suggest firethorn *(Pyracantha)* to train on the fence. *Pyracantha* are evergreen, with masses of hawthorn-like yellow, orange or red fruit. There is also a low-growing variety, *P.* 'Santa Cruz', with small red berries, to a height of 90cm (36in).

Commonly called japonica or flowering quince, *Chaenomeles japonica* is ideal for this situation, with glossy green deciduous leaves, thorns and red or orange flowers in spring, followed by hard yellow fruit. There are many other good quince varieties, but most of them will grow to 2m (6ft) high. *Viburnum davidii* is evergreen, with shiny dark-green, deeply veined leaves and small white flowers in late spring, followed by interesting metallic-blue fruit that last throughout the winter. Male and female plants are needed for fertilization to guarantee fruit.

If there is space for one more shrub, then plant the Christmas box *(Sarcococca humilis)* with its fantastic winter perfume from the tiny pink-white flowers. It is evergreen and the flowers are followed by shiny blue-black berries. It grows to 60cm (24in) high, but do try to open the soil around the roots with grit and compost.

I have an area of dry stony soil that is overlying broken rock in full sun and I would like to grow plants for summer colour. Will plants succeed here?

The short answer is yes. For maximum colour I would concentrate on annuals and perennials, with an occasional dwarf shrub such as *Convolvulus cneorum*, with its silky silver-green leaves and pink buds opening to funnel-shaped white flowers with a yellow centre in late spring and summer and growing to 60cm (24in) high.

The Californian poppy *(Eschscholtzia californica)* is an annual and can be sown directly where it is to grow. Sow the seed thinly in late spring and it will flower the same summer, with single orange flowers and a few that are white, yellow or red. Another annual that will love these conditions is the Livingstone daisy *(Dorotheanthus bellidiformis)* and patches of direct-sown seed will provide a carpet of fleshy leaves and bright daisy flowers.

African blue lily *(Agapanthus* variety 'Cherry Holley') is a perennial and a 'must' for this situation, with its strap-like leaves and large heads of dark-blue trumpet-shaped flowers in summer and again in early autumn. It is quite hardy, growing to 75cm (30in) high. Red valerian *(Centranthus ruber)* is perennial and revels in a poor soil, self-seeding readily. The white, pink or deep-red flowers appear from spring until late summer. Dead-heading will help to keep it flowering and tidy the plant up.

I want to have a Mediterranean area in the garden. How do I go about making it, and what should I plant in it?

When I think of Mediterranean gardens I think of a patch of shade, fragrant smells, earthenware containers, grey foliage and hot dry air. You can't do much about the air, but the rest is possible. The site chosen should be in full sun and sheltered from biting cold winds. Avoid low-lying areas that are subject to frost or soil in need of drainage. Seaside gardens are ideal as they are usually frost-free with light, free-draining soil.

If your soil is light and stony you are lucky, but if not dig the topsoil 30cm (12in) deep, then fork over the subsoil to allow the water to drain quickly. If the area is small, lay 10cm (4in) of clean broken stone in the base. Mix grit and gravel into the topsoil as it is being replaced, to form an open, free-draining soil that will warm up quickly. A layer of landscape fabric laid on the soil surface and covered with a 5cm (2in) layer of clean gravel will reduce the need to weed. The lighter the colour of gravel, the more light it will reflect back onto the plant foliage. The gravel will also keep the surface of the soil dry around the neck of the plants and prevent them from rotting.

A shady area is essential to move into when it gets too hot and can be provided by a suitable small tree on the sunny side of the garden or by a pergola over part of the Mediterranean area, draped with vines, honeysuckle or wisteria. A small water feature close by, with the sight and sound of running water, will complete the stage setting.

High temperatures help to release the aromatic oils from the foliage of lavender, artemisia and cotton lavender *(Santolina chamaecyparissus)*, all of which are silver-leafed. Spanish dagger *(Yucca gloriosa)* – with its stiff, sharply pointed, arching leaves and enormous flower spikes of bell-shaped creamy white flowers in autumn, which grow to 2.5m (8ft) – has a hot look. Thyme can be allowed to spread at will over the gravel, releasing its aroma as it is walked on. The sun rose (*Cistus* x *corbariensis*), with its small red buds opening to white flowers in late spring and summer and growing to 90cm (36in), loves dry gravelly soil, sending its roots far and wide in search of water.

If there is a wall in the Mediterranean area facing the sun, give it a splash

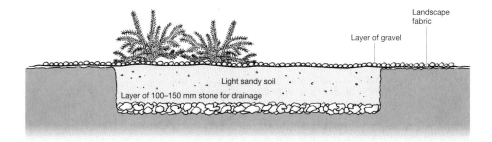

Mediterranean bed made to order

of terracotta-coloured paint and grow some fruit against it, such as a fig (variety 'Brown Turkey'), a Peregrine peach or an outdoor vine. Containers of all shapes and sizes are great and allow you to have temporary plantings of tender plants outside for the summer, moving them to a frost-free conservatory or glasshouse in winter. Plants such as aloes, agaves and echeverias are stunning in pots. Don't forget the *vino*.

The whole of my garden is wet in winter and stays damp in summer. Are there any herbaceous plants that will enjoy these conditions?

This garden sounds very like a bog garden and, as such, it is easier to deal with than a soil that is wet in winter, becoming hard, cracked and dry in summer. There are interesting and colourful herbaceous plants that will enjoy the constant moisture, spreading and multiplying each year.

Gunnera manicata is an enormous perennial with dark-green deciduous leaves up to 2m (6ft) long and prickly stalks. It is not fully hardy and in cold areas may be protected by breaking the leaves over the crown of the plant in the autumn. Astilbes all love damp soil conditions, and put out flowering plumes in white, pink, mauve, red and crimson in summer. *Euphorbia palustris* has green and yellow flowers in spring and spreads rapidly. The milky sap is an irritant on the skin, so always wash your hands after handling it.

Plantain lily *(Hosta)* is a lovely plant for soils that don't dry out and, while most of the varieties are grown for their foliage – which is available in shades of green, blue and variegated – the lavender-blue or white flowers on long stems above the leaves make a good show in summer. Candelabra primulas love moist conditions, and the early summer flowers are carried in a series of whorls on long stems above the foliage, in yellow, orange, pink, red, crimson and mauve. Then there is my favourite, the giant cowslip *(Primula florindae)*, with 90cm (36in) high stems, each carrying up to 30 pendant tubular, sulphur-yellow fragrant flowers in summer.

The willow gentian *(Gentiana asclepiadea)* grows to 75cm (30in), and in late summer to early autumn the arching stems carry clusters of trumpet-shaped white or blue flowers. For a tall, elegant perennial, try *Ligularia przewalskii*, with its 2m (6ft) high stems with spires of yellow flowers in mid- to late summer and large, deeply cut leaves. Others that will thrive in the constant damp are the monkey musk *(Mimulus luteus)* with yellow flowers, *Filipendula purpurea* with its bold foliage and rosy red flowers in summer, and *Rodgersia podophylla* with its creamy white summer flowers and large palmate leaves that colour beautifully in autumn.

Always be careful when you are weeding, as many of these plants will seed all around the parents, multiplying rapidly and, in the case of primulas, producing many more colours.

WALLS

Walls are great for growing plants against, training plants up and allowing plants to drape over. When properly trained on a wall, plants can show off to best advantage their flowers, fruits and berries, and the wall provides that extra space for growing, when the garden is bursting with plants.

Some walls are unsightly and need plants to hide them, so evergreens will be more useful than those that lose their leaves in autumn. A beautiful old stone wall may benefit from the odd plant to soften it, in which case the ideal plant will be compact and not likely to run riot, covering the whole wall. The position of the wall is crucial to the well-being of the plants. In the northern hemisphere south-facing walls will be in full sun when it is at its hottest, while a north wall will be cold with poor light conditions. East-facing walls get the morning sun, which is lovely except after a frost, when the flowers of plants such as camellia thaw too quickly and scorch. A wall that faces west is my favourite, well sheltered from cold easterly winds and from the sun when it is at its hottest. It will be bathed in evening sun, retaining its heat into the night.

When planting at the base of any wall extra care with the soil preparation is needed. Frequently all the debris of building work, such as bits of bricks, mortar and offcuts of wood, are dumped there and lightly covered with topsoil. If a path or hard surface comes right up to the base of the wall, then remove a large enough area to allow you to dig a hole at least 60 x 60cm (24 x 24in) and as deep as you can, but not less than 45cm (18in).

The strip of soil at the base of the wall will always be drier than the rest of the garden, sheltered from rainfall by the wall and with any moisture being absorbed by the porous building materials, so add lots of moisture-retaining compost and rotted farmyard manure to the planting hole: 60g (2 oz) or a handful of balanced fertilizer or bonemeal, mixed through the soil as it is being worked in around the plant roots, will get it off to a good start. Water the area well after planting.

I have a walled-in garden. Can you suggest plants suitable for growing on the four walls, facing north, south, east and west?

You have mentioned north first, so I will start with that. It is a colder wall and is good for all the frost-tender early flowering plants. There are no extremes of temperature, and after a frost the plants are slow to thaw out and the buds, flowers and new growths of plants such as pieris and camellia are not scorched. The climbing hydrangea *(Hydrangea petiolaris)* is a rampant deciduous self-clinging shrub. The dark-green leaves turn yellow in autumn, while in summer large heads of white sterile and fertile flowers cover the plant and, if it likes the site, it will grow to 15m (50ft) high. The silk-tassel bush *(Garrya elliptica)* is evergreen and free-standing, not needing any support. Long grey-green male catkins are produced in winter and early spring. The variety 'James Roof' is male, with silvery-grey 20cm (8in) long catkins.

Camellia such as 'Inspiration', *C. japonica* and the varieties of winter-flowering *C. sasanqua* will love a north wall, provided the soil is acid and is not allowed to dry out, especially in autumn, when it can cause flower buds to drop. Another good climber is the chocolate vine *(Akebia quinata),* which will hold its leaves in winter in mild climates, taking on a purple tinge. The brownish-purple male and female flowers are vanilla-scented and appear in early spring, followed by 10cm (4in) long, sausage-shaped purple fruit.

Fremontodendron 'California Glory'

Warm south-facing walls encourage early growth and flower and allow the plant a long growing season, with the shoots well hardened and ripe by autumn. The Californian lilac *(Ceanothus)* is available as a deciduous or evergreen shrub and most varieties flower in summer. *C. arboreus* 'Trewithen Blue' is evergreen and flowers in late winter and spring, with masses of fragrant, mid-blue flowers. *Fremontodendron* 'California Glory' is a fast-growing evergreen shrub with 5cm (2in) buttercup-yellow flowers from spring to autumn. Prune it regularly to prevent it growing away from the wall, and avoid getting the powder from the leaves in your eyes. It loves a dry soil and will not survive in wet ground. Fruit trees on dwarf root-stocks trained against a south wall will produce well-ripened fruit, with less risk of the flowers being damaged by frost. Apples, pears, plums, cherries, peaches and figs will all carry good crops.

East-facing walls are tricky in spring when morning frost, followed by early sun, can kill the flowers of lots of hardy plants such as camellia, rhododendron and the fruit recommended for a south wall. Virginia creeper *(Parthenocissus quinquefolia)* will self-cling and scramble all over a wall, climbing to 20m (65ft), its leaves colouring beautifully in autumn. Evergreen pyracantha and choisya, especially *C. ternata*, will hide unsightly walls and can be kept in check by regular pruning.

West-facing walls may be draped with clematis of all sorts, although some of the species, such as *C. montana, C. alpina* and *C. tangutica*, can be very vigorous. The climbing honeysuckles will provide summer colour and fragrance, and *Wisteria floribunda* and *W. sinensis*, with their long racemes of purple or white early summer flowers, are a memorable sight covering a wall. The Chilean potato tree *(Solanum crispum* 'Glasnevin') is covered in clusters of deep purple-blue flowers in summer and autumn and is a vigorous climber, which needs to be pruned hard to keep it under control.

Can you recommend shrubs that will grow up a wall without any support and that won't be too aggressive?

Shrubs to fit your bill are among the best plants for walls, requiring no training or tying-in to supports, and generally fending for themselves. Those with fragrance may be planted close to opening windows and enjoyed from inside the house.

Wintersweet *(Chimonanthus praecox)* is an upright deciduous shrub, flowering in winter with pendant, fragrant yellow flowers stained purple on the inside. The variety 'Grandiflorus' has large, 5cm (2in) deeper yellow flowers. Grow it on a south-facing wall. Golden bell *(Forsythia suspensa)* forms an arching shrub, with clear yellow flowers in early spring on the bare branches, and can be pruned immediately after flowering.

Chaenomeles x *superba* 'Etna' is deciduous, flowering in spring and early summer with dark scarlet flowers and growing to 2.5m (8ft) against a north wall. *Magnolia liliiflora* is deciduous, flowering in late spring and early summer with purple-pink goblet-shaped flowers, and will do best on a south- or west-facing wall. The bottle brush *(Callistemon citrinus)* also needs a south- or west-facing wall, producing its crimson 'brushes' in early summer. The lemon bottle brush *(C. pallidus)* has creamy yellow flowers. *Euonymus fortunei* 'Emerald 'n' Gold' is evergreen, with bright-green foliage with yellow margins and, if planted at the base of a wall, will grow up to 1.5m (5ft) without support. It will succeed on any wall.

Can I have suggestions for yellow-flowering plants for a red-brick wall?

What a sensible question! Nothing looks less interesting growing on a red-brick wall than some of the Japanese quinces or the red-flowering lobster claw *(Clianthus puniceus)*. A good strong yellow flower will contrast nicely with the brick, and my first choice would be a rose. There are plenty to pick from, but I love *Rosa* 'Golden Showers', which is a climber with glossy dark-green foliage and a mass of double, bright-yellow flowers that are really fragrant; it repeat-flowers all summer and autumn. Beside it plant a pineapple broom *(Cytisus battandieri),* with its silvery grey leaves and pineapple-scented racemes of golden-yellow flowers in mid- to late summer – allow the rose to scramble through the broom.

One more would be the Mount Etna broom *(Genista aetnensis),* which is again deciduous, with weeping branches laden with fragrant golden-yellow flowers in mid- to late summer. To cover the lower stems of the other plants grow a winter jasmine *(Jasminum nudiflorum),* with its bright-yellow scented flowers in the dead of winter. All these and you will be saying, 'What red-brick wall?'

I have a three-year-old Virginia creeper that is a heap at the bottom of the wall. How can I train it to climb?

You haven't named the variety of creeper and there are a few, such as *Parthenocissus inserta,* which climb by using tendrils and would find it difficult to grip a wall. A more likely cause, however, is that your plant *should* adhere to walls using its sticky pads, but when you bought the plant the lower pads had dried out and couldn't hold on. It is a good idea to hold the young growths temporarily to the wall with tape, Blu-Tack or lead-headed nails. Once they secure themselves, they will carry on without help. I would advise you to cut your plant back by two-thirds in the spring to encourage new growths, and to attach them to the wall when they are still young. If you talk to your plants, tell this one to get a grip!

Are there any good evergreen climbers suitable for a trellis garden?

Yes, there are. *Clematis armandii* has large, leathery, dark glossy green leaves and flowers in early spring. The flowers are fragrant and white, and the variety 'Apple Blossom' has flowers tinged with pink. *Clematis cirrhosa balaerica* is also evergreen, with finely divided leaves that are bronze-tinged in winter and pale yellow flowers speckled purple on the inside.

There is a vigorous evergreen honeysuckle *(Lonicera henryi),* with dark-green leaves and purple-red flowers with a yellow throat in early summer, followed by purple berries. There are lots of ivy (*Hedera helix* and *H. hibernica*) varieties, but they are more at home on a wall. *Rubus henryi* is a vigorous evergreen with pink flowers in summer, but is mainly grown for its glossy dark-green, three-lobed leaves, which are white-felted on the underneath.

SEASIDE

Coastal gardens get a name for being difficult, and the combination of salt-laden and strong winds does restrict the number of plants that can be grown. Having said that, there are advantages to gardening at the seaside – not least of which is the freedom from heavy frosts.

Please, please recommend trees that will survive close to the sea.

I can suggest some that will not only survive, but thrive and you will be proud of them.

Top of the list is the strawberry tree *(Arbutus unedo)*, which is hardy, although young plants can suffer from a hard frost. Evergreen, with glossy leaves and shredding red-brown bark, its small white flowers appear in the autumn and the warty, red 'strawberry' fruit appear the following autumn. It will grow to 8m (25ft) high. Hawthorn *(Crataegus laevigata)* will tolerate wind and salt, and in severe exposure will be bent at the same angle as the prevailing wind. The white or pink flowers are produced in spring, followed by red fruit that provide food for birds in winter.

Whitebeam *(Sorbus aria)*, with its dark-green deciduous leaves that are white on the underside, is a handsome tree and the white flowers are followed by clusters of deep-red berries. Keep the tree well staked, as the root can be less than adequate for storm conditions. *Griselinia littoralis* may be damaged by frost, but will tolerate all that a coastal garden can throw at it. It is evergreen, with apple-green leathery leaves and inconspicuous yellow flowers in spring. Excellent as a hedge, it will make a good-sized tree in a mild area.

We have a seaside garden and need a windbreak now that a wall has been removed. Please help by suggesting suitable types of plant.

Where space allows, you should plant at least three rows of plants. The idea is to filter the wind, rather than try to block it, as the wall would have done. The blast would have come over the top of the wall and caused turbulence on the garden side, for a distance of two and a half times the height of the wall. The outside row of plants closest to the sea can be sycamore *(Acer pseudoplatanus)* and rowan trees *(Sorbus aucuparia),* mixed with a few holly *(Ilex aquifolium)* and Austrian pine *(Pinus n. nigra).* Don't be tempted to plant big trees, as small 60cm (24in) high bushy plants will grow away more quickly. The inside two rows may be a mixture of deciduous and evergreen shrubs, to provide shelter and at the same time add colour and interest to the windbreak. Plant some or all of these in cultivated soil and prevent weeds from growing around the plants.

Elaeagnus pungens 'Maculata' is evergreen with attractive variegated foliage, while *Escallonia* 'Pride of Donard' is evergreen with large dark-green leaves and bright-red flowers in summer. All the hebes are tolerant of seaside planting, so plant a mixture and leave space for some tamarisk *(Tamarix tetrandra),* which are deciduous and pink-flowering in late spring. *T. ramosissima* – again pink – flowers in late summer.

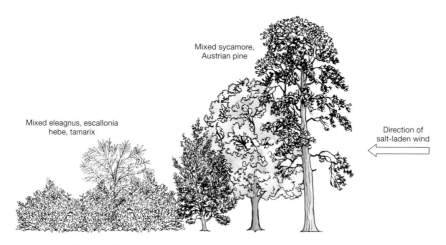

Mixed sycamore,
Austrian pine

Mixed eleagnus, escallonia
hebe, tamarix

Direction of
salt-laden wind

Form a wind break by planting trees and shrubs tolerant of the conditions

What can I plant as a windbreak 200m (600ft) up a hill facing the sea and the north?

I would love to recommend that you move house, but the view probably offsets the problem of gardening in these conditions. You will have to establish a windbreak gradually, and the first line of defence needs to be very tough. I am thinking of gorse, (furze of whin) *(Ulex europaeus),* which is as tough as they come, tolerating all you describe and poor soil as well. It also makes a good deterrent hedge for animals and is in flower all year round. Blackthorn *(Prunus spinosa)* grows in western Siberia, so it should be happy with you, with its white flowers in early spring followed in autumn by black 'sloe' berries. Behind that, plant the sea buckthorn *(Hippophae rhamnoides),* with its grey-green foliage and orange fruit in autumn (both male and female plants are needed for fruit).

HEDGES

Shrubs that are used for formal hedging are usually clipped or pruned at least once a year, although an informal type of boundary can be achieved by allowing the hedge to develop naturally, with the minimum of cutting. Hedges serve a garden well, filtering and slowing down the strongest of winds and providing shelter, screening and privacy. They can be used to divide up the garden and, in the case of low dividers, are aesthetic as well as practical.

What other plants, similar to box, will form a low hedge for edging a vegetable garden?

I'm glad that it is not going to be box, as a hedge of box is really a hotel for snails. They love to hide in it, and neither you nor the birds can get at them.

Cotton lavender *(Santolina chamaecyparissus)*, with its aromatic grey-green leaves and small bright-yellow flowers in summer, enjoys a sunny site and makes a low hedge 60cm (24in) high. Some of the rounded hebes make excellent low hedges, although they tend to spread to 60cm (24in) and need to be kept clipped. *Hebe* 'Red Edge' has small grey-green leaves, the new foliage margined with red, and lilac-blue flowers in summer. It grows to a height of 45cm (18in) and spread of 60cm (24in). *H. cupressoides* 'Boughton Dome' forms a dome-shaped hedge, with conifer-like pale-green leaves. I have never seen it in flower. It reaches a height of 45cm (18in).

Lavender *(Lavandula angustifolia)* variety 'Munstead' is compact and dwarf, with aromatic grey-green foliage and deep-purple flowers in summer. It grows to 45cm (18in) high. *L. a.* 'Nana Alba' has white flowers and is dwarf, growing to 30cm (12in) high. Clip the plants regularly to keep them bushy. Lavender is a fairly short-lived hedge, good for about seven years. Its aromatic foliage will disguise the smell of the carrots, keeping them free of carrot fly.

What can I plant to form a tall evergreen flowering hedge?

The plant I would recommend over all others is *Berberis* x *stenophylla*. It will grow to 3m (10ft) high, with dark evergreen, spine-tipped narrow leaves and clusters of deep-yellow flowers all along the arched branches in late spring, followed by blue-black fruit in autumn. If unclipped, it will spread out as well as up. Escallonia is nearly as good, and I would plant the variety *E.* 'Iveyi', growing to 3m (10ft) high, with glossy dark-green leaves and masses of fragrant, pure-white flowers in late summer. Laurustinus

(Viburnum tinus) will also grow to 3m (10ft), with dark-green leaves and white flowers in late spring. The variety *V. t.* 'Eve Price' has pink flower buds opening to white.

What will form a really thorny hedge, thick at the base, that will keep dogs out of my garden?

Stray animals can be a real nuisance, but I must warn you that the best way to keep any hedge thick at the base, with no gaps, is to clip it regularly and not to allow any weeds to grow up and choke the lower growth.

Japanese bitter orange *(Poncirus trifoliata)* is a deciduous shrub with green shoots and large sharp spines. The dark-green leaves turn yellow in the autumn and the white, fragrant flowers appear in early summer. The small green-orange fruit are not edible. Plant it 90cm (36in) apart for a quick, thick hedge. All the berberis are spiny, but the variety that I would recommend is *Berberis gagnepainii lanceifolia,* with its dark evergreen, very spiny leaves and bright-yellow flowers in late spring. It forms a dense hedge 1.5m (5ft) high.

A good rose is the Ramanas rose *(Rosa rugosa),* with its stiff upright, prickly stems, dark-green deciduous leaves and large single, fragrant pink or carmine-red flowers in summer and autumn, followed by fat orange-red hips. Prune half the shoots each year at ground level to encourage strong, dense shoots from the base. Blackthorn *(Prunus spinosa)* also makes a dense deciduous hedge, with white flowers in spring. However, it needs to be cut every year to keep it thick at the base.

SMALL PLANTS

Two sayings that are not normally used in reference to plants are 'small is beautiful' and 'size matters' – and yet this is what gardeners with small gardens need to believe. A small, mature tree or shrub is a thing of beauty, complete in every way and fitting the scale of its surroundings, where a large plant would be awkward and look out of place.

Is there a small tree that I can plant beside the patio to provide some shade in the afternoon?

The tree does not need to be evergreen, so I am recommending two deciduous trees that can be purchased and planted as sizeable plants, providing shade in the first summer.

Sorbus vilmorinii has arching branches and enjoys a rich, well-drained soil in full sun, with a height and spread of 5m (16ft). The fern-like, dark-green leaves are made up of leaflets that turn purple-red in autumn. The white flowers appear in spring, followed by dark-red berries that turn pink and finally white.

The snowy mespilus (*Amelanchier* x *grandiflora* 'Ballerina') is a great tree and good value, with a mass of white flowers in spring followed by new bronze-green foliage, turning green and then taking on autumn tints of red, gold and purple. The purple fruit are small, but sweet and juicy if cooked. It will form a bushy tree 6m (20ft) high.

Are there any really small conifers suitable for a rockery?

Yes, there are, but when choosing remember that there is a difference between a slow-growing conifer and a dwarf conifer. You want to buy a dwarf conifer, which will never get large; a slow-growing species will be

Juniperus communis 'Compressa'

fine for a few years, but will eventually become too big and outgrow its allotted space.

Thuja orientalis 'Aurea Nana' forms an oval-shaped conifer with gold-green foliage that turns bronze in winter and sits on flat, upright stems. It likes a deep, well-drained soil and grows to 60cm (24in) high. The Japanese cedar (*Cryptomeria japonica* 'Vilmoriniana') grows as a tight ball, with pale-green foliage in summer becoming bronze-purple in winter. It may be clipped if necessary, and grows to a height of 60cm (24in).

For me, the best of all the dwarf conifers is the dwarf common juniper (*Juniperus communis* 'Compressa'), which is spindle-shaped and grows at a rate of 2cm (¾in) per annum. The blue-green foliage is aromatic and the maximum height in a reasonable time is 90cm (36in), with a spread of 45cm (18in), making it ideal for troughs, containers or the rockery.

What small trees can we give to each other to celebrate 25 years of marriage?

Congratulations! Whatever you buy, make sure the trees are container-grown with good root balls – that way they will continue to grow and flourish for the next 25 years.

Full-moon maple (*Acer japonicum* 'Aconitifolium') is a deciduous bushy tree with green leaves that are deeply lobed and turn a brilliant deep red in autumn. The flowers are deep purple in spring and abundant every year. It will do best in partial shade and will grow to 5m (16ft) high.

Silver birch (*Betula pendula*) is ideal for a silver wedding anniversary and, while most varieties of birch grow to be large trees, the variety 'Youngii' is a weeping form that will grow to 8m (25ft). It is dome-shaped and deciduous, with yellow male catkins before the leaves, which turn buttercup-yellow in the autumn.

We would like to grow a chestnut tree. Do they all grow to an enormous size, or is there one suitable for a small garden with neighbours on either side?

You are in luck – there are two that I can recommend. The bottlebrush buckeye (*Aesculus parviflora*) is a shrub with typical green chestnut leaves, bronze when they first open, and panicles of white flowers with long stamens followed by the conkers, although the shell is smooth. It grows to 3m (10ft).

Red buckeye (*Aesculus pavia*) makes a small tree with green chestnut leaves and red stalks. The panicles of red flowers appear in early summer, followed by smooth-skinned fruit. It grows to 5m (16ft) high.

Red buckeye (*Aesculus pavia*)

Can you recommend a few permanent plants for window boxes? I am not fit enough to change them every few months.

Dwarf plants will certainly grow in these conditions, but they will soon run out of food if you plant them in a general potting compost, which will become exhausted and need to be replaced. Ask at the garden centre for a 14-month potting compost, which contains a slow-release fertilizer, and plant them in that.

Heathers will do well, but choose dwarf varieties such as *Erica cinerea* 'Eden Valley', which flowers all summer and into early autumn with deep pink and white flowers, growing to 20cm (8in) high. *E. darleyensis* 'White Glow' is compact, flowering with masses of white flowers in late winter and early spring, at 25cm (10in).

There are many ideal gaultheria, and wintergreen *(Gaultheria procumbens)* is a dwarf, creeping evergreen shrub, with dark-green leaves smelling of wintergreen and white or pink flowers in summer, followed by aromatic deep-red fruit that last all winter. This plant will tolerate shade and will trail down the side of the box, growing to 15cm (6in).

Euonymus fortunei 'Kewensis' forms a mat of dark-green leaves with pale-green veins, growing up to 10cm (4in) high. There are lots of varieties of thyme, such as *Thymus* 'Doone Valley', with green leaves spotted with yellow, red flower buds opening pink all summer and growing to 10cm (4in) high. And don't forget the dwarf bulbs that will reappear each year, such as crocus, snowdrops, scillas and the grape hyacinth *(Muscari)*.

Crocus

SHADE

There is a limited selection of plants that will grow in deep shade, but many plants prefer a site in light or dappled shade where they are out of the glare of the sun and their roots remain cool.

What shrubs will grow under an evergreen tree, where the tree roots are close to the surface?

This is an inhospitable site, not only heavily shaded but with bone-dry soil exhausted of nutrients by the tree roots. When planting, prepare the planting hole by making it larger than the root ball of the plant and incorporate some old farmyard manure and bonemeal. Water the hole before planting and again after the planting is complete.

Larger shrubs that will succeed include spotted laurel (*Aucuba japonica* 'Crotonifolia'), with variegated evergreen foliage and red fruit, growing up to 3m (10ft) high; and *Camellia japonica* and its varieties, with glossy dark-green leaves, flowering in spring and early summer in a selection of colours and growing to 4m (13ft) high.

Lower shrubs, such as any of the skimmia, sarcococca and ruscus, will do well. Carpeting plants, such as perwinkle (*Vinca major* and *V. minor*), with their blue flowers in late spring and summer, and *Pachysandra terminalis*, evergreen with small white flowers, will spread quickly, finding spaces between the tree roots.

What herbaceous plants will succeed in a border shaded for most of the day by a high hedge?

The border must be on the cold side of the hedge, so growth will be late in the season and it will take longer for the soil to warm up. Keep the back row of plants at least 60cm (24in) from the hedge, to allow you access for clipping, and well away from the hedge roots.

Astilbe 'Fanal' has dark-green foliage, panicles of crimson flowers in early summer and grows to 60cm (24in). The Lenten rose *(Helleborus orientalis)* has evergreen leaves and the nodding, saucer-shaped flowers are available in white, cream and ageing to pink in winter and spring.

Hostas will all do well, including variegated varieties, such as *H.* 'Gold Standard'. The toad lily *(Tricyrtis formosana)* has arching stems of deeply veined leaves and star-shaped white, pink or purple-pink flowers, spotted red-purple on the inside in early autumn. It grows to 90cm (36in) high. *Geranium macrorrhizum* 'Ingwersen' has light-green aromatic foliage that turns yellow in autumn and soft pink flowers in early summer, growing to 60cm (24in).

A good plant for the back of the border is the foxglove *(Digitalis purpurea)*, which is really a biennial but will fit in well and, if not dead-headed, will self-seed readily and grow to 1.5m (5ft) high.

GENERAL PROBLEMS

One of the nice things about gardening queries is the way some of the problems that crop up are common to a lot of gardeners and have a straight-forward answer.

I have a cherry tree, the roots of which are coming up through the lawn. Can I remove them?

Cherries have a habit of behaving badly, with surface roots that, as they thicken, lie on the lawn rather than underground, making grass-cutting difficult. It is usually only a serious problem with mature trees and the loss of a few roots will not cause a setback to the plant. Cut the root as close to the tree trunk as possible, making a clean cut and removing as much of the root as you can, without damaging the grass. Infill the shallow trench with old potting compost or fine soil and sow some grass seed. The problem won't go away and more roots will come to the surface, but they won't be a nuisance for another few years.

(PG) The problem with roots in lawns is that if the woody part becomes quite large, it can do fairly serious damage to lawnmower blades, so you may wish to consider raising the soil level very slightly. Do be aware that if you do this, it is only safe to raise the soil by no more than about 5cm (2in). If you raise it more than this, the tree itself is likely to be put under a lot of stress. One way is to cover the area with a thin quantity of soil and then place landscape fabric on top of this, before you mulch it with your favourite mulching material, which will then hide the landscape fabric. If you do decide to use a chemical to treat the shoots, do make sure that you sever them from the tree first, or even relatively small quantities of the weedkiller could have quite damaging effects on the main tree.

I have a variegated poplar, but over the past two years the leaves have all become green. What is wrong with it?

Populus candicans 'Aurora' has leaves splashed with white, cream and pink on a pale-green background, and while it is not my favourite plant, it is a common tree in gardens. As a deciduous tree, it will grow to 15m (50ft) and this is part of the problem. The attractive foliage is carried on the young shoots, with the older stems producing green leaves, so it is necessary to prune it every year to encourage new growth. I suspect that your plant hasn't been pruned or is too large to prune. Poplars are also prone to canker, which can eventually kill the tree.

How can I stop cats using my cherry tree as a scratching pole?

This is a common problem, where the cat reaches up and scratches the tree trunk with its claws. It will always go to the same tree and eventually all the bark within its reach becomes cracked and rough. It can make smooth-barked trees look unsightly, and in some cases canker spores enter the wounds and will cause even large trees to die.

If the cats are visitors, they may be discouraged by coating the tree trunk in Vaseline or one of the grease bands normally used to stop caterpillars climbing a tree. Alternatively, or if the cats are your own, the tree trunk may be wrapped in rabbit wire to protect it, but loosen the wire as the tree trunk swells or it will cut into the bark. Cherry trees are prone to canker and this type of wounding is more serious for them than for less prone trees, such as birch or lime.

When is the best time to transplant conifers?

There are two ideal periods for moving evergreen plants. Mid-spring, when the soil is warming up and is still moist, with more rain to come, is a good time. Having said that, if it is cold and windy, or if it has been a dry spring, wait until the weather improves. At the other end of the year, in early autumn, the soil is still warm and rain can be expected at any time.

Move the plant in such a way that it doesn't know it has been moved, retaining as many roots as possible with the ball of soil intact around them. Within reason, dig a ball of roots of the same spread as the head of the conifer, and have a well-watered planting hole (larger than the ball of roots) prepared for the transplant. Dig in some bonemeal, firming the roots in the soil and making sure there are no air pockets. Form a depression on the surface around the plant to prevent water running off, and mulch with bark. Water the soil in around the roots and, if there is a cold, drying wind, form a tent of horticultural fleece to cover the plant and stop it perspiring, allowing it to settle in and the roots to take up water. Stake a larger plant to keep it steady in its new position.

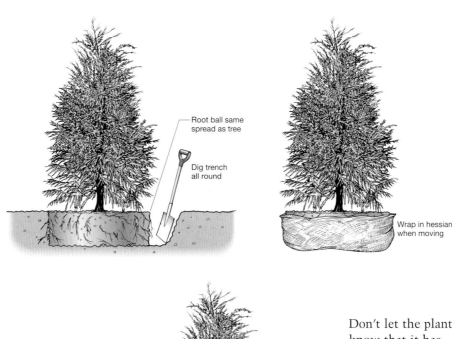

Root ball same
spread as tree

Dig trench
all round

Wrap in hessian
when moving

Don't let the plant
know that it has
been moved!

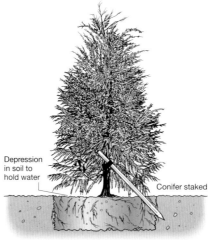

Depression
in soil to
hold water

Conifer staked

Will ivy kill a tree?

It is generally accepted that a tree in good condition, growing strongly and
with a good root system, has nothing to fear from ivy. In fact, evergreen ivy
offers winter protection for birds and its berries are a good source of food for
them. However, it can look unsightly and, if the tree is old and has a poor
root system or rot in the main trunk, then it may cause the tree to blow
down, with the mass of evergreen leaves acting like a large sail in a gale.

Once ivy becomes established it is securely held to the trunk and branches and is difficult to remove. If time allows, and the tree is not in the public
eye, then the main stems of the ivy may be cut at ground level. Eventually
the ivy will die, lose its leaves and loosen its grip on the tree. The stump of
the ivy may be treated with a brushwood killer, painting the chemical on to
the wounds as soon as the ivy has been cut.

Our garden is full of ash-tree seedlings. What can I do with them?

The first thing to decide is whether you want to give them to friends who have space to plant them or whether you want to dump them. They are cheap to purchase and, as such, have no value. If you can find a home for them, they can be dug up after leaf fall (taking care not to damage their brittle roots) and bundled together. Heel them into damp soil, peat or sand, covering the roots to prevent them drying out until they are ready to be replanted.

Otherwise, dig them out at any time and dump or burn them. Don't try to pull them up as the root will break, allowing them to regrow. Larger than 45cm (18in) and they will be too hard to compost, but they will go through a shredder. You will have no need for regrets, as there will be plenty more next year and the year after.

Are there any small trees that can be grown in containers?

Yes, there are, but a lot depends upon the size of the container. There are some large earthenware pots and even bigger plastic containers available, as well as half-barrels, which hold up to 100 litres (22 gallons) of compost. When potting, keep the compost about 15cm (6in) below the rim, to allow for watering and top-dressing with fresh compost each spring.

Japanese maples *(Acer palmatum)* make excellent trees for containers and, by repotting when necessary into ever larger pots, can spend most of their lives containerized. The variety 'Chitoseyama' only grows to 2m (6ft), with deeply cut crimson-green leaves that turn a bright purple-red in autumn. *A. p.* 'Shishio' grows slightly taller, to 2.5m (8ft), with bright-red new foliage turning green in summer and back to deep red in autumn before leaf fall.

Stag's horn sumach *(Rhus typhina* 'Dissecta') is a deciduous tree with velvety shoots resembling a stag's horns and finely cut pinnate leaves, which change from green to brilliant red, orange and purple in autumn. The clusters of deep-crimson fruit also appear in autumn. It grows to 2m (6ft) high. *Prunus* 'Amanogawa' is a narrow, upright flowering cherry tree with semi-double, fragrant pale-pink flowers in early spring. It will eventually grow to 7m (22ft), but can be kept containerized for many years.

There are a few crab apples that will succeed for a long time in a large container, and *Malus* 'Jewelberry' is one of the best. The white flowers open from pink buds in spring and are followed by masses of red fruit, even on young plants. It will grow to 5m (16ft) high.

When you visit a large specialist nursery with specimens in containers, you see a vast range of trees, from oaks to cotoneasters, containerized and looking healthy, but they are potted on regularly. One of the keys to trees

looking good in containers is their rate of growth. With fast-growing varieties the container quickly ends up being all root. Smaller trees of the legume family seem to do particularly well – examples include *Gleditsia triacanthos* 'Sunburst', *Robinia kelseyi* and *Cytisus battandieri*. The last is often grown as a wall shrub, but it is superb when grown as a standard tree. It has pineapple-scented, bright-yellow flowers and grey-green silky leaves.

Other suitable trees that are not legumes are *Crataegus prunifolia* and *Amelanchier laevis*. The former is a good robust yet attractive plant with a compact, rounded crown that will tolerate cutting back or shaping, if required. It has long-lasting showy fruits and good autumn colour. It has an Award of Garden Merit. The latter is covered in fragrant white flowers in late spring, which combine well with the young pinkish foliage; it forms a good multi-stem specimen, too.

Trees that tend not to do so well are members of the *Prunus* and *Malus* genera. Types of *Prunus* tend to have long roots and relish deep, fertile soil, while some of the more vigorous members of the *Malus* genus tend to grow fast and will run out of steam.

There are three tree stumps in my rear garden – how do I remove them? The access is only 1.2m (4ft) wide.

You haven't said how large they are, but I presume they are too big to dig out by hand. You can drill holes in the surface of each stump and pour in a proprietary chemical to hasten the decay of the timber, but these work best on freshly cut stumps, and even then they take a long time to have the desired effect.

A stump-grinder is a bit like a large chainsaw and one of the smaller machines will easily fit in through the rear gate. It grinds the stump down to well below soil level, leaving the lower roots. This is a job for a professional and makes such a noise that you should disappear for the day and return to a level site.

Each year the flower buds on my camellia drop off in the autumn and I have no spring flowers.

If the camellia is otherwise happy and healthy, this has probably been caused by dryness at the roots in late summer or autumn, just when the buds are starting to swell. Plants in containers are very prone to this, as they often suffer from a lack of water. If the camellia was planted in a very peaty compost, it may have dried out in the summer and the compost is then difficult to rewet. This year water the plant regularly and apply a deep surface mulch of leaf mould to the moist soil around the camellia.

Camellias also dislike limy soil, which causes yellowing of the leaves and stunted growth.

I bought a red hydrangea, but it has flowered a poor mauve-purple colour. Will it flower red next year?

Hydrangeas are very sensitive to the acidity or alkalinity of the soil and the flowers will change colour according to the soil in which they are growing. They react in the same way as litmus paper: pink flowers in a limy soil and blue flowers in an acid soil. In very limy soil the flowers will be red, and in very acid soil, where there is available iron and aluminium salts, the plant will have deep-blue flowers.

There are colouring compounds that can be watered into the soil to provide the elements that the hydrangea needs, in order to give the correct flower colour. However, it is a bit hit and miss, and at best you may end up with a deep-pink hydrangea.

I have an outdoor fuchsia that gets frosted each spring. How can I protect it?

I'm not sure that I would bother. If the frost is not severe, the plant will soon produce more foliage that will grow away quite happily and the fuchsia will be in flower by June. A very heavy frost will kill the plant back to the base, but it is likely that it will grow away from ground level.

If you want to have early flowers and a large plant, you can make a wigwam of canes and horticultural fleece and cover the fuchsia during periods of frost, but it will then be necessary to harden the plant off, as the growth will be soft and liable to suffer from cold winds.

I have some Japanese acers in containers and each year the ends of the branches turn grey and die. The compost is not dry. Are they diseased?

This is more likely to be caused by frost or biting-cold winds killing the tips of the branches. The discoloration will spread down to the first pair of side shoots and then stop. The damaged bits may be cut off or, if they are thin, snapped off. Move the plants to a sheltered side of the house during winter and spring.

In my experience Japanese acers, although incredibly beautiful, are also extremely temperamental and even minor extreme conditions seem to

make them suffer from this condition, which is commonly known as acer scorch. It often starts off with the leaves becoming scorched around the edges, then crumpling up and going completely dry and brown. Once this has happened, the branches often die back and may develop a whitish discoloration in the process. If the soil or compost is either too wet or too dry, acer scorch is likely; similarly if the weather is either too windy or too sunny, it becomes a common problem.

You may find that it is easier to keep acers in good condition if you grow them in open ground, as the fluctuations in moisture levels around the roots are more likely to be pronounced in a container-grown plant than in one that is growing in open ground.

How can I make the spiky leaves of *Yucca gloriosa* safe for children?

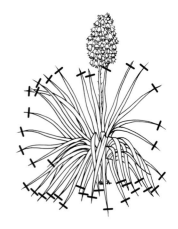

This is a spectacular shrub with stiff, arching leaves and enormous panicles of bell-shaped creamy white flowers in late summer. It is called 'Spanish dagger' for good reason, and it is not just children who are at risk from the needle-sharp, pointed leaves, although they are generally closer to them. Bending over to weed brings your face and eyes into danger, and if you back into a plant you won't sit down for a few days!

The solution is to blunt them by clipping off the tips of the leaves, removing less than 1cm (½in) using secateurs. This will do no harm to the plant, but will make your garden a safer place in which to work and play.

I want to kill a big pampas grass and an equally large New Zealand flax that are taking over the garden. How do I go about it?

It sounds like a case of the right plant in the wrong place and offers a lesson for the rest of us to heed. Always check the ultimate height and spread of plants before purchasing and planting them.

Pampas grass *(Cortaderia selloana)* can make a clump 3m (10ft) high with a spread of 2m (6ft), and the recommendation for rejuvenating an old plant is to light a fire around it to burn off the tangled foliage and debris. To eliminate it completely, light the fire on top of the plant in spring and keep it going – but under control – until it is no more.

New Zealand flax *(Phormium tenax)* can be treated in the same terminal way, but if you can cut the foliage down to knee height the fire won't be so dangerous. Make sure that plants close by don't suffer scorch damage, and don't be tempted to use diesel or waste oil as they will contaminate the soil.

Before replanting, dig in farmyard manure and general-purpose fertilizer, as the soil will have been exhausted of nutrients.

I have a rosebed that is only eight years old, but I don't like the roses. Can I replant it with new rose plants?

No, definitely not. The soil in the bed has grown roses for eight years and will be rose-sick. The existing roses will continue to grow where they are, but new roses will very quickly suffer from rose sickness, with loss of vigour. The exact cause is not known, but depletion of nutrients and soil-borne fungi seem to play a part in the deterioration of the new plants.

If the bed is small it may be worth your while digging the existing soil out to a depth of 45cm (18in) and replacing it with fresh loamy soil that has never grown roses. The excavated soil may be used elsewhere, but not for roses.

Please recommend ground-covering plants for a north-facing steep bank of heavy soil.

This is most likely to be a cold, wet site for much of the year, and cold and rock-hard for the rest of the time, so anything that you can do to improve the soil conditions – such as adding grit and humus in the form of compost or farmyard manure – will help.

Even if that isn't possible there are still plants to carpet and hold the bank. A shrub that has the ability to make the bank disappear is *Rubus tri-color*, a prostrate, evergreen spreader with dark-green leaves and its young shoots covered in red bristles. The white flowers in summer are followed by edible red fruit, like a raspberry. Clip it hard each spring to encourage new shoots and it will grow to 60cm (24in) high and will spread for ever, rooting along the stems as it travels. Green-leafed ivy will also tolerate these conditions. The Persian ivy *(Hedera colchica)*, with its dark-green leaves, will spread rapidly. Clip it every spring to make it spread to cover the whole bank.

The large- and small-leafed periwinkles *(Vinca major* and *V. minor)* are evergreen with blue flowers in summer and will carpet the bank, rooting along the stems as they spread. *Pachysandra terminalis* is a spreading evergreen perennial, with glossy dark-green leaves and small white flowers in summer, growing to 20cm (8in) high.

Rose of Sharon *(Hypericum calycinum)* makes a great, showy evergreen shrub with bright-yellow, saucer-shaped flowers in summer and autumn. It spreads by runners and grows to 60cm (24in) high.

I only have space for about three shrubs. I would like year-round interest, if possible. Suggestions, please?

Since I am always preaching about not packing plants into a bed and giving them space to grow, I will suggest that you stick to three shrubs, but you can choose your three from my four!

The Mexican orange blossom *(Choisya ternata)* has to be included – even the name is interesting. It is evergreen, with dark-green aromatic leaves and masses of pure-white fragrant flowers in late spring and again in late summer and autumn. It will grow to 2.5m (8ft) in height and spread, without becoming leggy.

Mexican Orange Blossom (*Choisya ternata*)

Hebe x *andersonii* 'Variegata' is my favourite hebe for a sheltered site, with long dark, evergreen leaves with grey-green centres and creamy white margins. Large spikes of violet flowers are produced from early summer through to autumn and often into winter, when they become pale violet. It reaches a height and spread of 2m (6ft).

Mahonia lomariifolia dislikes drying winds, but otherwise is happy in most situations. It has 60cm (24in) long pinnate, dark evergreen leaves with up to 41 sharply toothed leaflets, which look marvellous in sun or rain. The spikes of golden-yellow flowers are fragrant, last from late autumn through most of the winter and are followed by blue-black berries. It grows to a height of 3m (10ft) and spread of 2m (6ft).

You must have a rose, and *Rosa glauca*, which used to be called *R. rubrifolia*, is a vigorous species rose with grey-purple foliage and single cerise-pink flowers, with pale-pink centres and golden stamens in clusters in summer followed by red hips in autumn. After leaf fall the red stems of the new growths make a show all winter. It grows to 2m (6ft) in height and spread.

Could you make space for four?

How can I propagate a *Paulownia tomentosa* that has to be removed to make way for an extension?

The empress tree or foxglove tree are its common names, and since it is native to China and the flowers resemble a foxglove, both descriptions are equally charming. I love this tree: firstly because where I live it suffers from spring frosts on the early flowers, and yet I manage to get it to flower most years; and secondly because of the enormous leaves that it produces if it is cut to ground level each spring and then allowed to grow away on a single stem, making 3m (10ft) by autumn.

Paulownia is a very easy tree to propagate and you have a choice of three methods. Seed will germinate easily, if sown in early spring in a heated greenhouse. Sow the seed on the surface of the compost and, as it needs light, don't cover it with paper. Germination will take place in under 10 days. Semi-ripe cuttings of side shoots can be taken in mid-summer, choosing firm wood and pulling them off the main stem with a heel attached. Use hormone rooting powder and root in a gritty mixture in a frame.

Paulownia can also be propagated by root cuttings taken in mid-winter and rooted with bottom heat, in a temperature of 18°C (65°F). Roots 2cm (¾in) thick and 10cm (4in) long are stood upright in pots of moist compost,

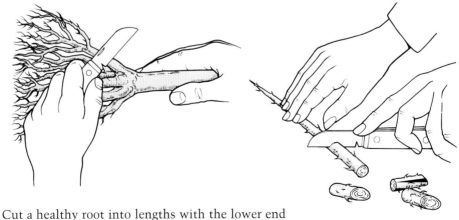

Cut a healthy root into lengths with the lower end
cut diagonally to prevent them being inserted upside down

with the thick end of the root at – or just below – the surface of the compost. New growth will appear on the root and it will quickly grow away.

What is the difference between a softwood cutting and a hardwood cutting?

Propagating by cuttings – where a piece of plant is removed and encouraged to produce roots, making a new plant – is simple to do, costs very little and provides you with a lot of satisfaction when it starts to grow.

You propagate softwood cuttings in late spring and the early part of summer, using young shoots before they become woody and hard. By mid- to late summer the stems will have hardened up and the cuttings are termed semi-ripe. Softwood cuttings wilt easily, so they need to be kept in an enclosed moist atmosphere, where cuttings of plants such as weigela, philadelphus, hebe and fuchsia will root with hardly any losses. Take the cuttings early in the day, before the sun has time to heat the foliage up, causing them to wilt and lose water. Place the material in a polythene bag away from the sun until you are ready to use it.

Cut immediately below a leaf and remove the soft tip of the shoot

Trim the cutting, using a sharp knife, below a node or leaf joint and cut off the lower two leaves. The cutting should be about 7.5cm (3in) long. Apply hormone rooting powder or liquid to the base of the cutting, before inserting it in an open compost of equal parts moist sphagnum peat and coarse grit in a tray or flowerpot. Keep the leaves of the cutting above the compost and water them in with a fine spray. Cover them with clear polythene to create a moist atmosphere and you will soon notice that the cuttings are growing; some will have rooted in two to three weeks. Softwood cuttings are soft, short and quick to root.

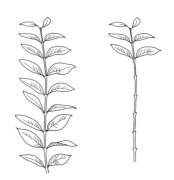

Remove the leaves that will be below the soil to prevent rotting

Hardwood cuttings are taken in late autumn or winter. The material chosen is fully ripened, healthy stems of the current year's growth, about 25cm (10in) long, cut straight across at the base just below a bud or leaf joint; the unripe wood at the tip is removed with a sloping cut above a bud. In this way you will know which end is the base for inserting in the soil. With evergreen cuttings of plants, such as escallonia, remove the lower leaves. Dip the base of the cutting in a hormone rooting powder formulated for hardwoods. These cuttings are rooted outside, with no cover, although a sheltered, well-drained part of the garden is best.

Make a slit trench by inserting the blade of a spade vertically into the soil and levering it, to leave a slit 15cm (6in) deep. A layer of grit in the base will keep the cuttings well drained. Push the cuttings into the trench, pointed end up and spaced 15cm (6in) apart, then firm well with your foot. Finally, loosen the surface of the soil to allow water to penetrate. Keep the area weed-free, water as necessary and, if the cuttings have lifted up in the ground after a hard frost, firm them in again. They should be rooted by the following autumn. Hardwood cuttings are hard, long and slow to root.

If I grow the white abutilon from collected seed, will the new plants have white flowers?

Abutilon vitifolium variety 'Album' is a lovely deciduous shrub with grey-green, vine-shaped leaves. It is fast-growing to 7m (22ft) and produces masses of large white flowers in early summer.

Yes, the plants will have white flowers, although they may have a pink tinge as they open. The trouble with open pollination (where there is no control over cross-pollination) is that there is every chance that a few plants may not flower white and are likely to be blue or mauve. If you intend giving them to friends, allow the young plants to flower, which they will do in their second year, and dump any wishy-washy colours. You may even produce a really good new colour. They are easy to grow from soft-wood cuttings in early summer, and these plants will be exact replicas of the parent.

PRUNING

There is no great mystery about pruning – common sense and knowing your plants will see you right most of the time. There are plants that require regular pruning to encourage growth, flowers and fruit, but there are many others that never need to be pruned, unless they are out of shape or have grown too large and are crowding neighbouring plants. Examples are daphne, hebe, hamamelis and magnolia. Diseased and crossing branches must be removed, and if there are too many branches causing overcrowding, they should be thinned out by pruning.

When should I cut a eucalyptus to keep it small and have the young foliage for flower arranging?

The best time to pollard or coppice any of the eucalyptus is as soon as any risk of frost has gone, which may be as late as late spring. The main stem is cut at ground level during spring in the first year, and the strong side shoots that appear are allowed to grow. The following spring they are all cut at

ground level and, if there are too many new growths, these may be thinned out by cutting again at ground level. Remember that if too many shoots are allowed to grow, the plant will become a thicket and take up too much space. The cider gum *(Eucalyptus gunnii)* will retain its juvenile, penny-round silvery-blue foliage on the young growths, while on the older branches the leaves become grey-green and lance-shaped.

There is a very old flowering hawthorn tree in my garden. Can I prune it into shape?

The common hawthorn or may *(Crataegus monogyna)* is one tough plant. It can survive in extremes of soil and climate and makes a fine boundary hedge that is strong enough to be animal-proof. As a tree, it suffers little from pests or diseases and offers shelter and food for birds. Its spring flowers, white and fragrant, are followed by dark-red fruit.

Hawthorn is a plant that can get away with being a bit misshapen, and since yours is old it can be forgiven a few abnormalities. Removing any dead branches is the first job, but be careful of the thorns, which are vicious. It is probably not worth trying to encourage new growth as a means of shaping, as it will make very little, but if there are any obviously 'out of place' branches these can be cut back or completely removed.

Providing the tree is not decayed and is sturdy, you might think of using it as a living support for a climber. It will have the ideal framework for a clematis or rose to scramble through. Choose a variety that won't swamp the tree and make it look top-heavy. *Clematis alpina* 'Frances Rivas' is not too vigorous and will drape itself over the outer branches, trailing down with bell-shaped blue and white flowers in spring, followed by fluffy seed-heads. The Old Glory rose *(Rosa* 'Gloire de Dijon') flowers in summer and autumn with creamy apricot, fragrant flowers and requires little pruning.

We have a large bay tree about 10m (30ft) high. Can I prune it without killing it, and how severe can I be?

Bay or sweet bay *(Laurus nobilis)* is a bit of a wimp. It doesn't like cold, drying winds and just loves a quick snip and clip, but since the leaves are large and leathery it prefers you to use scissors or secateurs rather than shears, as they leave foliage cut in half, which then discolours.

A bay tree is tolerant of severe pruning, but it takes a long time to recover and you may have to wait for two years for it to send up new shoots from older wood; even then the shoots are slow to grow, leaving the bare stumps visible for some time. I get the feeling you would love to drastically reduce the size of this tree and a better option may be to propagate from it. Do this by rooting semi-ripe cuttings in early autumn in a frame and then remove the tree completely, replacing it with a new young plant. This time keep it under control by clipping it into shape every spring before the new growth begins.

When and how do I prune climbing roses that are very old, with all their growth high up on the wall?

The aim with pruning is to form a strong framework of branches, thereby encouraging new shoots to grow from the base of the plant. The shoots are trained as near horizontally as possible by arching them over, and it is from these stems that the short, flowering side shoots grow.

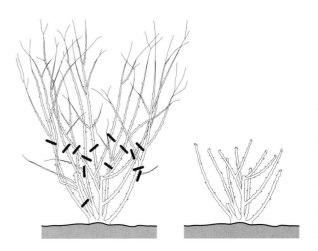

Where all the main stems are old, with no strong new side shoots and the growth is high up, it will be necessary to remove 30 per cent of the main stems as close to the ground as possible. Use a pruning saw and wear tough gloves, and try to cut the whole stem out without leaving a stump, which could encourage dieback. Remove weak or diseased stems first. To encourage the climber to throw up new shoots, water and feed with a rose fertilizer during the growing season.

Pruning may be carried out from autumn until early spring. If there are any long shoots, these can be shortened in the autumn before the winter winds blow them about. As the new shoots appear, train them to arch over before they firm up. Life is a lot easier if there are horizontal wires attached to the wall, which the shoots can be trained along and tied to. If the new growths are not allowed to become tangled, they are easier to remove at pruning time.

During the summer, constantly dead-head the old flowers, cutting at the first pair of leaves below the flower to encourage the repeat-flowering varieties to keep up their display.

When and how do I prune lavender? I have a 10-year-old hedge that has gaps. There are a few younger plants that are in a shrub border and are leggy.

Lavender is a short-lived plant, and by the age of 10 it will be woody at the base and will not break readily from hard, woody stems. In a low hedge you will find that some plants will grow away and others won't, so there will be even more gaps after pruning. I would be tempted to remove the old hedge and dig the area over, adding some compost. Don't add any fertilizer, as lavender love a poor, free-draining soil. Plant the new plants 30cm (12in) apart and prune every year. In a warm climate they may be pruned in autumn, but in cold areas dead-head after flowering, removing the flower stalk to tidy the plant up for the winter, and then prune them in the spring.

After planting, prune the new plants hard to encourage growth. In later years remove most of the previous season's growth to keep the plant bushy. Lavender plants in mixed beds are treated in the same way, but they will do better if they are not shaded by other plants.

My escallonia hedge is too high – can I cut it back by half, to 1.2m (4ft)?

An escallonia hedge 2.4m (8ft) high is probably quite wide as well and will probably benefit from a 'short back and sides'. It is a tough shrub and can tolerate hard pruning, breaking from the base of even thick, old branches that have been cut at knee height. Remember that it is an evergreen shrub and the foliage is liable to frost damage in the spring. This seldom does any lasting damage and new leaves will soon reappear. In frost-prone areas cutting hard will open the centre of the hedge from the sides and top, and the frost will be able to penetrate, killing the normally protected centre of the shrub.

Try to do the annual prune in mid-summer after most of the flower is over. If you leave the pruning until all the flowering is finished, it will be too late in the summer for any side shoots, which carry next year's display of flower, to grow. Escallonia are shallow-rooting and will benefit from a deep dressing of farmyard manure as a surface mulch around the plants.

I have a buddleia that is much too large for the space where it is planted. How, where and when do I prune it?

The butterfly bush does form a large plant and pruning will not reduce its size, except in the short term. You may have to consider transplanting it, giving it more space by removing other plants or enlarging the bed it is planted into. Your buddleia will need to be pruned every year, but the time of pruning will depend upon the species.

The butterfly bush *(Buddleia davidii)* is pruned in spring, after the risk of frost is over, and last year's growth is removed to within 5cm (2in) of the old wood. It self-seeds all over the garden and flowering seedlings are to be found along the banks of railway tracks and on derelict sites in many cities and towns. If the dead flower heads are removed immediately after flowering, you won't have to weed out inferior seedlings.

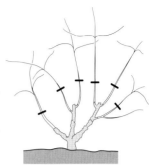

Buddleia alternifolia has long, arching stems with clusters of fragrant lilac flowers in summer, flowering on last year's branches. It is pruned in midsummer to remove crossing and diseased branches.

Buddleia globosa (orange ball tree) is evergreen in mild areas and the rounded clusters of orange flowers appear in summer on the previous year's stems. Prune in late winter before the shrub commences to produce new leaves. It can be pruned hard and will grow away quickly.

How do I go about pruning a strong-growing three-year-old wisteria that has never flowered?

Even when pruning has been carried out correctly and everything is going to plan, it can be the third year before a wisteria commences flowering – nevertheless it is worth the wait. It is a vigorous twining climber with beautiful pendant racemes of pea-like flowers in late spring and early summer. The flowers may be deep purple, violet-blue, pink, apricot or white. Wisteria are hardy, but they flower better if they are grown in a sunny, warm, sheltered area. Feeding them high potash and low levels of nitrogen will encourage flowering and prevent excessive growth.

Pruning of wisteria is done in two stages: in summer eight weeks after flowering and again in winter. By the third year there should be a framework of branches, and in summer the current year's laterals and their side shoots are cut back to 20cm (8in), or to six buds from the main branches. In winter these same laterals and side shoots are further shortened to within two or three buds of the main branches. It is these pruned spurs that will produce the flowers next spring. Old neglected plants may be pruned hard. They will grow away, with new shoots from the base of the plant, but it will take a few years for them to return to flowering.

What are the rules regarding the pruning of clematis?

For a start, there are far too many rules, and as a result a lot of clematis are either overpruned or not pruned at all. For pruning purposes there are three groups of clematis.

Group 1 includes those species and varieties that flower early in the season on growth made the previous year, such as *Clematis montana* and

C. alpina. Also included is the evergreen *Clematis armandii*. This group of plants is only pruned if they have become a tangled mass or are overgrown. Prune immediately after they have finished flowering. Cut long shoots back to a healthy pair of buds and thin the plant out, if it is congested. If all else fails, a big old plant may be cut almost to ground level and it will regrow.

Group 2 comprises large-flowered hybrids that flower in late spring on growths made the previous year and then flower again in the autumn on the current year's growth. It includes *Clematis* 'Lasurstern', 'The President' and 'Nelly Moser'. Prune in late winter or in early spring before the new growths appear, keeping a framework of older branches to support the new shoots. They may be pruned hard, but you will sacrifice the first show of flowers, although the autumn flush will be so much better.

Group 3 is made up of all the *Clematis viticella* species, *C. orientalis, C. tangutica* and varieties such as 'Ernest Markham', 'Ville de Lyon' and 'Bill Mackenzie'. They flower in late summer on the current year's growth. Cut hard to within 30cm (12in) of the ground in early spring when the buds are breaking into leaf. Prune to just above a pair of healthy buds.

My brooms are leggy, with all the flowers at the top. What am I doing wrong?

Brooms *(Cytisus scoparius)* will become leggy if they are not pruned annually. They flower on the previous year's growth and should be pruned in early summer, immediately after flowering. This prevents seed forming, which weakens the plant. Cut above the older wood, removing all the flowering branches. Cutting into old wood will probably kill the plant, so it is better to discard old leggy plants and buy new ones. If it is any consolation, brooms are short-lived plants, even when they are pruned.

Most of my shrubs are making lots of shoots but very little flower. Do I need to prune them?

Occasionally shrubs will have an off year and not produce flowers, instead putting all available energy into growth. Spring-flowering shrubs that suffer from a heavy frost often lose the potential to flower, but if all the shrubs in your garden are making excessive growth, and none of them are flowering, I suspect that the problem is cultural. An imbalance of nutrients, where the available nitrogen level is very high in comparison to the phosphate and potash levels, will cause plants to grow, producing lots of new stems and foliage. This is often at the expense of flowering.

Feed all the non-flowering shrubs at three-week intervals during summer and autumn with a high-potash, low-nitrogen fertilizer, such as tomato fertilizer. If you apply a high-potash liquid foliar feed to the shrubs, it will be immediately available and will therefore slow growth down and encourage bloom. The analysis of fertilizer is shown as N for nitrogen, P or P2O5 for phosphate and K for potash.

Pruning will encourage more growth. If, however, the plant is a bad shape or has straggly branches, they may be shortened back to a bud that is pointing in the direction in which you want the new shoot to grow.

We have a 1.5m (5ft) *Elaeagnus pungens* 'Maculata' with mostly plain green leaves instead of variegated leaves. Can we cut them out?

Yes, you can remove any branches with all-green leaves, cutting them as close as possible to the main stem. The problem is caused by the shrub producing branches that have gone back to the original green. This is quite common on plants that mutated from green to variegated, then were propagated as cuttings and are now trying to revert.

If the green-leafed branches are not removed, they will grow faster than the variegated shoots and will eventually take over, suppressing their rivals. Pruning back hard into old wood is risky, as new shoots may not break from the base and the resulting shock to the plant may cause any that do grow to be green. Apart from pruning out reversion, elaeagnus does not normally require much cutting but, if it is necessary, it is best to prune in late summer.

COLOUR AND SCENT

In many catalogues plants are described by their flower, and other attributes (such as leaf colour, bark colour and fragrance) are scarcely mentioned, yet it is plants with these extras that provide most interest in the garden from late autumn until early spring.

Can you recommend trees with good autumn colour?

There are so many that it hardly seems fair to leave any out, but I will describe my favourites, starting with an ornamental cherry *(Prunus sargentii)*. The young leaves are red, quickly turning to dark green, then in early autumn they become brilliant orange-red and finally a deep red. Unlike most cherry varieties, its leaves don't drop at the first hint of a frost but persist on the tree, finally carpeting the ground but still retaining their colour. A bonus is the pale-pink flowers in spring, highlighted by the young red foliage. It is not a small tree, growing to 16m (50ft), but there is a narrow upright form, *P. s.* 'Columnare', which only spreads to 3m (10ft).

The Katsura tree *(Cercidiphyllum japonicum)* is grown for its autumn colour. The tiny red flowers appear in spring but are hardly noticeable. The young, bronzed, rounded leaves are prone to damage from late spring frosts. In early autumn the leaves turn to brilliant red, orange and yellow and, when they fall or get a touch of frost, there is a powerful aroma of home-made fudge. The autumn colour will be at its best if the tree is grown in an acid soil. It will grow to 16m (50ft) or more, but the weeping form *C. j. pendulum* has slender branches and grows to just 6m (20ft), with an ultimate spread of 7m (22ft).

I will restrict myself to one maple *(Acer rubrum)*, which is commonly called the red or scarlet maple and that sums it up. My favourite is the variety 'October Glory', with incredibly red early autumn foliage and growing to 15m (46ft). Where a smaller tree is needed, *A. r.* 'Scanlon' may suit. This grows to 12m (37ft) and is columnar in habit, with autumn colours of orange, red and crimson.

A smaller tree is the Persian ironwood *(Parrotia persica)*, growing to 8m (25ft) although, for good autumn leaf colour, it needs to be grown in an acid soil. The green leaves turn to a patchwork of orange, bright red and purple-red. Clusters of small red flowers appear in late winter before the leaves open. There are many excellent trees that I haven't mentioned, including those that turn yellow in autumn, such as the birches *(Betula)* and the hornbeams *(Carpinus)*, and some that, every few years when the soil and weather conditions suit, can be quite spectacular.

I have seen a birch tree with a really white trunk, but I don't know what it is called. All my silver birch have dirty grey bark.

Silver birch *(Betula pendula)* grown from seed can be very variable in bark colour and even a good specimen has, at best, cracked silvery white bark. Erman's birch *(Betula ermanii)* has creamy-white bark with a pink tinge. The variety *B. e.* 'Grayswood Hill' has pure-white bark and will grow to 20m (70ft). *Betula utilis* var. *jacquemontii* has good-quality smooth white bark that colours quickly, and some varieties are particularly white and a talking point in any garden such as 'Grayswood Ghost' and 'Silver Shadow'.

Over the years bark becomes engrained with dirt and green algae, but if you scrub the main trunk every autumn with water and a stiff brush, or use a pressure hose with the pressure reduced, this will remove all the dirt and loose bark and the surface will come up looking a pristine white.

Betula utilis var. *jacquemontii*

Please recommend shrubs other than willow with winter bark colour.

The dogwoods have to top the list, especially *Cornus alba* 'Sibirica' with its red winter shoots and *C. a.* 'Kesselringii', displaying dark-purple stems. *Cornus sanguinea* 'Winter Beauty' has orange-yellow stems that are bright red towards the tips, while *Cornus stolonifera* 'Flaviramea' has bright yellow-green shoots.

A plant that I love to hate is *Rubus cockburnianus*. It is a bit like an overgrown bramble, but with stiff, erect and very prickly stems. Its saving grace is that the stems are covered with a brilliant white powdery deposit (bloom) in winter. It is vigorous and spreading, growing to 2.5m (8ft) high. *Leycesteria formosa* has unusual pendant white flowers with purple bracts in summer and autumn, followed by purple berries. The young bamboo-like shoots are sea-green, forming a thicket that will grow to 2m (6ft).

All these shrubs are deciduous and show their stems well in winter. If they can be planted with the low winter sun behind them, they will light up the garden in a way that flowers never can. The best-coloured bark is on the young stems, so each spring cut the stems close to the ground, and feed and mulch to encourage maximum growth during the summer, ready for next winter.

Are there any shrubs that I can rely on to produce autumn leaf colour every year?

I know exactly what you mean – there are shrubs that impress you with their autumn display, so you buy one and five years later you are still waiting for it to perform for you.

The smoke bush (*Cotinus* 'Flame') won't let you down. Its pale-green leaves turn bright orange-red in early autumn and it grows to 5m (15ft). The variety 'Grace' will make the same size, with purple foliage that turns to bright see-through red in autumn. They will do best in full sun in a sheltered site. Another shrub for a sunny position is *Fothergilla major*, with its fragrant white flowers in early spring and glossy dark-green leaves, which turn the most wonderful shades of yellow, orange and bright red in autumn. It will grow to 2.5m (8ft).

I have an *Enkianthus campanulatus*, which should turn into a Joseph's coat of many colours in autumn, but so far it has managed to look so poorly that if I didn't like the creamy yellow, bell-shaped flowers in early summer it would have had a ride in the wheelbarrow by now! On the other hand, the oak-leafed hydrangea *(Hydrangea quercifolia)* can't do enough for me. In autumn the mid-green leaves turn the most startling purple and hang on the plant for ages.

All the Japanese acers *(Acer palmatum)* are certain to show their true colours in autumn and it shouldn't be possible to pick one over all the others … but I will: *A. p.* 'Osakazuki' will be a brilliant red every autumn.

I would like to grow shrubs with flowers that are long-lasting when they are cut, for use in the house.

Some flowers will last for ages when cut, while others are on their way out before you can get them into water. Conditioning will prolong their life and there are some general rules that you can follow.

It is best to pick flowers in the early evening, when transpiration is at its lowest and the shrub has built up its nutrient level through sunlight on its foliage. Place the cut flowers in a bucketful of water and leave them for at least an hour to absorb as much water as possible. Before arranging, bruise the base of the stems with a hammer; hard woody stems, such as rhododendron, may have the bark scraped off the lower stem to provide a larger surface area for the absorption of water.

Forsythia is a great shrub for cutting and the long branches of golden-yellow flowers in late winter are a great standby. If flowering stems are cut as soon as the buds appear and stood in a frost-proof area with good light, they will come into flower much earlier than those outside. Cutting the flowering branches is the way to prune forsythia, as it flowers on the new shoots produced the previous season.

Snowy mespilus *(Amelanchier canadensis)* makes a dainty cut flower, with its small white flowers in early spring appearing before, or at the same time as, the young bronze foliage. It is best to cut the stems before the buds open rather than when they are in full flower as the petals of opened flowers quickly drop. Roses are a must for the flower arranger and when cut fresh from the garden, the flowers will last for a long period. The large-flowered bush (hybrid tea), cluster-flowered bush (floribunda), climbers and shrub roses are among the best.

The Mexican orange blossom *(Choisya ternata),* with its fragrant white flowers in late spring and again in autumn, lasts well, and its leaf is dark green and aromatic. *Hydrangea macrophylla*, the common hydrangea, has enormous mopheads of flowers and will last for a long time, if the leaves are removed and the stems plunged into water for 30 minutes after cutting. Camellia flowers last well indoors, and the glossy foliage sets off the deep reds and pinks of the *C.* x *williamsii* and *C. japonica. Hebe* 'Gauntlettii', with its long racemes of pink-purple flowers in late autumn, and *H.* 'Great Orme', with pink flowers fading to white in mid-summer, also last well as cut flowers.

I want to grow plants for winter perfume. Will they need protection?

The plants I am recommending are hardy, although the flowers will all do better if they are not buffeted by strong winds and knocked about by hailstones.

Christmas box *(Sarcococca)* is a wonderful genus of evergreen, winter-flowering shrubs with tiny white, very fragrant flowers in the dead of winter. They enjoy a well-drained soil in deep shade. *S. confusa* has white flowers followed by black fruit, while *S. humilis* only grows to 60cm (24in) and the white flowers are tinged with pink. Chinese witch hazel *(Hamamilis mollis)* is a deciduous shrub that flowers in mid- to late winter with very fragrant, golden-yellow, spider-like flowers; it grows to 4m (12ft) high. *H.* x *intermedia* 'Jelena' has coppery orange flowers.

Daphnes are in a class of their own when it comes to winter perfume.

Christmas box
*(Sarcococca
confusa)*

The two I couldn't do without are *Daphne mezereum*, deciduous with pink-purple clusters of fragrant flowers in winter and early spring and growing to 1.2m (4ft), and *Daphne odora*, an evergreen shrub with purple and white fragrant flowers in mid-winter and growing to 1.5m (5ft).

Don't forget the snowdrop *(Galanthus elwesii)*, with its white flowers with green markings on the inside and a scent of honey. The fragrance is not powerful, but on a still winter's day, with a watery sun, it is worth seeking out. And wintersweet *(Chimonanthus praecox)* is a lovely name for a lovely plant that flowers over a long period in winter. The sulphur-yellow flowers are fragrant, appearing before the leaves, and are stained purple on the inside. It makes a big shrub, reaching 4m (12ft), and loves a sunny site.

If you have space to plant another shrub that will grow in most conditions, add *Viburnum farreri* to your list. It used to be called *V. fragrans*, which suited it perfectly. It is deciduous and produces very fragrant, white or pink-tinged white flowers from late autumn through to early spring. In wet weather the clusters of flowers may be damaged. It grows to 3m (10ft) in height.

Will I be able to extend the colour in my herbaceous border into late autumn and winter?

The selection is limited, but at this time of year a little colour goes a long way and you won't be expecting a riot of colour. Depending upon the weather, there are some early autumn herbaceous plants that will flower well into the winter.

The Japanese anemones *(Anemone hupehensis)* are reliable for late colour and will spread rapidly. The variety *A. japonica* 'Bressingham Glow' has semi-double rose-pink flowers. The American pokeweed *(Phytolacca americana)* flowers in early summer but produces impressive clusters of shiny black-purple fruit in autumn, growing to 1.2m (4ft). The fruit are toxic, so don't plant it where children play.

Red-hot poker *(Kniphofia caulescens)* has spikes of yellow flowers that open from salmon-pink buds in autumn, and flowers at 1.2m (4ft) in height. All the kniphofia need a moist soil in summer to ensure good flower stems. Helianthus, rudbeckia, solidago and helenium all make an excellent late show in shades of yellow and, if the weather is mild, can still be flowering in early winter. Michaelmas daisy will flower until the first frost, as will the toad lily *(Tricyrtis formosana)*, with its unusual white-pink flowers spotted purple and a yellow throat. This plant loves a sheltered sunny site.

For leaf colour that will look good all year, plant some of the newer varieties of New Zealand flax *(Phormium)*, such as 'Maori Chief', with its evergreen, sword-like pink and red striped leaves, or 'Maori Sunrise' – pink and apricot with bronze margins to the leaves. My favourite is *Phormium tenax* 'Dazzler', with deep red, orange and pink stripes on a bronze background.

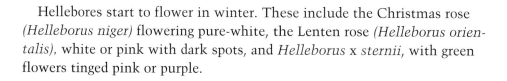

Hellebores start to flower in winter. These include the Christmas rose *(Helleborus niger)* flowering pure-white, the Lenten rose *(Helleborus orientalis)*, white or pink with dark spots, and *Helleborus* x *sternii*, with green flowers tinged pink or purple.

BERRIES

Berries are a bonus with many plants, where they are not the main attraction, as in the case of fuchsias. With other plants, such as pernettya *(Gaultheria mucronata)* and snowberry *(Symphoricarpus x chenaultii)*, the berries are the main reason for growing them, the flower being small and insignificant. Berries may be large or small, sweet, sour or poisonous, and colours range from white to black and most shades in between. Since they contain the reproductive part of the plant, they are ideal for increasing your stock of plants. Indeed, birds have a habit of doing it for you by spreading seed all over the garden.

What trees can I grow to provide the birds with food?

I always think of birds needing food in winter and, while they are most in need in cold weather when there is less food available, they are glad of fruit and berries at other times of the year.

The rowan tree, mountain ash and whitebeam belong to the genus *Sorbus*. They all carry abundant crops of berries from autumn onwards. The trees are deciduous and highly ornamental, with leaf, flower and in many cases autumn-leaf colour. Sorbus with pinnate leaves, such as *Sorbus aucuparia*, prefer an acid soil, while the whitebeam *(Sorbus aria)* will succeed in acid or alkaline ground. For a heavy cropper I would plant *Sorbus aucuparia* 'Cardinal Royal', while for large fruit plant the service tree *(Sorbus domestica)*, with individual fruit up to 3cm (1¼in) across. While all the sorbus are beautiful, there is no reason why you shouldn't have the best and still feed the birds. Plant a *Sorbus sargentiana*, with pinnate leaves that turn brilliant red in autumn, large sticky red buds in winter and huge clusters of white flowers, followed by bright red berries for the birds.

Crab apples are ornamental, providing fruit for the birds as well as a good show of flowers. *Malus* 'Golden Hornet', with golden fruit, and *M.* 'Red Sentinel', with dark-red fruit, hold their crop for most of the winter before the birds find it to their taste. Cherries are another good food crop for birds and often, in late autumn, large wild cherry trees *(Prunus avium)* seem to be moving, there are so many birds feasting on the fruit. The bird cherry *(Prunus padus)* produces small, shiny black fruit that birds love.

Another good garden tree that provides masses of fruit is the cotoneaster. My favourite is *Cotoneaster cornubia*, semi-evergreen with bright-red fruit and growing to 6m (20ft). Hawthorn (Crataegus) is a close relative and, as a hedgerow plant or as a specimen tree, is a good source of food in winter.

I have space for only one holly. Can I still have berries, or must there be two for pollination?

It all depends on the variety planted. Most varieties of holly carry the male and female flowers on separate plants, so one of each is required for fertilization to take place. If there are hollies close by in the hedgerow or in a neighbour's garden and they are the right sex, then one plant on its own may produce berries.

There are varieties of holly that are self-fertile, with male and female flowers on the same plant, and one plant is therefore capable of producing berries. *Ilex aquifolium* 'J. C. van Tol' is self-fertile, with smooth, spine-free dark-green leaves and abundant bright-red berries. *I. a.* 'Pyramidalis' is simi-

Ilex aquifolium 'J. C. van Tol'

lar, but with pale-green leaves.

Do be careful when choosing varieties of holly, because some of them are trading under false pretences – 'Indian Chief' is female; 'Golden King' is also female; while 'Silver Queen' is a male holly.

Will my purple-leafed hazel produce nuts? There is only one plant.

The purple-leafed hazel (*Corylus maxima* 'Purpurea') is a filbert nut, and the difference between a filbert and a hazel is the length of the outer wrapping, called the husk. With a filbert this is longer than the nut, while on a hazel the husk is only half the length of the nut.

Yes, it will produce nuts and will hopefully carry an abundant crop. It will grow to 6m (20ft) high and the dark-purple leaves will make as good a show as a purple beech. Not only are the leaves purple, but the male catkins and even the husks are as well.

The male and female flowers are carried on the same plant – the male flower easily recognized as the long catkin distributing clouds of pollen in late winter before the leaves appear, but the female flower is tiny with prominent crimson stamens and is subject to frost damage, which could ruin a potential crop.

Are the berries of the honeysuckle poisonous? We have three young children.

The berries of honeysuckle *(Lonicera)* may cause a mild stomach upset if they are eaten, but a large quantity would have to be swallowed to cause sickness. As such, they are not considered to be poisonous, and two or three ice-creams and a bag of sweets would cause the same symptoms.

There are garden plants that are very poisonous and you should check out all your plants. If in doubt about seeds, berries of fruit, remove them until the plant is given the all-clear.

I have a hedge of sea buckthorn (*Hippophae*) and there is not a single berry. The hedge is three years old and growing well. Does it have a sex problem?

It sounds very like it, for both male and female plants are required for pollination and you would appear to be missing one of the partners. The tiny racemes of greenish-yellow flowers appear in spring and, with the aid of a magnifying glass, you will be able to spot stamens (male) or stigmas (female). If your whole hedge is planted with male plants, then you never will have the lovely orange berries. If, however, they are all female plants, then all that is needed is a few male plants dotted through the hedge or planted close by. One male to every 10 female plants should be sufficient. When it comes to buying male plants, purchase them from a reliable source, or when they are in flower in spring check that they are indeed male. The last thing you need is more of the same.

Hippophae rhamnoides is at its best when grown in full sun in a well-drained sandy soil and is a great plant for the coast, where it will grow anywhere above high tide.

Sea buckthorn (*Hippophae rhamnoides*)

HOUSE
PLANTS

Anne Swithinbank

On *Gardeners' Question Time* Eric Robson always introduces me to the audience as 'The lady who knows more about house plants than house plants know about themselves'. This may or may not be true, but I have been fascinated by the challenges of growing indoor plants since before I can remember. Initially my love of house plants grew because my bedroom was the only territory over which I had complete control, and therefore most of my plants had to grow in pots. Later, having become used to surrounding myself with greenery, I always felt faintly uneasy in plantless rooms. While I fully appreciate plants as part of a landscape – whether natural or in the garden – I also enjoy them purely for themselves. As such, I am only too happy to watch them develop and flower in pots right under my nose.

Although I can understand the logic of dropping sentimentality and consigning faded house plants to the compost heap, I cannot bring myself to do it. They bring me so much pleasure, I feel obliged to repay that debt by nursing them back into another round of flower and foliage. Besides, I become attached to them and enjoy the sense of achievement when plants thrive long-term and bloom year after year.

Of course I enjoy outdoor gardening as well. The best move we ever made was to Devon just over two years ago, where I am gradually getting to grips with our large garden. We've had a lot of fun struggling with wild hedges, overgrown apple trees and a boggy slope. At the moment, we are putting up a greenhouse and creating a kitchen garden area. Although we tend to use the garden as a workshop to fuel the articles I write for *Amateur Gardening, Gardeners' World* magazine and the *Western Morning News*, it nevertheless remains a very personal space for us, our children and attendant dogs, chickens, guinea pigs and rabbits.

POSITION

Most of us choose our house plants because we like the look of them, rather than with a specific indoor location in mind. Visits to the garden centre are lethal and many is the time I have called in for a bag of potting compost and come away with an armful of irresistible new plants. Sometimes friends and neighbours offer spares, or lovely young plants crop up at craft fairs and charity sales.

The result of these casual acquisitions is a selection of plants from all over the world, which will only thrive if stood in just the right place. They need to receive something approaching the light and temperature to be found in their ancestors' natural home. Most plants need what is widely described as 'good, but not direct light'. This means that there will be adequate light for good, even growth and to promote flower buds, but no exposure to the harsh summer light that shines into a south- or west-facing window from midday onwards. The morning light received by an east-facing window is lovely and soft for plants, and in my last house a great crowd of them were positioned in my east-facing office to benefit from this. By using a mantelpiece, the floor and various stools and pedestals, I was able to create an attractive tiered group.

It is sometimes necessary to move plants according to the season, so that an African violet, for instance, catching as much winter sun as possible on a south-facing windowsill would migrate to one facing north or east from spring to autumn, to avoid the harsh summer sun.

Temperature and humidity are also relevant. Place a cyclamen in a dark, warm room and it will soon wilt and die. In a cool, bright place it will flourish. Many plants would rather spend the winter at a regular 13–15°C (55–60°F) than have to put up with temperatures fluctuating wildly from 10 to 21°C (50–70°F). Although it seems obvious that tropical plants will thrive in a warm temperature, they often dislike the dry air that comes with it. They also take exception to cold draughts. So for long-lasting plants, a house-plant-keeper has to be detective-like in his or her approach to find the best place for every plant.

My weeping fig loses its leaves from the side facing the wall.

Weeping figs *(Ficus benjamina)* grow to tree-like proportions in tropical countries and have become popular in houses and office buildings for their height, glossy foliage and attractive weeping habit. A quick flick through the most recent booklet listing the top varieties of pot plants on sale at the Dutch auctions (the origin of many house plants in this country) reveals 13 different cultivars, some with variegated or golden foliage. House plants even meld with sculpture, as these figs are available with woven or plaited stems. Tall plants are not cheap to buy and can cause consternation when leaves start to drop. In general they need good light, with a few hours of direct light every day, and do best at temperatures of 13–21°C (55–70°F).

Due to their size, large weeping figs invariably end up standing in a corner or with their backs to a wall, thus receiving light from only one side. Although evergreen, plants will shed a few older leaves from the inside of the plant, most falling towards the end of winter. But more leaves will fall from the side receiving less light, until in extreme cases the back of a plant becomes bare, twiggy and dead.

One tall office building in London keeps its magnificent weeping fig on a slowly revolving dais, so that it receives all-round light. This may not be practical in a living room, but turning the fig every few days will ensure that light reaches all parts. Or site it where light can reach the plant from two directions. Dry air spells death for weeping figs, of which the first symptom is undue leaf drop, so keep these plants well away from radiators and other heat sources. Raise the humidity by placing the pot on a wide saucer filled with moist pebbles, so that it is sitting on the pebbles and not in the water. Place other plants around the base to form a group and they will all benefit from the moisture rising from the leaves and potting compost.

Dryness at the roots will also cause leaf drop. Due to their size, weeping figs usually inhabit large pots and, when the surface of the compost begins to dry out and watering is appropriate, they need a lot in one go to soak through all the compost.

Plants that have lost a lot of foliage towards the bottom and back can be regenerated by encouraging the top shoot to root by air-layering (see p. 78). Or treat the shoot tip as a large cutting (15–18cm/6–7in long), which, with luck, will root in a warm place inside a polythene bag out of full sun. In my experience, figs are sensitive to hormone rooting compound and do better without it. Those who have failed with variegated or gold-leaved cultivars might find the plain-leaved kinds easier (and, to my mind, more beautiful).

My daughter chose a pretty primrose to keep in her bedroom. The flowers are fading and the plant seems to have shrunk. How can she keep this pet plant going?

Primroses are at their most enticing during winter, when their bright, jewel-coloured flowers are welcome and their prices well within pocket-money range. They can be regarded as short-lived pots of colour to be thrown away afterwards, but, given the right treatment, will last for years.

I guess this primrose has been living in a warm place with insufficient direct light, which is why it has stopped growing. Give the plant a short holiday of three to four weeks in a bright, cool place (a frost-free greenhouse, porch or on a windowsill). Apply a well-balanced liquid fertilizer at every other watering and wait until healthy growth starts and new buds form. The plant can then be returned to its young owner for another spell in the bedroom. This can be repeated until spring, after which the plant can be rested all summer in a bright indoor spot or lightly shaded outdoor place (in which case, protect it from slugs and snails). Late spring is a good time to repot it into a slightly larger pot. If there is more than one crown of growth, these can be split apart and grown separately.

Why do my cyclamen, which are bright and perky when I buy them, turn black and collapse within three weeks?

Many cyclamen meet the same fate, which is caused by warm, dark conditions or overwatering – or both. This is a shame, because indoor cyclamen, whose parents originated from the south-east Mediterranean and North Africa, are potentially long-lived and tales of tubers kept going for 40 years or more are not uncommon.

First, it is important to buy a healthy plant. Always hold them up and look into the forest of stems arising from the tuber. Never buy if there are signs of grey mould (rotting). On bringing a plant home, find it a bright, preferably cool position (13–18°C/55–65°F) in the house. Mine thrive successfully on or near windowsills facing south and west during winter, but I find they need moving to a shadier north- or east-facing window when the light intensifies in spring. When plants stop flowering in spring (yes, they should last this long), stop watering them and let them dry out in their pots. Leave to rest in a dry, preferably bright place until the middle of summer. Small pink buds on the top of the tuber show that growth is ready to start and, following a good soak, new leaves will quickly appear. Apply a liquid fertilizer every two weeks or, after a couple of seasons, repot, usually into the same (washed) pot, as most cyclamen are happy in a maximum pot size of 13cm (5in). Once the old compost has been crumbled away from the tuber, there will be plenty of room for new. I use a 50:50 mix of John Innes no. 2 and a soil-less compost.

Lots of people like to water their cyclamen from the bottom, by standing the pot in water. However, I water from the top, but never directly onto the tuber.

Is it a good idea to stand plants outside for the summer?

The answer to this is, rather unhelpfully, yes and no. Some house plants need the increased light and humidity available outdoors in order to thrive, make healthy growth and flower well, so there is a definite benefit to putting them out from early summer until early autumn. Examples of these are aspidistra, cymbidium orchid, azalea, urn plants (aechmeas and other bromeliads), Christmas cactus, staghorn fern *(Platycerium)*, winter cherry

(Solanum capsicastrum) and *Jasminum polyanthum.* Other plants are more likely to suffer from a variety of upsets than they are to benefit. Delicate foliage is scorched by sun and desiccated by wind, or plants fall prey to slugs and are deluged by uncontrollable quantities of rain.

Plants that I do not routinely stand outdoors are *Clivia miniata* (prone to scorch), hoya (prone to overwatering) and dumb cane *(Dieffenbachia),* on account of its thin leaves. Always move plants into the shade first, to toughen up their leaves after a winter indoors. Remove their drip saucers, or these will hold water and cause waterlogging.

Some house plants look great in the garden and can be used as features. Bromeliads and *Begonia rex* can lend a tropical feeling to a garden. I copy Caribbean gardeners and hang my staghorn ferns from low tree branches, though I admit that cherry trees are less exotic than lychees. More by luck than judgement, I have experimented with aspidistras and found that they are so hardy that I plant some in the garden year-round. They make good evergreen ground cover and, so far, the slugs have left them alone. With an increasing interest in creating an exotic atmosphere in gardens, I suggest that by experimenting with spares of different house plants, you could well get a list of stalwarts that will make excellent container specimens for the summer.

My olive tree is producing long, spindly shoots and seems very miserable.

Only a few years ago it would be unusual to see an olive tree *(Olea europaea)* on sale as a house plant, but they are now quite commonplace and often accompanied by a small bottle of olive oil, strapped to the pot by way of inspiration. This plant sounds as though it has been placed in low light and, if the room is warm, it may have been encouraged to grow during winter, which will cause long, drawn, pale-green stems.

To succeed with olives, you only have to think of their natural habitat, on the dry, sunny hillsides of Spain and Greece. The solution to spindly growth is to prune this off in spring, cutting just beyond a healthy leaf. Move the plant to a bright position, choosing a cool porch or greenhouse (aim for a minimum of 3°C/38°F) if possible. Water only when the compost surface has dried out, and new, healthy shoots will soon sprout. Even sturdy olives occasionally need a long shoot or two pinched back in order to keep a tidy shape. Olives enjoy standing outdoors during summer.

I would like to grow bougainvillea and hibiscus indoors to remind me of sunny holidays abroad. How can I keep them healthy and in bloom?

You have not chosen two of the easiest subjects to manage indoors, but it is possible to succeed with these spectacular flowering plants. Light is all-important and both plants are going to need a bright position with at least four hours of direct light every day. Most good bougainvilleas that I know live in south-facing rooms. Ideally, plants should have a cooler rest during winter, but it may be hard to find a bright room where temperatures are consistently cooler. If in doubt, leave them where they are. Do not be tempted to place the plants in a greenhouse or conservatory where temperatures dip below 10–13°C (50–55°F). Bougainvilleas and hibiscus will not die at these low temperatures, but without early, brightness and warmth, it is hard to wake them up in spring and get them flowering again.

Now concentrate on watering. For bougainvilleas, the top half of the compost should dry out between waterings, as they hate to be wet at the roots. Also allow the compost surface to dry out before watering hibiscus. As soon as the plants become active in spring, apply a well-balanced liquid fertilizer every two weeks while growth is active, then change to a high-potash one when the flower buds form. Should plants continue to flower and grow during the winter, feed them monthly.

Success brings its own problems, because some bougainvilleas will try to put on 1.8m (6ft) of growth a year and hibiscus can grow into large shrubs, though there are compact varieties. Otherwise, pruning and training are the answer. Bougainvilleas can be trained around a wigwam of three or four slender 1.5m (5ft) canes poked in around the outside of the root and secured together at the top. Once a structure is in place, long side stems can be pruned back to short spurs holding two to three leaves or buds in early spring, as growth steps up a gear. Ungainly hibiscus can be reduced by half to two-thirds in spring. Or, for complete regeneration, cut the stems back to within 15cm (6in) of the base.

I adore gardenias, but without fail they drop buds, turn yellow and then black.

Gardenia augusta is rather special, with its sumptuous, fragrant double white flowers opening from furled buds against glossy green foliage. Ageing flowers turn creamy yellow, so that white and yellow are present together. In fact they are so lovely that writing about them makes me want to go out and buy one immediately.

Some house plants, having been positioned correctly, will cope well as long as some water and food come their way periodically. Not so gardenias, which are in the same fussy category as African violets. They either receive the specific care they need or go into decline. First, make sure that they receive bright light, but not harsh, scorching sun. Then think hard about temperature, because it is wild winter fluctuations that send the buds dropping and leaves withering. Aim for 15–18°C (60–65°F) with no cold draughts. The pots of new plants are usually full of roots, so take care that plants never dry out, yet allow the compost surface to dry out between waterings.

Gardenias are acid-loving (and therefore lime-hating) plants and need rainwater (or boiled, then cooled water) where tapwater is hard. Bring all water to room temperature before use. Reward plants in active growth with a fortnightly feed of plant food formulated for acid-loving plants.

Strong-growing gardenias that have filled their pots can be repotted into a larger size (10–15cm/4–6in, for instance) during late spring or early summer. Use an ericaceous compost, or you can get away with 50:50 ericaceous and John Innes no. 2, which is easier to water.

I like lush-foliage house plants like maranta, but they suffer from brown leaf tips. How can this be prevented, and can I snip the dead tips off?

Maranta leuconeura, like many other foliage house plants, does well indoors because it has evolved to suit the warmth and low light levels of tropical forest floors, in this case those of Brazil. There are various cultivars to choose from, with varying leaf patterns. All spread their leaves flat during the day, yet raise them edge-upwards for the night – hence their common name, prayer plant. It is a habit they share with closely related calathea and ctenanthe.

What is present in rain forests but missing from our sitting rooms is humidity, and it is dry air that causes brown leaf tips, and sometimes brown edges and whole leaves. Dry air also encourages spider mites, which are only just visible to the naked eye and suck sap from the undersides of the leaves. These cause even more drying and shrivelling.

Various tactics can be employed to raise humidity, of which one of the most vaunted is misting. I do not have time to do this regularly enough. Moving the maranta to the bathroom might work, because it is steamy there and much visited, so you would be more inclined to mist regularly in the bathroom than anywhere else. Alternatively, fill a wide saucer with gravel or small shingle and keep this layer moist, so that the plant sits on it and not in water. Grouping plants together also helps, because moisture is released from the compost and leaves, creating a micro-climate around the plants.

Brown leaf tips can be snipped off with scissors, but the damage caused to the leaf tissue usually causes another brown edge to form. The ultimate solution would be to place the maranta its own terrarium, fish tank or bowl, where enclosure would create plenty of humidity.

WATERING AND FEEDING

Having introduced a new plant to the house and worked out the best position for it, the next challenge lies in watering it correctly and providing enough food for it to grow. Even the most neglected outdoor plant can sustain itself on rain and soil, but an indoor plant is completely at the mercy of its owner.

I like to use rainwater when possible and collect a lot in water butts. Some plants, notably citrus, gardenias, azaleas and orchids, need it because they dislike hard water, and most plants seem to prefer it. Feeding is important, too, since fertilizer added to the compost is usually used up by the plant within six weeks.

I have no luck with house plants, which seem to die within a few weeks. I suspect I have problems with watering. Please help.

Correct watering is an art, but one that, with practice, can become almost second nature. There are various watering indicators on the market, but fortunately we've been born with our own, which are difficult to lose and rarely wear out. These are of course our fingers, and at the risk of sounding eccentric, I have unwittingly trained the longest finger on my right hand as a water sensor. One or two gentle prods into the compost at the top of the pot and I can make my mind up within seconds as to whether or not the plant is ready for a good soaking.

Most plants need more water when the compost surface has begun to dry out, to the point where moisture can no longer be squeezed out of the compost and it feels dry and crumbly. This means that air has been able to circulate between the compost particles and the roots can breathe. Where compost remains waterlogged, the roots die, the plant cannot take up water and wilts.

Having decided that a plant needs watering, I usually do so from the top, applying enough to soak right through to the roots at the bottom of the pot, so that a trickle emerges into the drip saucer. If this is not reabsorbed within half an hour, it should be tipped away. Some gardeners like to water from the bottom, by filling the saucer and allowing the plant to absorb what it needs, before throwing the excess away. If this works for you, then do it.

During winter, when plants are resting at low temperatures, specifically in cool porches and greenhouses, they can be allowed to dry out more, so that the top half of the compost dries between waterings. Whenever possible, bring water to room temperature to avoid giving a shock to the roots.

If watering is still a problem, try a growing system where clay granules are used instead of compost, using a watertight pot or container provided with a watering indicator. The granules are moistened with water and a specially available fertilizer and then left until the indicator shows that more water is needed. I have a *Begonia rex* and a staghorn fern that have been growing like this for at least six years. It is a system that works particularly well with plants prone to overwatering.

How can I keep my azalea going from year to year?

A healthy azalea, bought in mid-winter, should flower for three or four months. Look for a fresh, new arrival in the plant centre, full of bud and with just a little colour showing. Bright colours are tempting for the festive season, but I prefer the white-flowered cultivars for their classiness and ability to blend in anywhere. Stand in good light and away from the dry air surrounding radiators.

The secret of a healthy azalea lies primarily in its watering regime. These are lime-hating plants, which need rainwater where tapwater is hard and alkaline. If rainwater is not available, boil water in the kettle, pour it into the watering can and allow it to cool before use. The compost should never be allowed to dry out, because azaleas rarely make a full recovery after wilting. A well-balanced fertilizer or, even better, one for acid-loving plants can be added every three weeks during winter. Move plants to a shadier spot, such as a north-facing window, in early spring.

Follow these few rules and by late spring the azalea will have finished flowering, but be full of new green shoots. Now is the time to pot on into a larger-sized pot (10–15cm/4–6in, for instance) using ericaceous compost. Most 'plants' are really four individuals growing together and it is tempting to split them up, but I prefer to keep them as a group. Plants can stay indoors until early summer, after which they will fare better and set more flower buds if placed outdoors in a lightly shaded spot. Keep up the watering and feeding (at fortnightly intervals) and bring inside during early autumn.

This routine can be repeated year after year until the plant becomes old and leggy. Some azaleas respond to hard pruning, but it is usually better to start again with a fresh plant.

Despite all the advice, I still kill plants with kindness and overwater them. Are there any plants that can withstand this treatment?

Fortunately, if all efforts at correct watering have failed, there are a few plants that can tolerate being permanently waterlogged. One group is the umbrella plants or cyperus, which love moisture and thrive best when their pots are allowed to stand in deep saucers permanently topped up with water. They can even be grown in watertight containers full of pebbles. Add quarter-strength liquid fertilizer to the water on three applications out of four.

Starting with the smallest cyperus, *C. albostriatus* originates from southern Africa, reaches about 60cm (24in) in height and bears somewhat wider, paler green, grass-like foliage than the others. Some leaves arise from the base while others, which are really bracts, grow umbrella-like at the tops of long stems below the pale flower spikelets. *C. involucratus* (sometimes known as *C. alternifolius*), also from Africa, is a taller, narrower plant altogether, reaching up to 1.2m (4ft). Both these are easy to grow, though the latter may need some careful staking. Three slender green canes pushed down the side of the pot to half the height of the plant, with some green raffia around them to make a corral for the stems, will hardly be noticed. The tallest, at 1.8m (6ft), is the Egyptian paper reed *(Cyperus papyrus)*, which is slightly more difficult to grow, but forms splendid 'umbrellas' of fine, thread-like stems ending in small brown flowers. A warm, humid and bright bathroom would make a wonderful home for such a plant.

The cyperuses' love of water can also be harnessed for their propagation. In nature, they grow along waterways and their umbrella-like heads bend into the water. This can be mimicked by cutting off an umbrella with its stalk attached and inverting it into a pot of water. Roots and then shoots will grow, after which the new plant can be potted up to lead an independent life.

Carnivorous plants, such as the Venus fly trap *(Dionaea muscipula)* and the pitcher plant *(Sarracenia)*, like to stand permanently in rainwater and will thrive on cool, bright windowsills. In winter, let the water in the saucer disappear before refilling (though never allow the compost to dry out).

I have a soft spot for air plants and have bought several – some attached to driftwood, some to shells and others on their own. Sadly, all have died after a few months. Where did I go wrong?

Air plants belong in the genus *Tillandsia* and are of great character. There are numerous species, all epiphytic by nature, which cling precariously, their reduced root systems lodging into crevices in trees or even fixing themselves to aerial cables in moist, tropical climates. Epiphytes are plants which grow on other plants yet do not derive any nourishment from them. Most tillandsias originate from South America. Their leaves are covered by silvery scales which absorb water and nutrients as though they were blotting paper, and in this way the rosettes of growth expand, producing flowers and propagating themselves by means of seeds and offsets. It is no surprise that these highly specialized plants are a challenge to grow, but their care is not difficult, once it is understood.

Most air plants die through a combination of over- and underwatering. Be very fussy when choosing plants, making sure that they are plump and healthy. They need a position in good (though not harsh) light, but normal room temperatures should be fine. Plants are watered by misting them with rainwater in such a way that they should dry out within two to three hours. As a rough guide, mist daily in summer and when the air is hot and dry in winter. During colder, damper spells, reduce misting to two or three times a week. Add a half-strength foliar feed every month. Air plants are sometimes fastened to their support with glue, but staples and nylon fishing line are best. Spanish moss *(Tillandisa usneoides)* is an air plant – or rather many air plants joined together – that I have found easy to grow outdoors in the summer, in light shade. At least it never needs repotting.

There are so many house-plant fertilizers on the market that I am confused about which type to buy. When and how often should they be used?

Although there may appear to be an abundance of fertilizers on the market, it is surprising how similar most of them are. It is the way in which they are used that tends to vary most.

The three main elements essential for healthy plant growth are nitrogen (N), phosphates (P) and potassium (K), which are always noted in this order on fertilizer packets. Nitrogen encourages healthy stems and leaf growth and stimulates the production of chlorophyll, the green pigment that is essential in trapping light to use as energy for growth. Phosphorus is good for a healthy root system, while potassium specifically encourages flowers, fruit and a sturdy growth habit. They are usually expressed as a ratio, so 15:30:15 indicates that there is more phosphorus than nitrogen and potassium and is a good general-purpose food. Tomato-type fertilizers, which are balanced to encourage flowering and fruiting, are high in potash. These can be used to great effect on plants like the wax flower *(Hoya carnosa)*, which sometimes refuses to flower. Fertilizers tailored for leafy plants tend to be high in nitrogen. A high-nitrogen fertilizer can also be used on plants like hibiscus, which have become woody and need to make some fresh, flower-bud-bearing shoots. In this case the high-nitrogen feed can be followed with one high in potash. There are also many trace elements (such as iron, magnesium and manganese) which, though only required in small amounts, are nevertheless important for plant health.

The most popular way of feeding is by liquid fertilizer diluted into water, as directed on the packet. This is applied directly to the roots, and most healthy plants will benefit from being fed every two weeks during summer and perhaps once a month during winter. For small quantities of plants, liquid fertilizers marketed specially for house plants are ideal, since they are easy to dilute into small cans. But for those people with many house plants, containers and outdoor plants, then general-purpose fertilizers such as Miracle-Gro, Phostrogen or Chempak 3 are more versatile and will last longer. I usually make up a large watering can of fertilizer, then fill my smaller can from it.

Some fertilizers can also be absorbed through the leaves, a process known as foliar feeding. This can be applied through a sprayer or mister and is ideal for plants that need feeding during winter when the roots are less active, and for epiphytic plants like bromeliads and orchids, which, because they naturally grow in trees, have small root systems and are more used to obtaining nourishment via their foliage.

Slow-release fertilizers are ideal for busy people. These are added as tablets or sticks and gradually release nutrients over a period of three to six months (this will be stated on the packet).

In conclusion, I tend to opt for a versatile, general-purpose liquid fertilizer that can double as a foliar feed. It is usually bad to feed a plant whose roots are bone-dry. There is also little to be gained by feeding the roots of a sick plant. Some people mistakenly believe that they are applying a tonic, but sick roots will not be able to take up the fertilizer, which hangs around in the compost doing more harm than good. A weak foliar feed would be better.

My lemon tree suffers from yellow leaves, especially during winter. Sometimes the surface of the leaves turns black and sticky.

There are two problems going on here, so let's tackle the yellowing leaves first. Lemon trees (*Citrus limon* 'Meyer' is the most popular) are hungry feeders needing lots of nutrients to keep the leaves green, the attractive, fragrant white flowers growing and the fruits setting and ripening. I have tried giving citrus plants my normal feeding regime for house plants and it does not work. They need more, and performed much better once I had invested in a bottle of proper citrus-plant fertilizer (high in nitrogen, low in phosphates), which has to be applied to almost every watering. During winter my plant, which lives in a cold porch, has to withstand temperatures as low as 3°C (38°F). When temperatures dip low like this in winter, the root action slows right down and hardly any nutrients are absorbed, which is why the leaves turn yellow. Warmer temperatures or some foliar feed will work miracles.

Citrus plants are usually named cultivars grafted onto stocks, because seed-raised plants are notoriously slow to flower and fruit. Some of the stocks are not lime-tolerant and plants can suffer if watered with hard tap-water. Citrus, like orchids, are plants that really benefit from being given rainwater.

The stickiness and black deposits on leaves are directly attributable to pests living on the undersides of the foliage. Citrus are prone to scale insects, the honeydew secretions of which land on the leaves below and provide nourishment for sooty mould, which spreads to mask the leaf surface. There is no cure for the latter, other than eradicating the former. This can be achieved firstly by strict observation – one or two scale insects can be removed by hand. When the problem grows, they can be sprayed with a relevant pesticide. What is important is to repeat the process as recommended by the manufacturers. The adult insects may have been killed, but their hardened scaly bodies are often protecting many eggs. These will hatch to a crawler stage, spread out, then settle down to suck sap. When soft, they are prone to insecticides.

BF I had my honeydew eaten off my citrus by a plague of flies. Not to everyone's taste, but I guess that fishing maggots would give a reliable clean source. I found they ate the honeydew most avidly if I kept it syringed with water so that it was moistened.

I have been given a Venus fly trap, but I don't know how to look after it or what to feed it on.

The most important first steps are to stand the Venus fly trap *(Dionaea muscipula)* in a deep saucer filled 2.5cm (1in) deep with rainwater and then to find it a bright position in which to live. Plants can stand outdoors during summer (acclimatize by standing them in shade first), but in winter they need a minimum of 4°C (40°F). They do not like to be too warm in winter and are best maintained below 15°C (60°F).

During winter there will be little activity and plants may die back to small, over-wintering rosettes of leaves, which look as though they have curled up to hibernate. Cut away any dead foliage that might cause grey mould to colonize. In spring plants wake up and new leaf traps will grow. They are activated when one of the trigger hairs on the surface is touched more than once, causing the trap to shut. Within a short while it clamps shut on its prey and begins to digest it and absorb its nourishment through the leaf. It is not a good idea to play with plants too much, or they waste a lot of time and energy in shutting and opening again without receiving any food. Outdoors, or even indoors, they should attract plenty of flies naturally, but if you decide to feed them, then a stunned fly is better than a dead one. Do not apply liquid or foliar feeds. Should plants need repotting, a 50:50 mixture of peat and sharp sand is ideal. Ordinary potting composts containing fertilizer will not be appreciated.

REPOTTING

Some house plants are pot-bound when bought and, after settling in, will benefit from being repotted during their first spring or summer. Pots are sized according to the diameter across the top, and plants generally need to go up two sizes at a time, for instance from a 10cm (4in) pot to a 15cm (6in) pot. Clay pots look better than plastic and there is an increasingly tasteful range of pots for indoor use. Some outdoor pots can be used for house plants, but check to make sure that matching saucers are glazed to hold water. Roots should be moist before repotting and the outer ones can gently be teased away from the congested mass of the old root ball.

For compost, it is handy to keep a bag of John Innes no. 2 (a loam-based compost) and a bag of soil-less potting compost, whose main constituent might be coir fibre, bark or peat. I usually mix the two together in equal quantities by volume, which may seem like hard work, but I have my reasons. The John Innes recipe stays the same, but brands do vary as to the quality of their ingredients (especially loam) and I sometimes find the mix a little stodgy. On the other hand, soil-less composts are too fibrous for my liking and can be hard to manage when they are too wet or too dry. A combination of the two seems just right and suits outdoor containers as well. Sharp sand or grit can be added to improve drainage for cacti, succulents and bulbs.

What we call one plant often turns out, on closer inspection, to be three or four small plants growing together, giving a faster, bushier potful. This is so with miniature roses, azaleas, shrimp plants, gardenias and palms, and at potting time creates the dilemma of whether to split them up or leave them together. Splitting is probably best for the plants in the long term, but

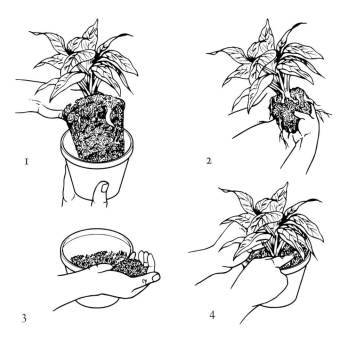

1

2

3

4

Remove the plant from its pot (1) and carefully tease out congested roots (2). Place some compost in the base of a pot (3) settle the plant in place and fill in around the roots with compost firming gently (4).

keeping them together is less risky and maintains the best display in the short term. It is best to judge each case on its own merit.

I have bought several ferns over the years, which have all frizzled up and died. Is there a solution to this?

Fresh young maidenhair ferns *(Adiantums)* and Boston or ladder ferns *(Nephrolepis)* look so tempting in the garden centres and can grow beautifully indoors when given the right treatment. Most are bought in 10–13cm (4–5in) pots and the scenario goes something like this. The fern arrives home, a saucer is found and the new owner decides on a position in the house, based on where the fern will look good and where it is likely to thrive (out of full sun and away from radiators, but where there is reasonable light for growth). Despite this thoughtfulness, the plant, whose roots make a solid wall around the inside of the pot, dries out faster than anticipated and the fronds turn brown and crinkled before anyone notices. This starts a downward spiral, which can result in a potful of crispy dead fronds.

Maidenhair
fern
(Adiantum)

The solution is to buy a larger pot and some compost at the same time as the fern. A specimen in a 10cm (4in) pot, for instance, would need a 15cm (6in) pot with saucer. The extra compost around the roots will hold water and keep them moist for longer.

I have owned several orchids, including cymbidium, which have grown and flowered well until I repotted them. After this, they seemed to shrink away and die. Where did I go wrong?

Most orchids need a special, free-draining compost and will not grow well in regular potting compost. The ingredients vary, but an orchid compost usually contains some bark, coarse peat, rockwool or foam mixed with perlite. Experienced orchid growers generally repot their plants every two years or so, but amateurs often delay repotting until their plant is so pot-bound that it stops flowering. I have to admit that one of my orchids has not been repotted for about 10 years. Although I may now lose the plant through repotting it, at least I have enjoyed 10 years of growth and flowering.

Orchids are either potted on because they need more room to grow – a process known as 'dropping on', because the plant does not have its roots disturbed at all – or because the compost has deteriorated and the plant is suffering. When the compost rots, it becomes stodgy and water-retentive, causing the roots to suffocate and die. So this process is more radical and involves getting rid of as much old compost as possible from around the roots and cutting away any dead roots.

Timing is important, because orchids will not take kindly to being repotted when they are dormant. Always wait until new growth starts. Begin by turning the cymbidium out of its old pot, then take a good look at the root system. To a novice, the roots may look sound, but only the white, firm roots with good growing tips are live ones. Those that are grey, soggy and with an outer skin that is easily pulled away are dead. Cut away all the dead roots. An orchid that has been left untended for a long period may have more dead roots than live ones. There may also be old and dead back-bulbs (old pseudo-bulbs with no leaves). Pull away the dead matter and if there are lots of leafless back-bulbs, remove some so that there are more active pseudo-bulbs than leafless ones. Having finished this, the size of the root system will be obvious.

Choose a pot that will leave a small gap around the roots. Put some compost (moistened the previous day) in the base, then settle the plant in the correct position and firm the new compost around the roots. Leave a good 2.5cm (1in) gap at the top for watering and expansion. The pseudo-bulbs should sit on the surface and the top of the roots should be covered. Water in, then leave until the pot feels light when lifted, before watering again.

If I buy a small plant in a 9cm (3½in) pot, which I know will probably end up in a 30cm (12in) pot, why can it not be planted straight into the larger one?

Imagine potting a tiny plant into a 30cm (12in) pot and watering it in thoroughly. The roots would be surrounded by masses of wet compost and it would take ages for air to reach the roots again. The plant would have to be very robust to grow under these circumstances, and most would wither and die. I know we do similar things outdoors in the garden, but there the soil is more open, there are worms and other roots to aerate the soil, and better light and humidity encourage stronger growth.

I would like my two cacti to flower. Instead, they just sit there looking scabby and horrible.

Well, at least you want to do something about it. I get cross with people who say they dislike cacti, then show me the most stunted and miserable collection of plants. Cacti are probably their own worst enemies, because they can survive on neglect and are known to have adapted to the harsh conditions prevailing in deserts and other arid regions. But we want our plants to thrive, rather than limp through their lives, and cacti can be extremely beautiful, both in form and flower.

Cacti need a bright position, and a cool windowsill or frost-free greenhouse provides the best home. Cool temperatures during winter enable a cactus to rest when there is insufficient light for healthy growth and, during this rest, they should only be watered if they appear to be shrivelling. Most of my plants go from mid-autumn to early spring with no water at all. But for the rest of the year they should be treated to regular waterings and the occasional dose of fertilizer (either well-balanced or a special cactus fertilizer, which usually contains more phosphates than nitrogen or potassium).

There will come a time when the cactus outgrows its pot, with its spines straining against the sides. Choose a clay pot that is slightly shorter and wider than usual, and either buy cactus compost or mix three parts of normal potting compost to one of potting grit. Spiny cacti are not the easiest chaps to handle. I suggest making a collar of several layers of newspaper and using this to ease the cactus from its old pot. Then take the old pot and use it as a template to pot into the new one: firm the compost around it, as if it were a root ball, then pull it out gently, leaving a hole exactly the same size as the old root ball (a bit like a reverse sandcastle). Now pick up the cactus with the newspaper and drop it into the hole. Top with some small shingle or pebbles and water in.

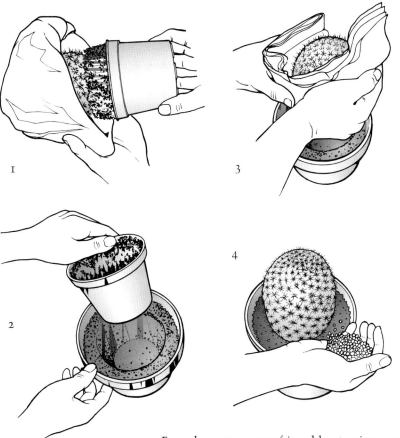

Ease the cactus out of its old pot using a collar of newspaper
to cushion the spines (1). 'Pot' the old pot into the new one
and remove to leave a hole exactly the right size for the roots
(2). Drop the cactus in (3), then top with shingle (4).

I have a number of unusual containers that I would like to use as vessels for house plants, but how do I get round the problem of there being no drainage holes?

The answer is to make a soakaway at the base of the container by filling it
about one-third full of pebbles. The expanded clay types are the best,
because they are light and clean. The plant can be potted into the container
in the normal way, but when watering, think hard about how much is needed
to soak the roots without causing waterlogging. Excess can trickle out of
the compost into the pebbles, but too much will back up into the compost.

Another method is to use a growing system (see p. 59) where the plant is
potted into absorbent clay granules with the old compost still on its roots.
True hydroponics systems require compost to be washed gently from the
roots, which are them potted into expanded clay pebbles. An indicator
shows the correct water level (usually to fill one-third of the container) and
special fertilizer is added to the water. If you want to be experimental, try

this with clay or other pebbles and, if special fertilizer is hard to find, use an ordinary well-balanced liquid feed at about one-quarter its normal strength. Chemical salts might eventually build up around the pebbles, but repotting would cure this, to an extent.

PRUNING AND TRAINING

While some house-plant growers have problems persuading their charges to grow, others are so successful that their main preoccupation lies in curbing their plants' exuberance. In the tropical rain forests where some of our plants originate, they grow to monstrous proportions (Swiss cheese plants, philodendrons and devil's ivy especially), and they can become a nuisance when they make themselves too much at home. Climbers can outgrow their welcome, too, sending long stems in all directions.

I have acquired several climbing house plants (hoya, stephanotis, passion flower and jasmine) over the years, but have difficulty in training them. Can you recommend elegant methods of coping with climbers?

These particular climbers are usually bought trained into a circular wire, which can serve them well for a couple of years. After flowering, long shoots grow, which can be tied into the hoop. As time wears on, however, older stems on the inside turn woody and there is congestion, so after flowering combine pruning, training and repotting.

Repot first, then loosen the plant from its hoop and take a good look at what is there. It may be possible to cut out all or part of some old stems in order to train in the new. This is particularly important with *Jasminum polyanthum* and the quick-growing *Passiflora caerulea*. Hoya and stephanotis are in the same family and both drip white sap from their cut ends, so put some newspaper down to protect surfaces. Neither of these needs heavy pruning and it is a good idea to keep as many old flowering stems of hoya as possible, because flower buds will grow again from the same stalks.

Next, take three long slender canes – say 1.2m (4ft) long if the pot is 15cm (6in) across – and push them in, evenly spaced around the edges. Draw in the tops and tie securely. If bamboo canes seem too straight and rigid, then rustic hazel sticks or even twisted hazel or contorted willow could be used. Look out for attractive metal cones that can fit into the tops of flowerpots.

Take the stems of the climber and begin to coil them as horizontally as possible around the support, tying them where necessary. I find the most effective fixing method (for indoor and outdoor plants) is green gardening string tied with a reef knot, with the ends snipped neatly off. If this is difficult, use soft twist ties. This way, there should be plenty of room for future growth.

I am fond of my Swiss cheese plant, but it is far too large and the aerial roots stick to the wall and poke their way behind the skirting board.

In tropical countries this South American giant will romp up to 20m (70ft) into trees, producing massive leaves with their familiar indents and holes and sending aerial roots in all directions. In the wild, these cling to tree trunks or hang in the air, acting both as stabilizers and as feeding roots. Should they locate the forest floor or a niche full of leaf mould, they produce fibrous feeding roots to help nourish the plant. In a sitting room these roots are unlikely to find a heap of well-rotted compost behind the television, but they will cling to wallpaper and pull it away from the wall and penetrate skirting boards. If they are causing a problem, and poking them back into the pot seems out of the question, simply cut them off. This will not harm the plant.

The other problem with Swiss cheese plants is that when they are happy, they outgrow an average house, blocking gangways and causing a nuisance. If this is the case, prune back as hard as necessary in spring or summer. Remember that the plant will sprout from just above the cut, so it is no use just lopping off the top 30cm (12in). If the plant is scraping the ceiling, reduce it to 75cm (30in) and have the fun of watching it grow back up again. Always cut just above a leaf, for it is from the leaf axil that a new shoot will grow. The tips can be rooted like giant shoot-tip cuttings and sections of healthy green stem, each bearing two leaves, will also root. Remove the bottom leaf before inserting into a pot of cuttings compost. Cover with polythene and keep out of full sun.

Give it a good home in a big container in a frost-free light place and get it to flower and fruit. The fruit, a 'Ceriman', is really delicious. I love it.

The stems of my tradescantia are 60cm (24in) long, but they are bare at the top. How can it be rejuvenated?

This is a familiar problem with trailing plants and the same technique can be used for goldfish plant *(Columnea)* and lipstick vine *(Aeschynanthus)*. The method could not be simpler. Take a sharp gardening knife or secateurs (scissors squash the stems) and cut all the stems back to the circular area at the top of the pot, though not into very old wood, during spring or summer.

Clean off any remaining dead foliage. The stems will sprout new growth and the plant will regenerate itself almost completely. Make sure that the plant is receiving some direct light every day, to stimulate growth. This drastic pruning method can be repeated until plants become tired and old. At the same time as pruning, take shoot-tip cuttings (see p. 75) and pot three up together, to grow on and eventually replace the old plant.

I have a Congo Cockatoo impatiens, but its single stem reaches 90cm (36in) tall and only the top 15cm (6in) is furnished with leaves and flowers.

Impatiens niamniamensis 'Congo Cockatoo' originates, as its name suggests, from tropical Africa. An intriguing plant, it bears busy Lizzie-type leaves and masses of brightly coloured orange and red hooded flowers, which, if you squint madly, do resemble a flock of parrots sitting in a tree, with the hooked red spurs looking particularly beak-like. Not surprisingly, then, it is commonly referred to as the parrot plant. Irritatingly, though, it does have a habit of growing up and up. Fortunately, cuttings root easily and plants sprout readily after pruning.

Impatiens niamniamensis 'Congo Cockatoo'

In spring or summer cut off the top 15cm (6in) and prepare the shoot tip as a cutting by trimming the stem below a leaf with a sharp knife so that it is 8–10cm (3–4in) long. Remove any flowers and the bottom leaves before dibbling it into a 9cm (3½in) pot of cuttings compost (50:50 soil-less compost and sharp sand or perlite), then water it in well and cover with polythene. Place out of the sun in a warm place and it will soon root. Prune the long stalk above a leaf to leave a stump about 8cm (3in) long. When placed in the light, this will soon sprout new stems and make a bushier plant.

My variegated parasol plant *(Schefflera arboricola)* has reached the ceiling. What do I do now?

Only the other day I was called to my neighbours' house, handed a pair of secateurs and asked to perform surgery on their schefflera, which they rescued from a local antiques centre. They stood by anxiously while I lopped most of their plant off, leaving a stump about 60cm (24in) above the pot. As I explained to them, it really does not make sense to cut any higher up, because the regenerative growth will arise higher, leading to an ungainly, unstable specimen. Their plant was sickly, as it had been badly cared for by its previous owners, so I was worried that it might die, sending my credibility into a nosedive. At the same time, I could not walk away and leave my poor neighbours with this ugly, straggling plant draped all over their kitchen. Luckily, the plant sprouted nicely, leaving my green-fingered reputation intact.

If a plant reaches the ceiling, the owners have already had years of pleasure out of it. A hard pruning might only have an 80 per cent chance of success, but I still think it is better to take a risk for a good result than put up with an ugly plant. If anything goes wrong, there is always the option of buying a nice new one. Bets can also be hedged by rooting cuttings (of the tip and of stem sections, each bearing two nodes) or by air-layering to root the tip before pruning.

What can I do with a miniature rose now that it has finished flowering?

I love miniature roses and find them hard to resist, as they are such good value. Compared to a bunch of flowers, they are going to last longer, even if the plant is thrown out after the blooms fade. But their prospects are good and they can easily be persuaded to flower again and again. I bought my last plant in mid-winter, which is the worst time of year for a rose, which is naturally a summer-flowering plant. However, these pot roses have been bred to survive well indoors and I enjoyed creamy double flowers with a flush of green for three weeks or so in my warm, bright kitchen. The plant would have lasted longer in a cool place, but I wanted to enjoy its blooms all the time.

After flowering, the stems and leaves began to show signs of botrytis (grey mould), encouraged by the warm conditions. I pruned the plant by a good two-thirds, leaving about 8cm (3in) of growth behind in the pot, then cleaned off the dead bits and put it in the cool porch. Here it stayed, resting until spring, when new shoots began to sprout. I potted it on into a larger pot and it rewarded me by growing strongly. By early summer it was lovely again, twice its original size and smothered with buds. After flowering, it will be cut back again and, with the boost of fortnightly liquid feeding, should produce yet another flush of bloom before autumn. In the absence of a porch, miniature roses make good patio plants and can be left outside during winter. The only problem is that they are more likely to pick up black spot and other diseases from roses in the garden.

PROPAGATION

There is nothing wrong with treating house plants like long-lasting bunches of flowers, keeping them until they go off, then relegating them to the compost heap and replacing them. Personally, this attitude is anathema to me, because I grow attached to my plants and enjoy nursing them through the ups and downs of their lives. Follow this to its natural conclusion and there is a desire to propagate a plant so that it can eventually be replaced by its progeny. Another motive for growing spares is to share them with friends.

Besides, if you love plants, propagation is fascinating, and among our house plants are some weird and wonderful methods involving leaves that sprout and stems that will root if cut into. Success does not depend upon lots of expensive equipment, but the luxury of a heated propagating case does help to root cuttings faster and bring on delicate young plants.

What is the best way to get ordinary shoot-tip cuttings to root without a heated propagating case, mist units and other fancy pieces of equipment?

The first step is to be organized. Find and, if necessary, wash and dry some 8–9cm (3–3½ in) pots. These will be the correct size to take four or five cuttings each of small-growing plants like shrimp plants *(Justicia brandegeana)*, goldfish plants *(Columnea)*, impatiens, Swedish ivy *(Plectranthus)* and snakeskin plants *(Fittonia)*. Prepare some cuttings compost by mixing together equal quantities by volume of soil-less potting compost with sharp sand, potting grit, perlite or vermiculite. This mixture will be weaker in fertilizer content than a normal potting compost and far better drained, so that water does not linger around the stems and vulnerable young roots.

Collect the cuttings material from the plant by cutting just above a leaf to take away shoots slightly longer than needed – 8–10cm (3–4in) long stems growing directly from an older stem can be pulled away with a 'heel' of older stems attached. These 'heel' cuttings are ready to insert, and the most attention they need is a little trimming. Make the ordinary cuttings about 8cm (3in) long by cutting neatly below a leaf or node, then removing the bottom leaves. Large-leaved cuttings can have their leaves cut in half to reduce moisture loss and make them easier to fit into the pot. Fill the pot with compost, firm gently, then dip the cut end into some hormone rooting compound and insert each cutting around the edge of the pot, making the holes with a pencil or plant cane.

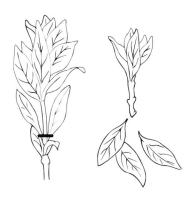

Shoot tip cutting

Water the cuttings in well, then stand the pot inside a polythene bag and loosely knot the top. Then comes the crucial part of deciding where they will root best. Good but not direct light and an even, warm temperature are best for rooting. Wait until the cuttings are well rooted before knocking the whole lot out of the pot, separating the plants and potting them individually into normal potting compost. Some plants, especially early in the year, benefit from staying inside polythene bags for another week or so after potting to keep them warm while their roots are growing.

My *Begonia rex* is much admired by my friends. How can I propagate several plants to give away?

I like *B. rex* too and maintain two different cultivars. My oldest plant, now 15, bears huge, rather stiff, puckered leaves that are almost black with silvery red markings. I regularly propagate these begonias by taking leaf cuttings.

There are several different methods, but I will describe the easiest, even though it yields only four or five plants per leaf. First, prepare a small seed tray with a large enough area to take a leaf lying flat. Fill it full of cuttings compost (50:50 soil-less potting compost and sharp sand, grit or perlite) and firm gently. Water the compost and let it settle. Next, cut off a healthy leaf about to reach its full size. Avoid old, moth-eaten leaves. Turn it over on a flat work surface and with a knife, make about six small cuts across the main veins that stick up on the underside, cutting each vein only once. Place the leaf, right side up, on the compost surface and weigh it down by placing stones here and there to help the veins make contact with the compost. Slide the whole tray inside a polythene bag, tuck the end under or knot it loosely, and stand in normal room temperature out of direct light. After about two months roots will have formed and new plants will begin to grow out of the cuts. Wait until these new plants are quite large (2.5–5cm/1–2in high) before potting them separately. The newly potted plants should be nursed along in polythene bags or in a heated propagating case until growing strongly.

I would like to try raising house plants from seed. What is available, and how do I go about it?

Growing plants from seed is fun, but if you have never done this before, I suggest that you start off with larger seeds (asparagus, banana, cordyline) and move on to the smaller ones later. The great benefit of raising house plants is that, unlike bedding plants, they can be sown later, in early summer, when light and temperature are naturally more stable and optimum.

I keep myself on the mailing list of several different seed companies and their catalogues provide me with a free and interesting read. House plants crop up from time to time, but will vary in their availability from year to year. A quick trawl through the catalogues at the time of writing revealed, in Mr Fothergill's Enthusiasts Collection, some tempting Begonia House Species Mixed, to be grown primarily for their foliage, although all will flower during the summer. Seeds of a dwarf-growing pomegranate (*Punica granatum* 'Orange Master') promise orange-scarlet flowers from within 12 weeks of sowing and edible fruits in perhaps six months. This plant would need a sunny windowsill and would best suit a conservatory.

Suttons were offering browallia, gerbera, cyclamen, calceolaria and coleus, which are really best raised in a greenhouse and moved indoors when performing. Bird of paradise *(Strelitzia)* is really a sunroom or conservatory plant, but cacti, sensitive plants *(Mimosa pudica)* and Cape primroses *(Streptocarpus)* are true house plants. D.T. Brown listed *Begonia rex*, the polka-dot plant *(Hypoestes)* and fairy primula *(Primula malacoides)*. Thompson and Morgan could provide *Begonia sutherlandii* (a dainty tuberous type that dies back in winter), stephanotis, various sorts of passion flower, ponytail palm *(Beaucarnea recurvata)*, living stones *(Lithops)* and more. The widest choice was probably held by Chiltern Seed, although their plants are not illustrated. For instance, four different kinds of indoor asparagus, including the wonderful foxtail type *(A. densiflorus var. Myersii)*, the jade tree *(Radermachera sinica)* and the good-luck plant *(Cordyline indivisa)*.

Sowing tactics vary from type to type, but because only small quantities of plants are usually needed, 9cm (3½in) pots and small trays should be adequate. Fill these with good-quality seed compost, pressing the surface down lightly, then water with a fine rose on your can. Leave to soak and the result will be a flat, moist surface for the seeds to fall onto. Fine seed can be sown thinly on top, then sprinkled lightly with compost or fine-grade vermiculite to cover it by no more than its own depth. Press lightly to improve contact between the seeds and compost. The tiniest, dust-like seed (*Streptocarpus*, for instance) does not need covering at all, but should be pressed in lightly. Large seed can be set onto the surface and either covered with compost or pushed into the surface individually. Only large seed should ever be watered lightly from the top, because tiny seeds will be washed down deeper than they could ever grow back from. There should be enough moisture in the compost, but if watering is necessary, stand the pot or tray in a large container to absorb as much as it needs.

Place the containers either in a propagating case or inside a loosely knotted polythene bag on a windowsill or other warm place. As soon as the seedlings appear, whisk the container out of its case or bag and wait until there is enough of a seed leaf to get hold of. The next step is to prick larger seedlings out into small, individual pots. Small seedlings are best spaced out in small trays first, or planted five to an 8cm (3in) pot. They can be potted separately after they have grown on. Some pot plants, like the Prairie gentian *(Eustoma)* and the polka-dot plant, can be left three to a pot permanently.

How do I propagate my rubber plant, which has grown too large?

Rubber plants (cultivars of *Ficus elastica*) do their best to grow into trees, as they would in their native lands (India and Malaya). Although they can be pruned, this makes them branch and, instead of a neat, single stem, you often end up with an unruly monster. Large plants can be beautiful, but only if the house is large enough to accommodate them. One of the best and most interesting solutions is to have a go at air-layering the growing tips, which is a bit like encouraging the cuttings to root while still attached to the mother plant (See diagram opposite).

Select a point on the stem of a healthy shoot about 45cm (18in) from the tip and remove a couple of leaves to expose the stem. White, sticky sap will drip out, so protect the carpet first. If there is no support, push a plant cane in and secure the stem to it. Cut along the bottom seam of a polythene bag to make it into a sleeve and, bunching the leaves together, slide it over the tip until it surrounds the area where the cut will be made. Using gardening string, bunch the bottom of the bag tightly around the stem below the position of the cut, then bind the string to hold it and tie tightly.

Using a sharp knife, make an upward cut from about 1cm (½in) below a leaf or leaf scar, ending just under it. The cut should penetrate about halfway through the stem. This is the tricky point, where the top seems to want to fall away, so make sure that it is well secured to its support. Wedge the cut open with a piece of matchstick or sphagnum moss, then bring the bag up around the cut and fill it with moist cuttings compost. Pull the top of the bag in above the cut and secure tightly with string.

The technical part is now finished, but it will take about eight weeks for roots to grow and it may be necessary to loosen the top of the bag and add water periodically. When roots are visible through the bag, cut below the roots to remove the whole shoot tip. Take the bag off carefully to reveal the new roots and pot them up. Air-layering can be tried with a variety of plants, including *Schefflera* and *Draceana*.

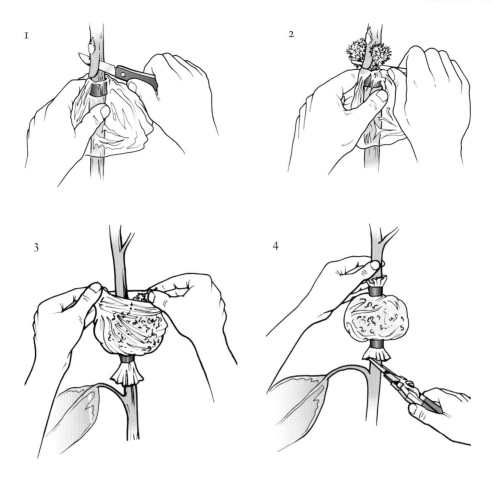

Air-layering a rubber plant

My friend cannot persuade her Christmas cactus to bloom. How can I take cuttings of my plant, which flowers every year, so that I can give some to her?

Take stem cuttings during summer by twisting away sections of three joints, which should come away cleanly with no need for trimming. Insert several into an 8–10cm (3–4in) pot of cuttings compost (50:50 soil-less compost and sharp sand or grit) and leave, uncovered, for them to root. Either grow on individually for a longer-lived plant or pot up three rooted cuttings together for a quicker, bushier effect.

No matter how many young plants you hand on to your friend, she will not persuade them to flower if the conditions are wrong. Good but not harsh light will encourage buds to form. Where this is not available, stand the plant outdoors in a lightly shaded position for the summer, but guard against slugs and snails. A high-potash liquid fertilizer applied during the summer should help the plant set buds during early autumn. Christmas cacti, which naturally inhabit jungles rather than deserts, produce their flowers as a response to shortening days. Some of them are upset by artificial light, which lengthens their day, so it may be worth moving the plant to a little-used room. When in bloom, everyone will want to enjoy the flowers, but changing the plant's orientation to its light source is said to carry pitfalls. The buds will try to turn towards the light and, in so doing, will apparently twist themselves off. I think this might be an old wives' tale, because I have carted my plants around mercilessly when giving talks and they have not dropped their buds, but it might be worth consideration.

I intend to use my interest in house plants to raise money for charity by selling plants at coffee mornings. Which plants would be particularly good at offering up plentiful offspring?

The delightful, easy-to-grow hen-and-chicken fern *(Asplenium bulbiferum)* from Australia and New Zealand is dainty, tolerant of most rooms (including, to an extent, dry air, though the compost must always be moist) and of cold temperatures (minimum 3°C/38°F). Plants will also thrive, though not

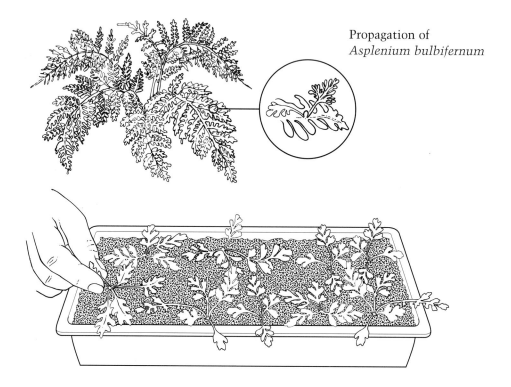

Propagation of
Asplenium bulbifernum

necessarily grow fast, in gloomy corners. Mature fronds produce many small bulbils, or baby ferns, which can be pulled off and firmed gently into good potting compost, where they will soon root and grow. Under ideal conditions of light and humidity (usually in a greenhouse), plants can expand from 2.5cm (1in) across to a spread of 90cm (36in).

Then there's the dinner-plate plant *(Pilea peperomioides)* from China, grown for its rounded, succulent leaves, each with a pale dot in the centre, held out on long stalks. After a while many offsets are produced around the base, which can be removed and potted separately with no detriment to the parent. The babies usually have their own roots and soon romp away.

Propagation of *Streptocarpus* by leaf cuttings

For flowers, Cape primroses *(Streptocarpus)* are ideal and are propagated by leaf cuttings, for which there are two methods. Select a healthy leaf, then cut it across the width to make two or three sections. Prepare the base of each by making the vein the point of a V-shape, then insert three sections into a 9cm (3½in) pot of cuttings compost. Water, cover with polythene and keep out of direct light to enable it to root. Alternatively, lay the leaf upside down on a board and cut either side of the long midrib with a sharp knife. Prepare a small tray of cuttings compost and make two long grooves in it to match the length of the leaf sections. Discard the midrib, pick up a rather floppy, long section and set it into the 'drill', with the cut ends of the veins downwards. Firm gently along the length, so that there is good contact between the veins and the compost, because this is where the roots will arise. Water in, then slide into a polythene bag to root. After several months young plants will have appeared; when these are large enough to handle, pot each one separately.

Although they are slow to produce offsets, *Clivia miniata* are easy to divide, grow and flower. The young plants will fly off the sales bench when you can show a mature plant in full bloom. Always make sure that plants are pest-free, are labelled and that you show what the mature plant looks like.

FLOWERS, AND NO FLOWERS

Keeping house plants healthy is one thing, but persuading them to flower again can be a challenge. In some ways it's a miracle that plants like stephanotis and orchids will bloom in our houses at all, when the environment must be so different from that of their natural habitat. Apart from annual plants, such as cineraria and calceolaria, most plants sold in flower are capable of repeating their performance, as long as they are well cared for and provided with the right conditions.

My clivia was beautiful when I bought it, but has not flowered for the last three years.

Clivia miniata produces bunches of (usually) orange flowers, mainly in spring, but sometimes during summer. Even when not in bloom, its strappy evergreen leaves are attractive. These plants originate from South African woodlands and dislike full sunlight, which scorches their leaves and turns them yellow. However, they do need to receive good light, with some gently direct light in order to flower. My plants thrive in many positions: some have done well in east-facing rooms with gentle morning light; several benefit from a north-facing position, but close to the windows; and yet more are sited in south-facing rooms, but some distance from the windows.

Throughout spring and summer clivias benefit from plenty of water, reapplied when the surface of the compost has dried out, and with liquid fertilizer added every two weeks. However, during late autumn and winter they can be rested by allowing them to dry out a lot more, though never becoming bone-dry and stressed. By early spring pale buds appear between the leaves of mature crowns of growth and this is the signal to give the plants a good soaking, to step up the watering to normal and begin liquid feeding again. Allow plants to produce offsets, pot on during summer to give them room to mature, and your reward will be large potfuls, with five or more sets of flowers.

Why won't my cymbidium orchid flower?

These can be among the most challenging of orchids to get to re-flower, but the elation at discovering flower spikes in early autumn or winter is worth the struggle. In order to flower again, the newer, unflowered pseudo-bulbs on the plant need to reach a certain size and maturity. This can only happen if the plant is watered correctly with rainwater, so that the roots are not waterlogged (they may die if constantly wet). The best way to tell whether a plant needs watering is to pick it up and, if light, apply water. Otherwise,

Clivia miniata

leave well alone. Feeding is important too, and either a well-balanced fertilizer applied at half-strength to three out of four waterings during summer or a weak high-potash fertilizer should work wonders. Light is important and, if left inside the house, there may be insufficient light to initiate flowering.

A shaded greenhouse will provide better light, or plants can be placed outdoors in a semi-shaded spot for summer. Cymbidium flowers are also initiated by a drop in temperature during late summer and autumn, so plants should be left outside or in the greenhouse as the evenings grow cooler, but before they become seriously cold and frosty. Let the plants feel the chill, then either leave them in a cool greenhouse or bring them inside to a well-lit position.

I am often tempted to buy a bromeliad and wonder how long their flowers last? Is it best to throw them away after flowering, or will they bloom again?

Bromeliads (plants in the pineapple family), like *Aechmea*, *Guzmania*, *Vriesia*, *Neoregelia* and *Nidularium*, either bear stunning flower spikes, consisting of glamorous bracts from which the true flowers are produced, or the leaves at the centre of the flowering rosette blush attractively for a long period either side of flowering. Most of the house-plant types originate from South American rain forests, where the plants cling epiphytically to the branches of trees. This is why many have comparatively small root systems and often make vase-like shapes with their leaf bases, which are adapted to hold water and nutrients for the plants – hence the common name 'urn plants'.

A fresh, healthy plant should remain colourful for a good few months, after which the choice of what to do with it is a personal one. Under nor-

Urn plant (*Aechmea fasciata*)

mal room conditions most bromeliads will take as many as six (or more) years to come back into flower. During this time the plant will at best bear interesting foliage, and at worst will irritate you by sitting there, growing very slowly and gathering dust. I have only ever persisted once, with the urn plant *Aechmea fasciata*, whose silver-banded foliage I do find attractive. What happens after flowering is that the old rosette of leaves slowly dies (this takes years rather than months). In the meantime offsets grow, which with good light, regular watering and feeding will slowly mature. I gave my plant summer holidays in the garden, then after six years the new offsets reached maturity and, to my absolute delight, pink 'buds' appeared, thrusting their way through two of the urns. These developed into massive heads of pink bracts from which purplish-blue flowers were produced sporadically, during a display lasting a good six months.

It is said that the gases given off by ripe or decaying fruit (usually achieved by placing an apple core in the urn) help make bromeliads bloom. This may be so, but the urns would still have to grow to maturity, which is what takes the time.

How can I persuade my African violets to flower?

These are demanding plants, which I don't even try to grow unless I have time on my hands to cater for their needs. So I don't grow them very often. A plant bought in its prime first needs the right position for it to remain in bloom. During summer a windowsill facing north or east is ideal, because good but not direct light is best. For winter plants prefer a bit more light and are best sited on a south- or west-facing windowsill. This must be draught-free and preferably double-glazed for constant warmth. African violets appear to like stippled glass, because even when facing south this seems to filter the light.

Watering should take place from below and even an inveterate from-the-top water like myself follows this rule. Only water when the plant is almost about to wilt from being too dry, as they hate to sit in soggy compost. The water should be at room temperature, and at every other application should have African violet fertilizer added to it, or half-strength general-purpose liquid plant food. Avoid splashing water onto the leaves, as in bright light this causes discoloration.

Attention to the above should guarantee a succession of blooms, with perhaps a short break between flushes – that is, until an individual plant becomes tired and starts becoming multi-crowned, or pushes up on a longer stem. Now is the time to take leaf cuttings in order to start again with new plants. Cut off a healthy leaf with the stalk attached and either sit two back-to-back in a pot of cuttings compost (kept in a polythene bag) or put them in water to root. When roots have grown from the leaf stalks, pot them up and wait for small plants to develop. When these are about 5cm

(2in) tall, they can be divided up and planted separately. Use soil-less or special African plant compost and, after potting the leaves and small plants, keep under polythene for two weeks each time while the new roots are growing.

From a flower show I bought a stunning ginger plant with tall, narrow leaves and stems topped with pink, shell-like flowers. I can't find it in any books and need to know how to care for it.

Curcumas are becoming increasingly popular for their long, elegant leaves and heads of pink or white bracts and flowers. Place in good light and water when the surface of the compost dries out, adding a well-balanced liquid fertilizer every two weeks. When the leaves show signs of dying off towards the end of summer, stop watering and feeding and allow the plants to die back. My first attempts at keeping curcumas through the winter failed because I kept them too cold, in a frost-free but unheated porch. They need a warm rest period, with a minimum of 10°C (50°F). Apply a little water just a couple of times during the winter to prevent the rhizomes from withering up completely. In spring the rhizomes can be potted into new compost and watered carefully to set them into growth. A heated propagating case will provide the even warmth they need to get going.

I have kept my poinsettia alive since last Christmas and it looks healthy. Now that it is autumn how can I make sure its bracts turn red in time for Christmas?

By now I will have been exposed as a fanatical house-plant grower capable of waiting patiently for six years for an aechmea to flower and painstakingly keeping other plants going from year to year. Yes, a plant has to be well and truly dead before it hits my compost heap, and yet I cannot summon up much enthusiasm for keeping poinsettias from one year to the next, although their foliage is quite attractive, even when not producing the red, pink, salmon or white bracts.

When bracts begin to look old and tired in late winter or spring, dry the plant out somewhat and do not worry if the leaves droop or fall. After about three weeks, prune the plant back by about two-thirds and water well. New growth will sprout, so stand it in good but not bright light, water regularly and apply liquid fertilizer every two weeks throughout summer.

Poinsettias (cultivars of *Euphorbia pulcherrima*) set bracts and flowers in response to short days and although some plants surprise their owners by bracting up despite being exposed to artificial light, most will need to have light excluded to ensure 14 hours of darkness out of 24 for eight weeks during the run-up to Christmas. Even when they colour up, bracts will probably be smaller than when the plant was bought, because it has not been subjected to the strict regime of lighting and temperature control of nursery-raised plants.

My mother-in-law's tongue has flowered. Is this unusual?

The tough, fleshy-leaved *Sansevieria trifasciata* can grow for years in the house and never bloom, yet when plants are removed to a conservatory or greenhouse they sometimes produce a long stalk (up to 75cm/30in) bearing small greenish-white flowers. This is probably triggered by exposure to better light and a drier, cooler winter rest. So yes, flowering is an unusual occurrence, especially if the plant is kept in the house. With its long marbled leaves edged with yellow, *S. t.* 'Laurentii' is the most commonly grown, but I believe this flowers less readily than the plain-leaved species. Incidentally, the flowers are fragrant, particularly during the evening.

How can I persuade my amaryllis to bloom again?

Amaryllis *(Hippeastrum)* are usually bought as dry bulbs, which after being potted and watered in, send up first a long flower stalk with buds at the end, then strappy leaves. The flowers are enormous and although hippeastrums could be described as rather vulgar, their speed of growth is awesome and it seems dreadful to consign such a thrusting plant to the compost heap. After flowering, keep the plant in good light and continue to water it, adding liquid fertilizer every two weeks. Now decide on one of two courses of action. Hippeastrums can be treated as evergreens, which if kept watered will continue to grow and, eventually, produce flowers. There will be little control over when plants bloom and this is likely to revert to the summer.

Alternatively, plants can be dried out and rested by withdrawing water in late summer. The foliage will die back and the bulb can then go dormant in its pot of dry compost. During autumn a flower bud should appear in the neck of the dry bulb, which is the signal to take it from its pot, shake off some loose compost, repot it into the same (cleaned) pot and water in. Only water again when the top half of the compost is dry. If the bulb refuses to produce a flower bud, try placing it in the heat of the airing cupboard, but do check on it every day. My mother has a habit of forgetting hers until pale, drawn flower spikes are winding their way past the flannels in search of light. If the large-flowered cultivars don't appeal, look out for the *gracilis* types, whose flowers are smaller, but more profuse.

Despite having lots of healthy green leaves, my hoya will not flower.

Several different species of hoya, or wax flower, are commonly grown as house plants. *H. bella* is a trailing type bearing heads of small flowers, while the twining stems of the larger *H. carnosa* like to climb. In the wild these plants are often epiphytic or semi-epiphytic, reflected in their rather small root systems and their dislike of being overwatered. *H. carnosa* and similar species often infuriate their owners by making masses of growth but no flowers. In my opinion, these hoyas are having far too good a time of it. They have been placed in a warm house in good light, with plenty of room for their roots and with plant food to live on. My solution is to move them into a slightly brighter position, allow the roots to dry out a little more between waterings, particularly in winter, and ease back on the feeding. Stop feeding completely during winter and apply only a little high-potash feed during summer. Hopefully the plant, sensing a change in its fortunes, might consider producing some flowers, just in case. A vulnerable plant invariably flowers well to produce plenty of seed in case it dies. Once the plant has flowered, leave the old flower stalks in place, because they will sprout more buds. Now some of the plant's benefits can be reinstated.

Are there any house plants that remain in flower throughout the year?

One of the best performers, capable of producing flowers non-stop without a break is the shrimp plant *(Justicia brandegeana)*. So much so that it is really hard to decide when plants should be cut back. There are also several cultivars of the crown of thorns *(Euphorbia milii)* that are rarely without a flower. Like the closely related poinsettias, it is the red or pale-yellow bracts that provide the colour. Some plants in the aroid family flower continuously, if not profusely. Peace lilies *(Spathiphyllum)* are reliable, as long as they receive enough light. Move them closer to a window during winter to form a good supply of sail-like white spathes. Flamingo flower *(Anthurium andreanum)* requires even warmth, good but not direct light and good humidity, but will reward you with a succession of waxy red spathes.

I admire the flowers of the hot-water plant. How can I grow this?

Hot-water plants *(Achimenes)* are so called because they were traditionally grown in stove houses, which relied upon hot water running through their pipes. They should not, however, be watered with hot water. Plants are started in spring by planting the tiny, maggot-shaped rhizomes four to a

9cm (3½in) pot. These are best started off in a heated propagator and, even there, will take several weeks to start sprouting. Once shoots are showing, take them out and place them in good light. After a while, pot on into 13cm (5in) pots. Water in, but allow the surface to dry out between waterings.

Most cultivars need support, so before the stems become too large, push four slim canes around the outside of the pot and tie string around them, cutting this to size afterwards. Continue to water and apply liquid fertilizer every two weeks and flower buds will soon form. The blooms are exotic, usually with blue, pink, salmon, red or purple as a background colour. They last all summer and well into autumn, but as the days shorten the plants begin to look miserable, and this is the sign to stop watering and allow them to die back. Keep dry and frost-free during

Hot-water plant (*Achimenes* 'Tango')

winter (ideally at 4–10°C/40–50°F). In spring it is time to turn the plants out of their pots, crumbling the compost to look for the rhizomes, which have usually multiplied. The cycle can then repeat itself. Where there are no rhizomes, this usually means that the plant was not healthy during its growing season, or the root ball was too cold in winter or too damp.

CHOOSING HOUSE PLANTS

Although it is likely that most house plants are bought on impulse, I am frequently asked to recommend plants for specific positions in the house, or to satisfy certain requirements.

Please recommend some house plants for a room where there is little direct light.

Dark rooms and gloomy corners are difficult positions for plants, most of which need medium-to-good light in order to make healthy growth. Yet there are one or two that, having adapted themselves to growing in dense forest or woodland, can survive and even flourish where light levels are low. My favourite solution to this problem is devil's ivy *(Epipremnum aureum)*.

In the wild this tough plant from the Solomon Islands scales tall trees, sending down skeins of growth and aerial roots (it is in the same family as philodendrons and monstera). In the house it will either climb or trail. I once owned a plant that, having outgrown its moss pole, sent long stems behind the piano, where it continued to produce leaves. The closely related goosefoot plant *(Syngonium podophyllum)* seems equally able to cope with gloom.

The dinner-plate plant *(Pilea peperomioides)*, creeping fig *(Ficus pumila)* and bird's nest fern *(Asplenium nidus)* can withstand low light for short periods, but tend to stop growing. The best plan is to rotate them, so that each has a turn of several weeks in the gloom, then periods of better light for balanced growth.

The ultimate solution to a dark corner is special lighting. For years I struggled to find lighting equipment that would provide the best light for plant growth at the correct distance from the plant, yet would look elegant enough for a living room. These are thin on the ground but are effective. The system I use enables me to grow virtually any plant I like, as long as I switch the light on and remember to replace the special bulbs when they go. Currently a tropical bamboo *(Bambusa vulgaris)* and a money plant *(Crassula argentea)* are basking in artificial light.

Can you recommend a tall plant for the living room, other than the ubiquitous weeping fig?

Some tall plants, like the figs, would grow into trees in their native countries. The unusual Australian bottle trees, for instance, form massive trunks of great girth, capable of storing water to see them through droughts. The Queensland bottle tree *(Brachychiton rupestris)* is usually sold like a bonsai, but when potted on and pruned, its branches elongate to make a graceful plant strung with large, elegant, five-lobed leaves. When it becomes too tall, simply lop it back by cutting the stem or stems to within two nodes (points where leaves are, or used to be) of the older growth at the base. This will reduce the plant from 2.5m (8ft) to 60cm (24in), but in good light it soon regrows. My own plant is just brushing the ceiling for the third time in 12 years. Other trees that grow fast include *Paquira aquatica*, which has a swollen trunk and wider, three- to five-lobed leaves. The jade tree *(Radermachera sinica)* can survive a similarly brutal growing and pruning regime.

Dracaena deremensis grows more slowly, but will reach impressive heights. There is also the option of training strong-growing climbers like philodendrons and grape ivy *(Cissus rhombifolia* 'Ellen Danica') against tall moss poles.

I travel a lot for work, yet like to keep a few plants. What will tolerate periods of neglect, or are there any watering devices that will help my plants survive?

Cacti and succulents enjoy a regular watering regime between spring and autumn, but a good soaking will last three weeks or so at a time. My personal favourites are the golden-ball cactus *(Echinocactus grusonii)*, which is endangered in the wild. It grows into a magnificent barrel cactus with golden spines. The powder-puff cactus (*Mammillaria bocasana* var. *rubriflora*) makes a colony of individual plants covered by silky, hair-like spines and freely produces lots of pink flowers in early summer. The old-man cactus *(Cephalocereus senilis)* is hilarious, being a tall columnar sort covered in long, wavy white hairs.

Among succulents, the partridge-breasted aloe *(Aloe variegata)* is handsome. Give this plant plenty of room in a large pot for the best results. But the ultimate in easy-care plants are the pebble plants *(Lithops)*. These mimic the pebbles to be found in their native Namibian desert regions and should not be watered at all between late autumn and early spring. You could go away for the entire winter and not be missed.

There are also watering devices that will help plants survive their owner's absences (see p. 178).

Pebble plants (*Lithops*)

Please recommend some scented house plants.

The classiest fragrant house plant is probably the gardenia (see p. 52), closely followed by stephanotis. Both have creamy white flowers offset by glossy green foliage. Jasmines (usually *J. polyanthum*) are hard to resist, but they are easier to grow in a cool, bright porch, green-house or conservatory and their perfume can be totally overpowering. For a fruity scent, the Canary Island broom *(Cytisus canariensis)* is delightful, with its small leaves and sprays of yellow, pea-like flowers in spring. It needs a cool, bright windowsill or can be grown under glass (minimum 3°C/38°F). Shear the growth back after flowering. Cherry pie *(Heliotrope)*, usually sold as bedding plants, can be potted on for a bright windowsill, where the purple flowers, redolent of cooked cherries, will delight every-one. Plants are best relegated to a frost-free greenhouse for the winter.

Gardenia jasminoides 'Fortuniana'

Aromatic foliage is largely the province of the pelargonium tribe, with neat, upright-growing *P. crispum* mouth-wateringly lemon-scented. The larger-leaved *P. graveolens* is rather sprawling for the house, while *P.* 'Mabel Grey' is almost over-whelmingly citrusy. Soft-leaved *P. tomentosum* smells of peppermint and neat *P. fragrans* of pine. All require a bright windowsill and will want a hard pruning in spring.

In summer my windowsill is sunny and hot. What will grow on it?

This sounds like a classic south-facing windowsill, where the sun will be too scorching for many plants. A range of cacti and succulents is the obvi-ous choice, but always pot them into attractive terracotta pots with match-ing saucers. Their roots will have more space and the effect will be more decorative. Look out for large-leaved, but low-growing *Kalanchoe thyrsi-flora*, whose leaves develop glowing red rims in good light. Cactus gardens in wide, shallow pans are great, with several plants grouped together and topped off with sand, gravels and stones.

Bougainvilleas love hot, sunny windowsills, where they will be encouraged to produce masses of their colourful bracts. Pretty, dwarf-growing kangaroo-paw plants *(Anigozanthos)* like the light, too, and will produce a succession of flowers shaped like small, furry kangaroo feet. The African shaving-brush plant *(Haemanthus albiflos)* makes a cluster of bulbs and responds to plenty of light by sending up lots of flower heads, which resemble white brushes dipped into yellow paint. Venus fly traps like the sun, too, and their traps often turn bright red in response.

The velvet plant *(Gynura aurantiaca)* will only retain its purple colour and grow strongly if kept in good sunlight. Grown for its foliage, the whole plant is covered by soft, purple hairs. Two more foliage plants, coleus *(Solenostemon)* and bloodleaf *(Iresine)* thrive on sunny windowsills. Plants need regular pinching out of their growing tips to maintain a bushy shape. Both can be propagated by cuttings when they become too large.

Please recommend the best orchids for a beginner to try indoors.

I used to recommend the moth orchid *(Phalaonopsis)*, which is certainly beautiful and lasts for months in bloom. Now, having tried a few, I consider orchids from what is known as the odontoglossum alliance as being the easiest to bring back into bloom every year. These are intergeneric hybrids resulting from species originally collected from the Andes, then hybridized extensively over the last 200 years. The results are the likes of *Odontoglossum, Odontioda, Odontocidium, Wilsonara* and *Vuylstekeara.*

I keep my plants in a north-facing position by the main door of the house, where they receive good but not harsh light, coolness in summer, plenty of fresh air (the door is open a lot during summer) and a minimum temperature of 10°C (50°F) in winter. Water them using rainwater when the pot becomes light in weight and add a half-strength liquid fertilizer every other watering. Only pot on when necessary, preferably during spring or autumn at times when there are no flowers but the plants are growing. Use an orchid compost based on bark chippings (see p. 67). The choice of flower size, colour and pattern is fantastic and it is tempting to buy more plants than you have room for.

Moth orchid *(Phalaonopsis)*

Which three house plants do you consider to be the most indestructible?

This is a dreadful question, because whichever plants I nominate, there will always be someone who has killed one. *Asparagus sprengeri* has fleshy tubers on its roots, which help it come back from the brink of death. I also consider *Begonia* x *corallina* 'Lucerna' to be tough. This cane begonia makes tall, straight stems, bears silver-spotted leaves and bunches of pink flowers. Finally, I think *Clivia miniata* is difficult to kill. On the runner-up list are the rosary plant *(Ceropegia woodii)*, money plant *(Crassula argentea)*, dinner-plate plant *(Pilea peperomioides)*, Swiss cheese plant *(Monstera deliciosa)* and rubber plant *(Ficus elastica)*.

As a persistent plant abuser, I find *Billbergia nutans*, aspidistras and most cacti pretty durable!

I live in a small flat, but would like to keep a number of different plants. Apart from African violets, which plants take up little space?

From the same family as African violets are the miniature sinningias, no more than 5cm (2in) tall, such as *S.* 'Pink Petite', lilac-blue *S.* 'Dollbaby' and others with *S. pusilla* in their parentage. They make small mounds of soft, hairy leaves above which rise the stalks of tubular flowers, which under ideal conditions (similar to those needed by African violets) can bloom all year. If you like hot-water plants *(Achimenes)*, then try eucodonias. E. 'Naomi', for instance, is started by planting the tubers in spring, just as for achimenes. The resulting plants have beautifully soft leaves and lilac flowers and are under 8cm (3in) tall. The plants die back for winter. A little larger is *Streptocarpus saxorum*. Unlike most Cape primroses, this is a stem-forming type and bears many small, rounded succulent leaves and masses of pretty blue flowers held out on fine stalks.

Pepper elders *(Peperomias)* tend to be on the small side. *P. caperata* is neat, with its deep-green crinkly leaves. Red stems bearing narrow spikes of tiny cream flowers poke through the foliage. The watermelon type *(P. argyreia)* is pretty, too. These plants look good growing as a pair in matching terracotta pots. The panamiga *(Pilea involucrata)*, from the nettle family (though it does not sting), is striking, with its bright-green and bronze, quilted leaves making low mounds over the pot. And although most pelargoniums grow large, there are dwarf and miniature varieties that fit neatly onto sunny windowsills. These are usually available only from specialist nurseries.

I would like my bathroom to look like a jungle. Which plants should I grow?

Bathrooms are usually good places for plants, because they tend to be warm and humid. Even if nobody is in the bath or shower, residual moisture lingers and rises from towels drying over radiators. Before the pleasurable task of deciding which plants to choose, give some thought as to how they will be arranged. I am not straying into the realms of DIY, but an attractive metal trough along a window bottom, shelves and plinths will avoid a cluttered look. Unless you are a fastidious cleaner, avoid plants that drop bits, which rules out a lot of flowering types.

Choose the plants according to their size, starting with large specimens. I will give you three to whet your appetite. A majestic Boston fern *(Nephrolepis exaltata)* will look lovely with its long fronds draped over a plinth or pedestal. Keep it well away from dry air, never allow the roots to dry out and feed regularly for healthy plants, but be aware that large plants reach a spread of 90cm (36in). For massive leaves, the fiddle-leaf fig *(Ficus lyrata)* is unbeatable and grows up on a good straight stem. And bananas are fun, especially those like *Musa* 'Purple Rain' with its dark leaves.

Now add some medium-sized plants, with exciting foliage colours. A red, orange, green and yellow-leaved croton *(Codiaeum)*, a stripy-leaved zebra plant (*Aphelandra squarrosa* 'Dania') and a tall, white-flowered peace lily *(Spathiphyllum)* will have impact. To stand on windowsills, shelves or in window boxes, use draping, silvery-leaved goosefoot plant (*Syngonium* 'White Butterfly'), long-leaved *Stromanthe sanguinea* 'Stripestar', silvery-patterned aluminium plant *(Pilea cadierei)* and long-lasting moth orchids *(Phalaeonopsis)*. If these all stay healthy, have a go with *Alocasia* x *amazonica*, which bears the most extraordinarily heart-shaped leaves with scalloped edges and veins picked out in white. This will only grow where there is stable warmth and high humidity. For a final touch, fix to the wall a staghorn fern growing on a slab of cork bark and hang skeins of Spanish moss *(Tillandsia usneoides)* from hooks in the ceiling.

I am quite style-conscious and would like to know how to use house plants without upsetting my colour schemes and the simplicity of my rooms.

To use plants without offending your simple tastes will require some rules. The easiest is to stick to green leaves and white, or perhaps cream, flowers. Use only plain terracotta pots, or stand all pots inside a variety of glazed white containers. Repetition also works well, so that instead of buying one white *Begonia elatior*, you buy three. White azaleas, moth orchids *(Phalaeonopsis)*, gardenias, miniature roses, hydrangeas, poinsettias, stephanotis, cyclamen, African violets and a lovely plant called *Clerodendron wallichii*, which I am sure we will be seeing more of with its dangling white flowers, will all fit the bill. Look out for foliage plants with green and white leaves, such as dumb cane (*Dieffenbachia* 'carina'), variegated Swiss cheese plant (*Monstera deliciosa* 'Variegata'), the trailing succulent *Sedum sieboldii* 'Mediovariegatum' and the cream-flecked polka-dot plant *(Hypoestes)*. There are many more, and you will soon have the indoor equivalent of a white border.

Being so style-conscious, it will be best to harden up or throw away those plants that are past their best, replacing them with new ones. This may seem extravagant, but many pot plants are reasonably priced and, with even basic care, will last much longer than a bunch of flowers. Otherwise you will need a resuscitation room, where plants can be nursed back to health without blotting the interior landscape.

I need a plant with personality to give to a friend for her office.

The gout plant or Guatemalan rhubarb *(Jatropha podagrica)* will certainly stand out from the ranks of usual office plantings. A strange number, this succulent grows from a swollen, woody base, sending up woody stems terminating in somewhat fig-shaped, thin leaves. Healthy plants produce bunches of small red flowers on long stalks virtually throughout the year. Good light is needed, but this jatropha can tolerate some dry air and likes warm temperatures. Plants that feel the cold in winter sometimes go dormant, dropping all their leaves and looking even more bizarre.

Alternatively, the ponytail palm *(Beaucarnea recurvata)*, with its woody stems and tufts of narrow leaves, has great presence. And bulrush *(Isolepis cernua)* will amaze your friend, with its mop of cylindrical, thread-like stems, which produce tiny flowers at the tips, so that it resembles a fibre-optic lamp. If these are too odd-looking, try the nearly black-leaved *Oxalis purpurea*, whose leaves fold up for the night and which produces pretty, pale-pink flowers in good light.

I would like to grow some different palms. I already have the parlour palm.

For many years the parlour palm *(Chamaedorea elegans)* and larger Kentia palms *(Howea)* were all that was readily available. Now the range is far wider, although some are too wide and stiff to suit normal rooms. My favourite small palm is the lady palm *(Rhapis excelsa)*, whose fan-shaped leaves are not hard or spiky, but usually end in blunt tips. These can grow quite tall, although progress is slow indoors. The beautiful yellow variegated version, *R. e.* 'Zuikonishiki', rarely exceeds 60cm (24in). The fishtail palm *(Caryota mitis)*, whose leaflets resemble the ragged tails of exotic goldfish, is slightly more difficult to grow, because it needs consistent warmth (above 13°C/55°F) and greater humidity.

I was given a bowl containing five mixed house plants, three of which died and two of which I have removed and potted separately. I would like to replant the bowl, which is 30cm (12in) in diameter and will stand in the light from an east-facing window.

Bowls are a good idea because plants benefit from the moisture being given off by their leaf surfaces and from the moist compost around them. Before repotting, empty the container thoroughly, wash it out, let it dry and then spread a layer of expanded clay pebbles or chunks of polystyrene at least 2.5cm (1in) deep in the base. When choosing new plants, remember that they must all like similar conditions of light, watering, and so on. One possible combination might include a maidenhair fern *(Adiantum)* and a dumb cane *(Dieffenbachia)* as the taller plants. Around them arrange an aluminium plant *(Pilea cadierei)*, a dark-green, glossy button fern *(Pellaea rotundifolia)* and a low-growing prayer plant *(Maranta)*, or leave space for a flowering plant, which can vary according to season. This could be a small red-hot cat's tail *(Acalypha hispida)*, with long red tassels of flowers, a Madagascan periwinkle *(Catharanthus roseus)*, a small gardenia, or anything else that takes your fancy. The main plants can be expected to last for at least two years before the bowl will need remaking.

I would like a trailing plant for a high shelf on my kitchen unit. The light in the kitchen is good.

The first plant that springs to mind is the succulent rosary vine *(Ceropegia linearis* subsp. *woodii)* from South Africa, whose trailing pinkish stems will reach great lengths, strung with small, silvered, heart-shaped leaves. This gem is easy to grow and makes small, but exquisitely structured, tubular flowers topped by fuzzy maroon crowns. Another succulent, the string-of-beads *(Senecio rowleyanus)*, from south-west Africa, is of bizarre appearance. Long, slender stems support spherical succulent leaves. Then there is the lipstick vine *(Aeschynanthus* 'Mona Lisa'), which will love the warm, humid kitchen conditions and good but not direct light. The tumbling stems of foliage are handsome, but clusters of maroon calyces and red, tubular flowers are the real attraction. It is obviously unwise to site any plants near to the surfaces where food is prepared, as dead leaves and so on will fall periodically from even the best-behaved plants.

I am a junior school teacher. What plants could I grow in the classroom that would be of interest to the children, as well as provide them with learning props?

The sensitive plant *(Mimosa pudica)* is a lively choice, because it moves. Look out for plants during early summer or raise them from seed. They are somewhat small and wispy, so I usually grow three to one pot. Touch the leaflets and they fold together neatly, but tap the whole plant and the leaflets close, the leaves bend downwards and the whole plant seems to be folding up. One can only assume this is a defence mechanism against grazing animals, and the plant will recover and stand upright again after half an hour or so. Pompons of pink flowers are produced towards the end of summer and should be at their best for the start of the autumn term.

Tradescantias are easy to grow, yield plenty of cuttings material and the cuttings root easily in water. When the roots have developed it is easy to see the root hairs, which are so vital to a plant for the take-up of water. And children are unfailingly interested in Venus fly traps, pitcher plants, sundews and other carnivorous plants, which are easy to keep standing in rainwater on a bright windowsill. I would also think about growing plants from different climates. Jungle plants could be arranged against a jungle-painted backdrop, cacti and succulents against a barren, desert landscape. There are plenty of points to make about how plants have adapted to their environment.

BG

My first office was open-plan. We decided to break up the space organically and so we sowed common morning glory *(Ipomoea purpurea)* in plastic coffee cups. We then positioned them between our drawing boards and trained them up strings that we fixed to the ceiling. They rapidly formed a vibrant, see-through screen, twining up the strings with their hairy stems and purple-blue flowers.

I belong to a local flower club and would like to grow house plants whose leaves I can use for my exotic flower arrangements. What would you suggest, and how can I succeed with them?

I am no floral artist, but I can imagine which leaves would be useful. There are a number of aroids (plants in the family Araceae) that can be grown from spring-planted rhizomes. One of the best and easiest is the golden arum or golden calla *(Zantedeschia elliottiana)*. Plant the rhizome about 8cm (3in) deep in a 15cm (6in) pot, water in, then water only when the compost surface has dried out; keep it warm and bright and shoots will soon appear. The heart-shaped leaves, capable of reaching 30cm (12in) long,

Pitcher plants
(*Sarracenia
leucophylla*)

are spotted with silver and, when the plants are well established (this may take another year), lovely yellow spathes are produced. Plants die back in winter and should be kept dry and frost-free until spring.

The large, fantastically marked, arrow-shaped leaves of tuberous angel wings *(Caladium)* seem fragile, but would probably last a few days in water. They need similar treatment, but must have a minimum over-wintering temperature of 13°C (55°F) when dormant. And a good stock of Swiss cheese plant *(Monstera deliciosa)* and philodendrons should yield a range of large, exotic leaves. Pot the plants on, feed regularly and place in adequate light to promote plenty of growth. Leaves can be removed individually from certain areas of stem, which can then be pruned off when bare. New stems will replace them.

Marantas and calatheas, particularly large-leaved sorts like cathedral windows *(C. makoyana)*, whose leaves have the effect of stained glass, will look good as long as their leaves remain unblemished by dry air. The foxtail fern *(Asparagus densiflorus* 'Myersii') yields those marvellous tail-like fronds of leaves, is simple to grow and regenerates well.

Caladium bicolor

Are there any plants, other than cacti and succulents, that do not object to hot, dry air?

Where hot, dry conditions prevail, we tend to look to plants that originate from arid regions and have adapted ways of surviving heat and dryness.

Leaves tend to be small and more needle-like, to reduce moisture loss over their surface area; sometimes they are covered with dense hairs. Roots might be succulent, as in the asparagus tribe. It is difficult to find lush, jungle-like plants that can tolerate hot, dry air, because these have evolved to produce leaves with large surface areas to absorb as much light as possible in shady, moist areas.

My first choice is the white velvet plant *(Tradescantia sillamontana)* from northern Mexico, whose grey-green leaves are covered by dense silky hairs. This silvery appearance contrasts brilliantly with magenta flowers. The pepper elders *(Peperomias)* are a little bit succulent, but a collection of these would tolerate some heat and dryness, although they may become a little distressed if placed in scorching hot sun. *P. obtusifolia* 'Variegata' has thick, oval leaves patterned with yellow and various shades of green. Bronze-leaved *P. caperata* 'Luna Red' is distinctive, with its neat, puckered leaves, which will root if cut off with the stalk attached and inserted into cuttings compost. A pineapple grown from a pineapple top is resilient and should grow well in warmth and good light. Miniature pomegranate *(Punica granatum)* and bougainvillea will revel in hot, dry air. Mother-in-law's tongue *(Sansevieria trifasciata* 'Laurentii') prefers dryness to moisture; it is tough, but hates to be wet at the roots.

I have read that house plants can be beneficial to health. Are there any that are particularly good at improving the environment?

I have always believed that plants are good for the spirits and I always feel happier working in a roomful of plants (especially ones I know) than in one that is barren. This may sound strange, but I never feel lonely with my plants around me. This general feel-good factor has now been taken a step further and it is generally thought that plants make indoor environments healthier. The premise is that interiors are becoming more sealed, in attempts to conserve fuel. Rooms are also more likely to be stuffed with furnishings and with synthetic materials that give off gases. The result is a concern that chemical vapours might become trapped inside buildings and affect our health.

Research conducted at NASA (the National Aeronautics and Space Administration) in the USA to cope with pollution in the Skylab spacecraft found that plants could purify the air. In simple terms, the pollutants enter the leaves and biodegrade in the compost. Water vapour is given off by the leaves to help raise humidity, which is of benefit to us, since most rooms are too dry. The rubber plant, ivy, pygmy date palm *(Phoenix roebelenii)*, Boston fern and gerbera were noted as being particularly good at cleaning the air.

I would like to grow some herbs on my warm, sunny kitchen windowsill. Which would be the best ones to start me off?

Ordinary culinary herbs like thyme, sage and rosemary do not grow well indoors in the long term, because it is too warm and there is not enough air circulation around the plants. If you can, grow the herbs in a window box or in pots outside on the window ledge. If there is no ledge, put up a couple of brackets for a window box.

For those with no garden and not even the prospect of a window box, the kitchen is better than having no fresh herbs at all. Pots of herbs from the supermarket are usually better value than cut fresh herbs, because they last longer. For the best results, grow herbs singly or just a few to a pot, because there is then better air movement and less chance of rotting. Congested plants can be potted on into a compost with added grit or sharp sand. Use clay pots whenever possible and do not overwater. Try any culinary herb, including basil, chives, parsley and mint. Once established, they can be cropped until there is virtually nothing left of them, then replaced with some more.

I need the colour of house plants most during the winter, when the garden is cold and muddy, many outdoor plants are asleep and daylight hours are few. What are the best plants for brightening up mid-winter?

I love cyclamen, which now come in several sizes, of which the middle-sized are my favourites. They seem just the right scale for small window-sills and carry such jewel-like, usually perfumed flowers above patterned foliage. Remember that they need a cool, bright growing position in order to thrive. Azaleas are also hard to resist, as long as you are prepared to water them frequently with rainwater. South African heathers are usually sold during the winter, but I class these along with azaleas, as they have me scurrying back and forth to the rain butt.

Far easier are the flaming Katies (cultivars of *Kalanchoe blossfeldiana*). These have succulent leaves and many heads of four-petalled, long-lasting flowers in red, pink, orange, yellow or white. Cheap to buy, they look good when grouped together for a larger display. Potted narcissus are great in late winter as a reminder that spring is on the way, but really need a cool, bright place to stand a chance of lasting longer than a bunch of flowers. Primroses are cheap and cheerful, but last well in good light. White moth orchids are a personal favourite and I once treated myself to three *Phalaonopsis amabilis* during early winter, which I plunged into pebbles in a large container. I gave them small quantities of rainwater every so often, with a half-strength liquid fertilizer roughly every other watering. They were still flowering nine months later.

My daughter is shortly to depart for university and wants some plants for her room. What would look good, be interesting and difficult to kill?

Had you asked me this about 20 years ago I would probably have said a yucca, but I never really liked indoor yuccas, even when they were fashionable. Instead, try a pale-leaved dracaena, such as *D. fragrans* 'Massangeana', whose broad leaves, striped irregularly with yellow down the centre, are softer than those of a yucca. The false castor-oil plant *(Fatsia japonica)* is sometimes grown outside, but also makes a splendid indoor specimen plant that is fairly difficult to kill. This can tolerate shade and fluctuating temperatures, draughts and picks up well if allowed to dry out. Moreover, its large, shiny lobed leaves are easy to wipe clean with a damp cloth, and make great silhouettes against plain walls.

Smaller and softer, the piggyback plant *(Tolmiea menziesii* 'Taff's Gold') will make a mound of softly hairy, variegated leaves. When they reach maturity, a young plant sprouts where the leaf meets its stalk and can be used to start off new plants. And the money tree *(Crassula argentea)* is meant to bring good fortune to those who rub its leaves, which bodes well for the student loan.

PLANTS UNDER GLASS

A glass porch or even a small lean-to attached to the house opens up huge possibilities for plant growing. Whatever is currently cluttering up such a space, turf it out and plan a magnificent display of plants. My own north-facing porch is only small, yet it is filled with flower and foliage all year round and makes an attractive entrance to the house.

When my new conservatory was finished I moved a lot of my house plants into it. Their leaves have turned yellow, look miserable and have not created the look I want.

The great advantage of owning a conservatory is that it widens the field of plants that you can grow. In general, house plants can cope with shade and warm temperatures, but a conservatory is usually brighter and cooler, which benefits a lot of flowering plants that would pine in the house and refuse to flower. My guess is that the house plants found the conservatory too bright and the nights too cool, which explains their yellow leaves.

Return the miserable house plants to the house, where they belong, and choose some exciting conservatory plants to capitalize on the conditions you have. Look at larger specimens first and, assuming that a winter minimum of 4°C (40°F) can be maintained, the Brazilian spider flower *(Tibouchina urvilleana)* is a strong contender. The soft leaves are lovely in themselves, but from mid- to late summer they are joined by large purple flowers with spider-like stamens. The Kahili ginger lily *(Hedychium gardnerianum)* produces its new shoots in late spring after a winter's rest. These grow to 1.5m (5ft) high and terminate in a column of perfumed yellow and orange flowers by the autumn. The balm mint bush *(Prostanthera melissifolia)* from Australia will be covered by small violet flowers in spring, while the Australian fuchsia *(Correa backhouseana)* opens its creamy bell-shaped flowers in winter. And citrus of all kinds look great. Add a few scented climbers, such as *Jasminum polyanthum,* followed by star jasmine *(Trachelospermum jasminoides)* and the smaller Regal Pelargonium 'Lord Bute' with its dark-purple blooms, plus miniature roses and gerberas.

My conservatory is like a furnace in summer, but I cannot afford to heat it much during winter. What will grow there?

This is a common problem, usually arising from a disinclination on the owner's part to leave vents and conservatory doors open when they are out. An unventilated and unshaded conservatory will become so furnace-like, especially if it is south- or west-facing, that little or nothing will grow in it. Even cacti and succulents suffer, becoming long, drawn and wizened by the heat. Fabrics will fade and plastics turn brittle in the heat. The solution requires some lateral thinking.

My advice is to grow nothing in the conservatory during summer. Keep a selection of potted plants outside and bring them in during the autumn, when temperatures are cooler. Ventilation is still needed in autumn and winter, but can be managed by automatic vent-openers. Your selection of plants should be of winter interest and, for an unheated conservatory, could include the following specimens. Camellias are ideal, because their early flowers will not be blighted by frost under glass, while the pink flowers of evergreen *Daphne odora* are highly scented. Bamboos *(Phyllostachys aureosulcata* 'Spectabilis' and *P. nigra)* can be brought in and will avoid the worst wind damage. Mimosa *(Acacia baileyana)* does well in a pot and will stay compact if pruned back after flowering each year. For dramatic foliage, grow the false castor-oil plant *(Fatsia japonica).* Large-leaved Persian ivy *(Hedera colchica* 'Dentata Variegata') will climb against a moss pole, and for aromatic leaves, choose myrtle. Imagine sitting among this lot on a sunny but cold winter's day when it is freezing outside, yet warm and comfortable under glass.

Please, please try guavas, and especially the strawberry guava. They are thirsty but ideal, and productive, too.

What can I grow in an unheated, north-facing porch?

Porches are usually (though not reliably) frost-free because they are protected by the house and warmed by the occasional blast of hot air as the door opens. There are lots of lovely plants to try. Despite my north-facing aspect, I grow the variegated New Zealand Christmas tree (*Metrosideros kermadecensis* 'Variegatus'), mainly for its foliage, though brilliant red flowers (mostly stamens) are produced in summer. Cyclamen will be happy here and so will the dainty succulent known as bride-and-groom (*Aichryson* x *domesticum* 'Variegatum'). The small paddle-shaped leaves edged with (and sometimes entirely) cream are arranged into rosettes on the stems, so that the whole plant looks like a miniature tree.

None of these plants will appreciate being frosted, so bring them into the house during seriously cold spells. Ventilate during mild winter days and water carefully, during the mornings, so that excess water has time to dry out before night-time. Adding flowering plants for summer is easy. These could include Cape primrose *(Streptocarpus)* and primulas.

How can I make the best use of my greenhouse so that it will be both productive and attractive throughout the year? I can only afford to heat it for short periods during the early spring.

The greenhouse, even though unheated, will be invaluable for over-wintering slightly tender plants like Indian shot *(Canna)* that are dormant in their pots, tender pittosporums, hardy banana *(Musa basjoo)*, holly fern *(Cyrtomium falcatum)* and large-sized agaves (these are more frost-resistant than smaller, younger specimens). Fix bubble-plastic insulation to the inside to keep the frost out, but always leave provision for ventilation, which is just as vital during winter as it is in summer. By adding some of the plants recommended above for unheated conservatories, the winter display can be made attractive. I suggest housing them partly on the staging, but with some standing on a bed running down one side.

In spring, turn the heat on and use a heated propagator to germinate seeds of early vegetable crops, bedding plants and summer-flowering glasshouse plants, moving them into the greenhouse, then pricking them out and growing them on. By mid-spring the bubble-plastic will need to come off and a light shading spray be applied to the outside of the greenhouse. Having experimented with several methods, I think application is easiest through a pressure sprayer fitted with a lance. The vegetables and bedding plants can be hardened off and planted outside in late spring. At the same time the winter residents can be moved out when all danger of frost has passed.

This will leave room inside for tomatoes and perhaps sweet peppers or aubergines. On the staging make displays of seed-raised Barberton daisy

(Gerbera), Persian violet (Exacum affine) and climbing *Mina lobata*. Fuchsias can be bought in as young plants and grown on for the summer. Summer-flowering bulbs and tubers planted in spring will give rise to the pineapple bulb *(Eucomis bicolor)*, blood lily *(Scadoxus multiflorus)* and tuberous begonias.

When the weather begins to turn cold in autumn, the summer plants can be thrown away, or (in the case of the bulbs and tubers) stored dry and frost-free in a shed, and the greenhouse thoroughly cleaned inside and out. Fix the bubble-plastic up, move the winter residents back in and the cycle can repeat itself, but with different plants grown each summer for variation.

I am planning a greenhouse and would like your thoughts on choosing, siting and equipment.

Always buy the largest greenhouse you can, because there will never be enough space in it. The next consideration is: wood or aluminium? Wood is usually prettier and installations such as bubble-plastic are easier to fix up, but maintenance tends to be more time-consuming. Aluminium can look utilitarian, but there are some attractive (though expensive) coloured finishes available. My old aluminium greenhouse was no beauty, but it was spacious and, once I had planted around it, it melted into its landscape. I carried out absolutely no maintenance (other than oiling the ventilation screws) for a good 10 years.

Orientation is usually dictated by the only site available, but, if there is a choice, everyone seems to disagree about which is best. This is probably a good sign and means that it really is not that important, as long as the greenhouse is not shaded by trees and buildings. For the record, I prefer the ridge to run east–west, so that the roof has a north- and a south-facing side.

The customer is usually in charge of installing the base and this requires some thought. A concrete base is practical and clean, but plan gaps for any beds that are needed. For at least the first few years, crops can be grown directly into soil along one side. However, you have to be prepared for a build-up of diseases that may one day prevent the growing of tomatoes year after year. My last greenhouse was 3 x 6m (10 x 20ft). I left a bed of soil right across the back, so that I could plant large subjects (jasmine, passion flower, Canary island broom) directly into the soil. Alternatively, a brick base and a flag path down the middle could be sufficient. This is the time to think of running services (water and electricity) to the greenhouse via an underground conduit. To have sockets for propagating cases and heaters and an electric light is invaluable. I always employ an electrician and a plumber to sort these out for me.

When ordering the greenhouse, check exactly how many and what kinds of vents are supplied. If necessary, ask for extra vents, or order louvres for the sides. Adequate side and top ventilation means that the air will circulate, heat up, rise and leave effectively. Personally I do not bother with automatic vent-openers. Most will not open at temperatures low enough for my liking and are difficult to override. As my greenhouses are usually run at a winter minimum of 4°C (40°F), I like to ventilate really well during the winter, but then I am usually on hand to make alterations throughout the day. Automation is useful for those who are away a lot.

Necessary equipment can be as simple as a heater of some sort (electric, paraffin or gas), a maximum/minimum thermometer to check the efficiency of heating and ventilation, a propagating case (nice to have) and a large and small watering can fitted with roses. The roof is a valuable source of rainwater for plants that need and prefer it, so fix up one or two water butts to fill from the gutters.

I grew my bird of paradise from seed seven years ago and I am still waiting for it to bloom. It lives in my conservatory in a 17cm (7in) pot and I am loath to pot it on, because I read that these plants flower better when pot-bound.

Well, they say a little knowledge is a dangerous thing! The plant might, eventually, flower better if pot-bound, but it needs to reach a good size first. To do this its roots need space and the plant definitely does need potting on. I would say that a bird of paradise (*Strelitzia reginae*) in an average conservatory would need to occupy a 45cm (18in) pot in order to flower well over a long period. So pot on during the next spring/summer growing period to a 25cm (10in) pot, then when this is full of roots, pot on again to the 45cm (18in) pot. Leave room in the top for expansion, because over several years root growth forces the plant higher, making watering difficult.

Plants in large pots need enough water at one time to reach all the roots. Make sure that the saucer is a generous size, otherwise there will be a disinclination to give the plant enough and the lower roots will suffer. Once established in its pot (after six weeks or so), the plant can be given general-purpose liquid fertilizer every two weeks during the summer. In warm conservatories (minimum 10°C/50°F) it is worth giving a half-strength feed during the winter, too.

Bird of paradise (*Strelitzia reginae*)

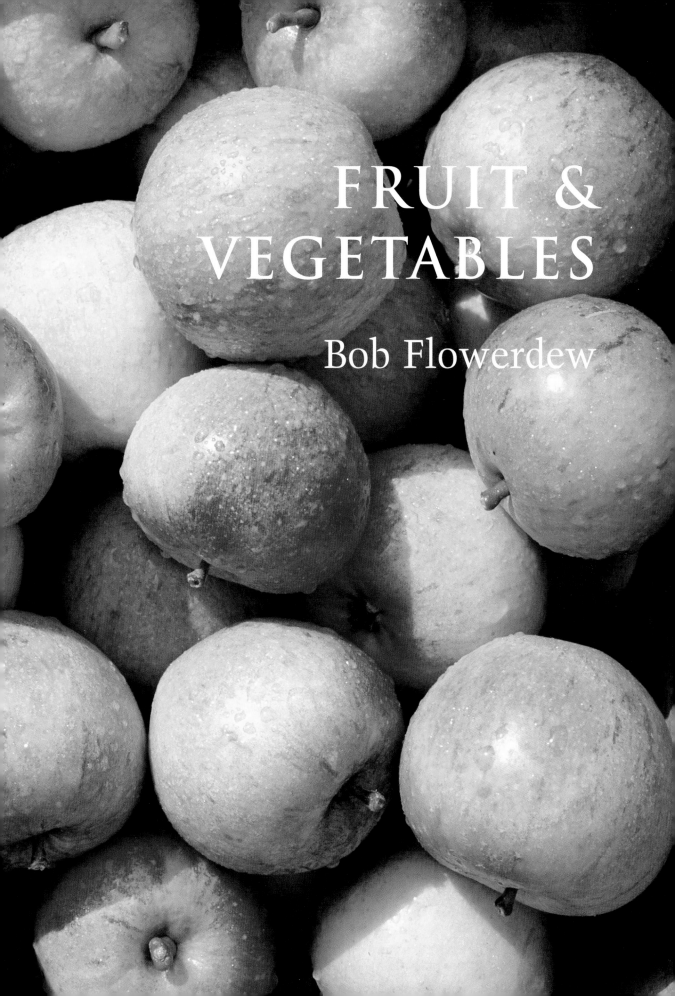

FRUIT &
VEGETABLES

Bob Flowerdew

Born a farmer's son, I always loved the natural world and would rather be outside if not in a library. I moved to this plot of just under an acre eighteen years ago and commenced growing every fruit and vegetable possible, to the highest organic standards and solely for home consumption. Likewise I keep chickens, ducks, geese and bees and several lazy cats. I wished to prove that all this could be done aesthetically and single-handedly, in one's spare time – this I achieved at great cost to my back and my social life! I started a consultancy and landscape gardening service, ran evening classes, taught at the local agricultural college, gave talks (still listed in the Royal Horticultural Society's Register of Speakers), published articles and wrote *The Companion Garden*, *Bob Flowerdew's Complete Book of Companion Gardening*, *The Organic Gardener*, *Bob Flowerdew's Complete Fruit Book* and most recently, *Bob Flowerdew's Organic Bible*. In addition to regular appearances as the organic fruit and vegetable expert for BBC *Gardeners' World*, my garden and methods have been featured on *Muck & Magic*, *Grow Your Own Greens* and *Gardeners' Gardens*. Nearly a decade ago I was asked to join the BBC Radio 4's *Gardeners' Question Time* panel as a guest and became part of their regular team where I concentrate on fruits, vegetables, organic methods and scented plants. In addition, I have been a question setter for BBC *Mastermind*, a literary critic for Radio 4's *A Good Read* and perform my own one man theatre show.

I Like gardening, scented plants, good food, cats, conversation, reading, etymology, outrageous ideas, public speaking, beautiful women, scuba diving and whinging on about the state of things.

I Dislike bad and bland food, over-done political correctness, anti-sexists and people whinging on about the state of things.

FRUIT

Which fruits have the fewest maintenance and watering requirements?

The more you want maximum yields of perfect fruits, the harder you have to work and the more water is required. If you want trained forms, then you make much more work for yourself than leaving them to grow naturally, but you get much better quality fruits and more variety in the same space. Initially all the different fruit trees and bushes require about the same amount of work to plant them – they all need watering and the weeds controlling under them for the first year – but after that they vary. Trees need staking for that first year, and those on dwarfing stocks will always need stakes to stop them snapping off at the grafting point. Most trees can be left unpruned to little disadvantage, but all the trained forms, such as espaliers, need to be tied onto frames and given regular careful pruning. They almost all benefit from thinning the fruits to prevent overcropping and biennial bearing, but unless trained will get too big to enable this.

Although they may all get attacks from pests or diseases, tree fruits are generally so productive that few problems need much attention. In order of reliable cropping, for least work, I rank apples first, then quinces, plums, pears, hazel nuts and mulberries, though these last get big! Soft bush fruits and vine fruits are even more reliable than tree fruits, but are much more prone to bird damage. Indeed, if you want any at all you need netting, or better still a cage – which is quite an expense and effort to make initially, though no regular attention is needed unless you live in a snowfall area, when you need to remove the net each winter.

Almost all the soft fruits need pruning every year, and if they are trained shapes they will need supports and tying in each year as well, but this is light work done safely at ground level. No thinning is necessary for most soft fruits, though gooseberries and grapes benefit from it. Red-, white- and blackcurrants are without doubt the least work for your effort; raspberries come next; and then the hybrid josta berry.

Are any fruits bird-resistant?

Birds will eat almost all fruits – after all, they are the rightful owners – although they do have their preferences. Cherries, redcurrants, tayberries and strawberries are great favourites; indeed, it is almost worth planting these as sacrificial crops so that the stuffed birds have no room for other fruits! Raspberries, loganberries and blackcurrants soon disappear, but blackberries are so productive that the birds rarely manage to eat the majority. All ripe tree fruits are eaten, but often the unusual ones, such as peaches, are not spotted for several years, then one year all the birds find out about them. Quinces are so hard that the birds leave them until they soften with the frosts. Medlars are likewise rarely eaten until rotten, but are barely worth growing anyway.

Some of the unusually coloured fruits last longer while the birds wait for them to ripen. Thus whitecurrants outlast red, and the delicious Japanese wineberry, which resembles a half-ripe blackberry, can stay almost unscathed. Alpine strawberries are often ignored, as is the miserable strawberry spinach, *Chenopodium capitatum*, which is disliked by the birds but not worth eating anyway. A bird bath provides the birds with water and reduces theft considerably, as they eat fruit for its moisture and not so much for food, as fruit is rather low in calories for bird metabolism.

Which fruits need pollination partners?

Not only must a fruit be compatible with its partner, but both need to be in flower at the same time. Often one will pollinate another but not be pollinated in turn, and some are just very choosy about who they want to mate with. Fortunately, many modern fruit varieties have been developed so that they do not need partners, but even so almost all fruits crop more heavily or give better quality fruits when given pollination partners, even those that are allegedly self-fertile. For example, the Conference pear frequently sets banana-shaped fruits on its own, but better pear-shaped fruits when cross-pollinated. Cherries are notoriously difficult, but the newer varieties are less so and on modern dwarfing stocks it is possible to fit in a pair where before only one would go. Pears are also finicky and many need a nearby partner. Most apples are awkward and need partners, but fortunately there are so many apple trees about that we can usually get away without planting partners ourselves.

When buying any fruit tree ask the nursery staff which of their other trees are suitable partners to go with it, or of course with a tree that you have already. Do go and cross-check in a reference book for that fruit before planting – just in case. If you have an unknown tree to pollinate, then try the wild form as they tend to be good pollinators. Almost all the soft fruits are much easier, as they are mostly self-fertile, but again a mixed group always crops more heavily than the same number of just one variety on its own.

How do I choose the right rootstocks, spacing and staking?

In theory you choose the right rootstock to suit the soil, site, micro-climate, variety and form of training required for your fruit tree or bush. In practice you rarely get much choice of rootstock on anything but apples; almost everything else is only offered on the most dwarfing rootstocks, to make small trees or bushes, or on a stronger rootstock for a bigger or standard tree. Even with apples, unless you go to a specialist you are lucky to find more than a couple of different rootstocks, varying marginally according to their vigour. It doesn't matter that much anyway, as in most cases the best rootstock is the more dwarfing one, as then the trees grow relatively compact and can be fitted into the smaller spaces of today's gardens.

The smallest rootstocks offer the possibility of growing more varieties. Thus a triple row of apple cordons can include dozens of different sorts in the space taken by just one or two standard trees – which can't even be picked as they get so tall. Of course you have to prune and tie in if you want cordon or other trained forms, such as espaliers. Fruit trees left relatively untrained and unpruned on dwarfing stocks just make smaller trees, the only problems being their need for staking all their lives and that, being so low-growing, it is hard to get anything underneath them.

Obviously you have to give the stronger-growing varieties and rootstocks more space, but almost all of us never give trees or bushes enough space, regardless of the rootstock, soil type or micro-climate. It is of paramount importance to give all plants more space, rather than cramp them.

Overcrowding makes for more work, poorer quality and less yield! Where the soil is richer or moister you need to give them more space to grow into, as they will grow bigger faster; where the site is poor or dry, then they will need more space to get their sustenance from! Ask your prospective supplier what distance they recommend for their rootstocks on your type of soil for the sort of tree you desire; if they can't give you a convincing answer, then don't trust their stock and go elsewhere. Moreover, whatever planting distances any of them tell you, take their maximum and add a quarter. It will pay dividends in the long run, with better growth; and in the short term you won't buy so many plants.

Trees on dwarfing stocks need staking all their lives, while standard trees only need support in the first year or so, but otherwise their care is the same. Most bush fruits need no staking, but do need wires or canes if they are to be trained to any form. Brambles and vines are invariably grown on wires but can be trained up strong stakes instead.

From which fruiting plants can I propagate my own replacements?

Almost all fruits can be grown from their seeds, but few ever produce anything like the parent, and they will take a long time to do so compared to taking a cutting or an offset. However, I have found that seedling alpine strawberries, Japanese wineberries, raspberries and black- and redcurrants almost always give useful specimens. All soft fruits can be very easily propagated by cuttings – currants and grapes especially so – while most of the brambles freely root their cane tips in autumn; likewise, raspberries and strawberries are soon increased by runners. However it is not wise to propagate *old* stocks of strawberries, raspberries or blackcurrants, as these three pick up virus diseases that severely hamper their performance; they are best bought in afresh, and repropagated every few years *before* they degenerate. Very few tree fruits can be grown from cuttings, though some antique apple varieties will root, but then they tend to grow too large for most gardens as they are not controlled by a dwarfing rootstock. You will probably succeed with cuttings from mulberries, quinces and citrus trees.

Which fruits can I grow in containers?

Almost all fruits can be grown in containers, but they take infinitely more time and effort than when grown in the ground and you have to ask if it's worth the effort. Watering becomes crucial, cold-weather protection for the roots is necessary and pests seem to be more of a problem when the plants are confined to containers. However, the advantages are terrific: you can get many more plants into the same space and, as they are movable, they can go into a greenhouse or similar for protection from the weather or birds during critical periods.

I strongly recommend that grapevines and figs are grown in containers; they come inside for an early frost-free start, go out when the weather warms, to return when the fruit ripens and then go out again for the winter. All the moving around is more than made up for in the quality and earliness of the crops. Likewise for peaches, cherries, apricots and nectarines, which are well suited to the same regime. Strawberries are easy and a few earlies in pots in a greenhouse are a real treat, but don't overplant patio containers; each strawberry plant in the ground needs at least 1sq m (1sq yd), so even a dustbin only just makes a decent-sized pot for one plant – try it and see how it does!

Are there any good companion plants for fruits?

There is less known about companion plants for fruit trees and bushes than for vegetables. However, it is well accredited that orchards with clover, alfalfa and other leguminous plants growing in the grass sward do better than those with grass on its own or bare soil. Pears, however, are exceptionally unhappy with grass growing underneath them and prefer to be mulched. Most important for the early flowerers, such as peaches and pears, are dead nettles and other earlier nectar and pollen sources to get the bumble bees going in time for the fruit flowers. Beds *of Limnanthes douglassii, Convolvolus tricolor* and *Phacelia tanacetifolia* are all useful as they attract and feed many pollinators and predators. Most of the pungent herbs are generally thought to be beneficial – garlic and chives especially so – and stinging nettles are believed to improve the keeping qualities of fruit growing near them.

How do I go about training shaped fruit trees?

This is the hardest of all questions to answer, as every case is different and in life no sample ever matches the illustrations. It is a pleasure to take a young maiden tree and create the desired shape from it over the years. It is also not really a job for the novice; the regular pruning of a shaped tree is hard enough to do properly – forming the shape as well is even harder. Where speed and excellence are needed, just buy it ready-formed! If you wish to do it yourself, then get a specialist book or three on the subject, as there are many aspects concerning style and method that can't be dealt with in this small volume.

Basically, instead of allowing the tree, or bush, to make its own shape, we determine that it will be but one, two or more limbs, each pointing and growing in a specific direction and manner. A cordon is the simplest form, being simply a tree restricted to only one branch, usually sloping between the vertical and 45 degrees. Espaliers can be two-limbed, as stepovers for railings, or have many limbs, all tiered horizontally. Fans are similar, but the branches radiate. Bushes are just small trees. Goblets are bushes with open centres. Grid-irons are like espaliers, but with vertical tiers and are usually only used for soft fruit.

In most cases the side shoots are pruned back to form fruiting spurs along the branches. It is not difficult to do, but requires patient, methodical work. From the first you choose which limbs are to be the final framework and remove all others, trimming back side shoots and tying ones going in the wrong direction to canes or wires to guide them the right way. You also need to encourage new limbs to form, or divide, to fill the desired shape, and need to check growth as well, to stop the new growths being all leggy with no side shoots, so you prune back different shoots by different amounts. Perversely it seems that the more you prune back a shoot, the more it grows compared to another in the same position. To balance two opposite limbs the weaker one is cut back harder during the autumn prune. But too much pruning weakens trees, so it's better to rub out buds, taking away the need to remove the shoot later on and encouraging the remaining ones to be stronger.

Apples and pears are relatively easy to train, as they do not mind being manipulated and most form spurs along their branches fairly readily (although not the less common tip-bearing varieties). Apricots are similar and are not difficult to train either, though they prefer a fan shape. However, plums, peaches and cherries are all much more work, with more tying in and removing numerous larger shoots on a continuous basis, or what is termed replenishment pruning. Indeed, the regular pruning of trained fans of these fruit trees makes for a never arduous but always available workload, if you want a retirement occupation. If you wish to practise training, then try redcurrants, as they are very forgiving and amenable and resemble apples in behaviour; gooseberries are similarly well behaved but rather thorny.

The important thing to understand is that sap pushes vertically up, so buds high up will break and grow much faster than buds low down – especially those at the ends of branches; thus you must always finish the lower tiers before allowing much more growth higher up the plant. By removing the highest shoots and the tips of lower shoots in winter you cause more of the lowest buds to break than would do otherwise and thus prevent bare branches at the bottom. So it takes a year to add a tier. Each year two more of the topmost shoots are allowed to extend unpruned and bent down the following season. Of course they do not always come where you want them. Where you want buds to break along a branch, you can cause this by bending it into an arc, so that the middle becomes the highest point; where you want more length, you can raise the tip up higher and buds will grow away from there. It's all simple really.

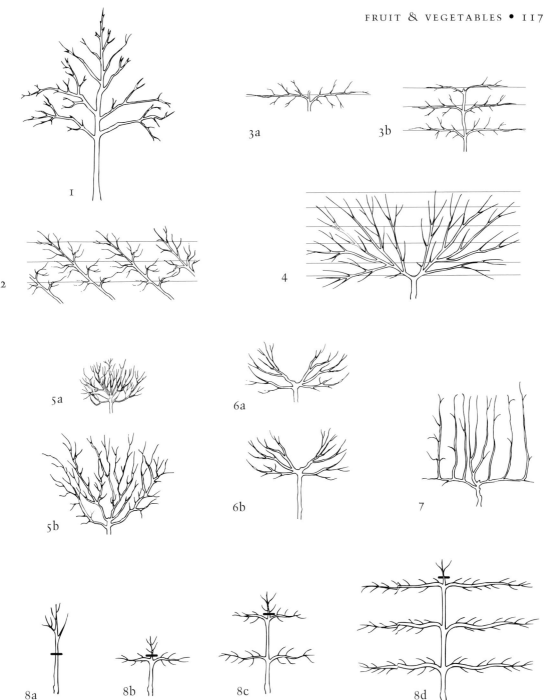

1. Standard trees are least effort to look after but get big
2. Cordons are more work but allow more variety
3a. Stepover espaliers have one tier so cast little shade
3b. Tiered espaliers are good for apples and pears
4. Stone fruits and figs prefer to be made a fan shape
5a. Bush trained fruits on dwarfing stock are compact
5b. Bushes on vigorous stock get bigger and yield more
6a. A goblet on a short leg gets the warmth of the ground
6b. A goblet on tall legs gets more air flowing through it
7. A gridiron shape on a wall can suit red currants
8. The ideal progression over four years of making an espalier from a maiden, seen in winter

What is the difference between winter and summer pruning?

Winter pruning is to establish the shape and form of the plant and to remove dead, diseased and rubbing growths while they are visible and the plant is dormant. For a healthy plant up to one-third of the top growth can be removed in winter, but it will all grow back. Winter pruning does not reduce the size of the plant because of the top growing back to balance the roots. Summer pruning will control the size of a plant; it is done to control vigour, and to encourage flowering and fruiting. With summer pruning less of the plant is removed and preferably in three stages.

When you prune back in winter the plant tends to push back new growth in proportion to the amount removed and thus it is good for forming a framework, but not so good for controlling the size of the plant or encouraging fruiting; in fact winter pruning usually reduces fruiting by removing fruit buds and encouraging strong growth covered in vegetative buds. When you prune in summer the tree is not dormant, you remove a lot of sap and

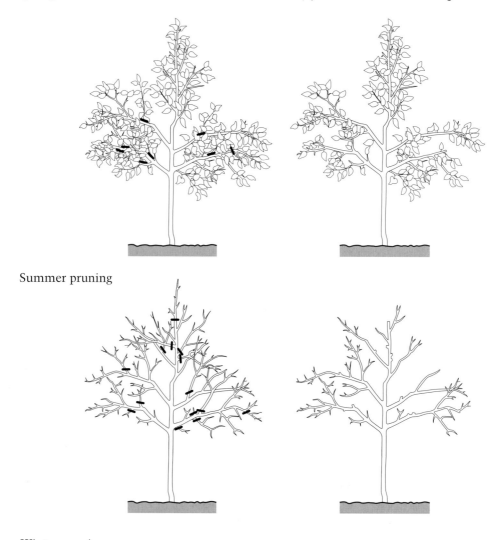

Summer pruning

Winter pruning

leaf with the young woody prunings and this checks the plant's growth and vigour. The check encourages vegetative growth buds to turn into flower buds so that the next year you get more fruit and less growth. And the removal of all the leafy growth lets in more air and light to improve this year's crop.

Ideally half to one-third of every side shoot is removed in three stages between early and late summer, except for those left to extend the frame-work. Each shoot is not pruned three times; instead, one-third of the shoots are cut back at a time and preferably the highest-placed ones are pruned back first. The light falling on the remaining leaves is now increased, as others have been removed, so the plant does not suffer unduly but redirects its energy to fruiting rather than growth, which is usually what you are after once the plant has been trained to its desired form. Good summer pruning thus maintains the size and shape of trained plants, as well as keeping up their productivity.

My apple tree's branches are covered in hundreds of vertical shoots.

This is what happens when a healthy tree has too much wood removed in one winter pruning. There are not many vegetative buds on the spurs making up the tips of an oldish tree, so when the tree's roots push back and try to regrow to replace all the missing material, the sap pressure breaks new buds all over the branches, which then give the tree a hedgehog look. The only cure is to summer-prune and remove the 'water sprouts', as they are called, in several stages, preferably over a couple of years, leaving a few that are well placed to become new branches. Just occasionally the same thing can happen if an old tree suddenly gets considerably more water or fertility than it has been habituated to. The cure is then the same but slower to take effect.

Why do I get such poor performance from a tree several years after planting?

The causes of poor performance are many: it may have too dry a spot, which will result in little growth; it may be too wet and the roots may drown each winter – in a heavy soil the roots may be confined in a hole full of water after every rain. The soil may be far too acid, too alkaline or just too poor. If the site is, or becomes, too shady, then a plant can become drawn or stunted. If a tie is left encircling the trunk it can choke a plant to death. If the specimen was planted from a container, then the roots may not have been teased out and are all trapped in their original place, where they now strangle each other. This last is often manifested by the plant bursting into life in spring to peter out and look miserable all summer. The roots may have been damaged or become diseased or may be being eaten by a pest. The first growths may be destroyed regularly by frosts, or the leaves may be falling too early after disease attacks.

Try giving the tree a really enthusiastic hard tug. If it doesn't come up, then weed underneath it, give it a couple of sprays with seaweed solution, add a thick mulch and feed the soil, and water it during dry spells; then it will surely grow. If after three years of this treatment it has not grown well, burn it.

BG Tree stakes can be detrimental to the growth of a tree, as they do not allow sufficient movement, which in turn helps root growth. The stem on a staked tree may also be thicker below the tie than above it – the opposite of what it should be. In addition, aftercare in the form of loosening the tie and checking for rubbing may be lacking. Ideally you should plant trees at a size where support is not necessary. If you do stake a tree (if it is over 2m/6½ft tall and in an exposed site), then the stake should not be more than one-third of the total tree height and should be attached to the trunk only at the top. To prevent adverse effects from the staking on the trunk's development, the stake should be removed after one growing season (ideally at the onset of the second growing season after planting).

A key factor in establishing trees is to make sure that the bare roots are not exposed to any frosts during the period of lifting in the nursery and replanting in its final situation. Even if the roots are subjected to light frost for a period of a few minutes, this has a marked effect on subsequent establishment and growth.

Why is my fruit tree growing well, but not flowering?

Sometimes if you are in a frost pocket all the flower buds, flowers or fruitlets are destroyed by a frost without you noticing. Sometimes birds such as bullfinches destroy the flower buds, but they rarely get all of them, so you would see those that do flower – and these usually set very well. Most likely the trees are too young, or they are too vigorous. When trees grow well they are in no mind to flower and fruit, as they want to use all their energy to dominate all the available space first. A give-away sign is branches growing very strongly upwards, often with leaves that are a dark green. First, stop feeding the soil if you have been. Too much fertilizer will not help but hinder fruiting! Next, bend the branch ends down with ties and canes. I find plastic bottles part-filled with water work well and allow the branches still to move freely. Sometimes dressing the soil under the tree with wood ashes provides extra potassium and can encourage flowering.

My trees grow well, but never fruit.

I assume they are flowering. If the trees are flowering but you still get no fruit, then you have a serious water shortage occurring at some time during the start of the season, the roots are choking themselves as they were not teased out, or you have not got a pollinator. The first can be rectified with mulches and irrigation, while the last cause can be eliminated by bringing in a flowering partner for pollination, leaving only the choked roots to worry about. And if the trees are growing healthily then that is unlikely, so to summarize: get a pollinator!

My trees fruit some years and then don't for many more. Why?

This is known as biennial bearing; the tree exhausts itself by overcropping one year and then has to take a year, or more, off. The solution is simple: after the June drop in early July *(sic)*, you must ruthlessly thin the fruits. Remove at least half, taking the poorest-placed, the crowded, deformed and diseased and leaving only the best. This reduces the load on the tree by lessening the number of seeds, which it takes a lot of resources for the tree to make. The sweet pulpy bit that we like is not expensive for the tree to make, so the remaining fruits will swell large and give a good crop. And so the tree will fruit each year as long as the fruits are always thinned – a rough guide is to leave no more than one apple, pear or peach to each hand-sized area of foliage.

My apples have brown spots in the flesh. Are they poisonous?

If these are bruises and are rotting, then yes, they might be. The fungal infections that come in on rots can be very bad for you, though fermentation by yeasts is not quite so dire. More likely, though, if the dots are spread under the skin throughout the flesh, is that this is bitter pit, caused by a calcium deficiency, and the tree is short of lime. Simply dress underneath the tree with ground dolomitic lime, ground chalk or calcified seaweed and rake it in – the effects will take a year or more to show. Sadly, though you might be able to eat apples with bitter pit, you will probably not want to, as they are not so pleasant.

PG
If trees regularly suffer from bitter pit, the developing fruits can be sprayed with a solution of calcium nitrate. This is generally available only through mail-order catalogues or from particularly good garden centres, and needs to be applied at regular intervals as the fruits develop. Do be aware that a few varieties, including 'Bramley Seedling' (which is one of the more prone to this disorder), may be injured by calcium nitrate and in this case it may be

worth putting it on at half the recommended strength. Your best way of dealing with bitter pit, however, is really to try and ensure that the trees do not overcrop, as this obviously makes them need more calcium, and that they are kept really well watered and mulched.

My apples have maggots and holes. How do I stop these appearing next year?

If the maggots are in the middle of the apple, the frass comes out of the flower end and a large entrance hole in the side tinged with pink is apparent, this is codling moth (see p. 297). If, however, the hole in the side of the apple is only pencil-lead-sized, then it is probably caused by apple sawfly, especially if the holes are worming their way in the flesh but avoiding the core. Sawfly are a worse pest than codling moth as they will leave the apple they started on and enter another, and even a third. These damaged apples often fall in the June drop or ripen prematurely.

The best method of control is careful inspection and early removal of any infected fruitlets, the clearing up of any fallen chats and the destruction of all of these as soon as possible, with the maggots within and before they have left to hibernate. Heavy mulches under the trees laid over a woven fabric or plastic-sheet layer traps the hibernating pupae above. They can then be exposed to the birds by raking the mulch aside in winter.

How do I store apples, and which keep the longest?

First, grow them without extra fertilizer, and if they are growing through grass stop cutting it in August so that it takes up spare nitrogen. Do not try and store any apples ripening before the end of September, as few of these will keep for long – better turn them into purée, juice, cider or dried apple rings. The best keeping varieties hang on the trees through October and are only gathered before a hard frost hits them. They need to be picked with exquisite care; one bruise, squeeze or blemish will cause them to rot. The little bit of stem, the pedicel, must stay in the apple as well!

Lay the apples in trays on a bed of crumpled or shredded newspaper and keep them in a frost-free, cool dark place that is not too dry. It is a good idea to prepare them first for storage by leaving them in a cool airy place for a day or two to sweat out any excess moisture, and then to put them out at night on a chill evening without frost and put them in store first thing in the morning before they have warmed. A garage or shed is a common storeplace, but is not good if there is any smell there, as the apples will pick up any taint! I find that a dead refrigerator or deepfreeze makes a perfect store; the temperature and humidity are constant and it is rat- and mouse-proof. The only modification required is to cut holes in the door or lid seal to allow some respiration. I find the best long-keepers are 'Granny Smith', 'Winston', 'Tydeman's Late Orange' and 'Brownlees Russet'.

My apples do well, but my pears are poor.

There are several likely reasons for this. The first is that you are in a bleak inhospitable spot, a shady spot or a frost pocket and the apples, which are tougher all round, can cope with the adverse conditions. They flower later than pears so miss more of the frosts, are less upset by cold winds, need less sun and do not need such autumn warmth to ripen their wood. Indeed, it is hard to grow any pears at all well in the maritime west of Britain, but local varieties of apple will do. Another possible reason for failure is a lack of a pollinator, as both fruits do best with good pollinating partners, even if the variety is theoretically self-fertile. There are more apple trees about than pears, so you can often rely on a neighbour's tree to do the job for you. Pears also need more moisture in the soil than apples, but cannot stand waterlogging. And a third very likely reason is allowing the grass to grow underneath the trees, as pears resent the competition far more than apples.

My apples and pears do well, but my plums are poor.

It is always possible that late frosts take out just the plum blossoms, but pears would usually be hit as well. A lack of suitable pollinators is another possibility. The stone fruits also like richer soil conditions than the pome fruits, so it may just be that your soil is a little hungry. Most likely it is another soil problem, though; pome fruits (as apples and pears are called) will grow on acid soils, as they do not need as much lime as stone fruits, such as plums, cherries and peaches. These stone fruits need a lot of lime in the soil and do not thrive where it is absent. A good dressing of a handful of lime per square metre (square yard) will do wonders – dolomitic lime or calcified seaweed even more so.

I want fresh cherries, but I'm told they're difficult to grow.

They are only easy to grow outdoors in drier regions, as rain on the flowers destroys them. If they set the fruit, the birds eat it. And cherries are big trees, even on most allegedly dwarfing rootstocks, and even the really dwarfing sorts do not stay that small. They can be kept trained on a wall or in a fruit cage, but resent it and are hard work. They are better off grown in a large pot, where they can be immune to the birds and weather and do not make such strong growth. You will need to buy a pair to ensure pollination.

The cooking cherries, morellos, are easiest to grow, as these will endure some shade and can be very simply pruned (unlike the others). Unfortunately, they are too sour to eat fresh.

My plums have maggots in most of them. What can I do about this?

Pick off and pick up any infected fruits and destroy them whenever you see them – they are often the first to start ripening. Spread thick mulches under the tree and rake these aside in winter to let the birds eat the pupae. And next year buy a plum-fruit moth pheromone trap and hang it up when the flowers appear, keeping it topped up with refills throughout the season.

Why do my pears turn black and fall off when small?

If pears are not fully pollinated they may fall as small fruitlets; similarly, if they are frosted, then the fruitlets may blacken and drop. However, if the pear fruitlets that fall are cut open and maggots or holes are apparent, then you have pear-gall midge. The best method of control is to collect and destroy all the fallen fruitlets and then lay a thick mulch, which is raked aside in winter to let the birds eat the pupae.

How can I grow peaches and apricots?

These are fairly easy to grow as free-standing bushes in the warmer, drier south-eastern counties of Britain, but in the colder, wetter regions they need to be on a wall, under cover or grown in pots. The last is a good solution, especially for peaches, which avoids leaf curl if they are taken indoors all winter; it also prevents the frost damaging their flowers in spring and they can then go out for the summer, avoiding most of the red spider-mite attacks, then back under cover when the fruits ripen. Apricots can be treated likewise, but are not too much work trained as a fan on a warm wall in the manner of an apple or pear espalier. Training peaches on a wall is harder work, as they need a lot of pruning and tying in.

The biggest problem in growing either fruit outdoors is frost damaging the flowers or fruitlets, and a temporary cover is often needed to ensure crops. Both fruits are greedy feeders – the peaches especially so – and both appreciate thick mulches, lime and regular watering. Do not try growing these fruits from stones: though they may grow happily, they will be variable and take 10 or 15 years to crop.

Are quinces and medlars easy trees to fruit?

These are very reliable and rarely get damaged by any pests, diseases or weather. They are usually only available on dwarfing rootstocks and make very ornamental small trees. They are self-fertile and the fruits store for a long time; indeed, the medlar has to be half-rotten before it ever becomes edible and the quince is so hard that it must be cooked. Both trees need little pruning or any other attention. *Cydonia*, or the true quinces, prefer a moist site but will do almost anywhere. Japonica quinces are lax wall shrubs, usually with red flowers; their fruits resemble true quinces and can be used in the same way to make jellies, but the plants are near impossible to train.

My fig tree always drops its fruit before it's ripe.

If the fig is in a pot indoors, then this may be due to a water shortage at some time, or possibly to a severe infestation of red spider mite. However,

Figs (*Ficus carica*)

if it's in the ground outdoors, then it is probable that it has tried to carry too many crops. Figs can potentially give three crops a year, but not happily so in England's climate. Small figs that form in late summer and autumn get slightly damaged by winter and then grow again in the spring. As they swell they prevent the spring buds from starting, but because they were slightly damaged their skin won't stretch and they usually split and drop off; or, if damaged, stay small and blackened. The existence of the over-wintered fruitlets thus retards the next crop, which may not ripen in time to catch the good warm weather and so it is lost as well. The answer is simply to remove *every* fruitlet – no matter how small – in November.

I want a better grapevine, as mine gets mould every year!

I think you have the right approach. It is easier to grow more resistant varieties than to struggle with such regular problems. Grapes get mildews on their leaves and berries, and rots as well, so resistant varieties are usually a better choice than the old, nondescript varieties that one often comes across. I love grapevines and have tried 40 or so varieties in my Norfolk garden, where it is a little too cold, damp and north-sloping for them to be happy, but nonetheless some prove reliable.

Best of all for outdoors is 'Boskoop Glory', a black grape that is good for eating or juicing; the 'Strawberry Grape' and 'Schuyler' are other reliable heavy croppers of dark grapes for juice. In a warm lime-free soil or in a container 'Siegerrebe' may not be as disease-resistant as some, but it's sweet rose fruits are so delicious that it's worth it. On a hot dry wall or in a cold conservatory 'Golden Chasselas' is remarkably reliable and trouble-free. In a heated greenhouse grow 'Muscat Hamburg' in containers – it really is worth the effort; 'Black Hamburg' comes a close second.

How do I grow good melons?

It is just possible to grow melons outdoors in a warm, sheltered south-facing garden, but they will not be very big or good. Their chances and quality will be vastly improved if they are grown under cloches or in a coldframe. Enriching the soil with as much compost as possible is essential, as are constant moisture and plenty of lime. Placing a coldframe on top of a fermenting compost heap is pretty close to ideal and can produce some prize specimens. In a greenhouse a hotbed, or at least a large container of rich compost, is vital.

The earliest you can sensibly sow indoors is March, and outside in a coldframe *in situ* wait until the end of May. Do not wet the neck of the plant where it enters the soil as they easily rot there. Red spider mite is often a pest, best beaten by introducing the predators; melons do not like their foliage being syringed to keep the mite down. You do not need to prune the shoots or thin out the fruits, but this can be done to control the number and size produced. Pollination by hand is rarely necessary. When the fruits ripen do not pick them too soon, but support them so they do not fall down, either!

Why do my four-year-old strawberry plants do so badly?

Strawberries are a crop that only does well for a few years and then needs to be replaced by new plants. This is inevitable, for as the crowns grow older, tougher and larger, the vigour deteriorates and they frequently pick up virus diseases. Thus it makes sense to start a new bed each year of roughly one-quarter to one-third of the total area devoted to strawberries, and to destroy the equivalent oldest part. The replacement plants should be grown from just a couple of the best of last year's new plants, which ideally should not be allowed to fruit and made runner, by deflowering them. Or buy in new certified virus-free stock, as this is worth every penny. Ideally the new plants should be got in before mid-August, as then they will be big and strong enough to fruit the following year – unlikely with commercial plants, which never arrive in time. With plants put in after August it pays to deflower them the first year, as they will give a bigger crop during the following years. Do remove the runners from all the plants except your selected breeders, as more runners formed means less fruits produced!

My blackcurrants are doing badly – why?

Blackcurrants do need a rich soil to keep up their yields. They also need to be pruned to ensure a regular supply of young wood, as that is the most fruitful. Ideally, one-third of all the bush's branches should be removed each year. As the best, most vigorous growths come from ground level, blackcurrants are planted deep and rarely grown on a single stem. Because of this they can become congested and this may cause poor crops. However, the most likely reason that yields are poor is because the bushes have become

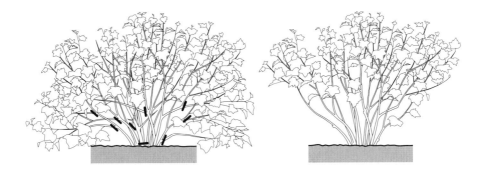

old and over a decade or so they inevitably catch a virus disease called reversion, which causes the crops to fail. This disease is spread by the big bud mite, which is often the first sign of infection; the big, rounded buds are obvious in late winter. The only solution to reversion is to burn the old bushes and buy in new virus-free stock, preferably to be grown in a different position.

Why are my raspberries so poor?

Raspberries need a moist soil, and they do far better in wetter regions; thick mulches also help them immensely. Dry soils can make them more prone to chlorosis, which shows up as green veins with yellowing in between. If the yellow is in blotchy patches, then they have mosaic virus and need burning. There is no cure for the virus, but new canes are cheap enough and will be surprisingly vigorous and productive if your old stock had degenerated. New stock is needed about every 10 years, as with blackcurrants. It is also a good idea to prune out all the old canes each year and to thin the new ones down to a hand's breadth apart, as this concentrates the growth into a few, which will fruit all the heavier accordingly.

Why do all the leaves disappear from my gooseberries?

They have been eaten by the gooseberry sawfly caterpillar. This is most often a problem in about the third or fourth year after planting. They first appear as a cluster of tiny holes in one leaf, then move out and decimate the whole bush. Catching them at an early stage prevents too much damage. The caterpillars can be shaken down onto a sheet and destroyed or killed with Derris dust on a dewy morning before the bees are about. Thick mulches under the bushes can be raked aside in winter to let the birds eat the pupae. They can even be knocked off with a jet of water and prevented from returning with a thick sprinkling of ashes or soot around the stems.

(PG) Gooseberry sawfly is certainly a common problem, but if when you say that the leaves have disappeared, you mean that there is nothing left and they have fallen to the ground, then I suspect that currant and gooseberry leaf spot is the most likely cause of the problem. This is most common in early summer and you may initially notice very tiny blackish-brown spots on the leaves of both gooseberries and occasionally currants. The leaves then turn brown and fall early, and the leaf drop is often so extensive that the plant is completely bare by mid-summer. The fungus responsible, *Drepanopezizsa ribis*, oozes its spores from the leaf spots and these may over-winter on the fallen leaves and be carried by both wind and rain. If you find this is the case, you should regularly remove the fallen leaves to decrease the chances of the problem recurring next year and spray with a suitable fungicide, such as Supercarb, Traditional Copper, Dithane 945 or Nimrod T. If possible, you should ensure that the lower surfaces of the leaves are also sprayed thoroughly.

Japanese wineberry (*Aristotelia serrata*)

Aronia 'Chokeberry Viking'

What unusual fruits are worth growing?

The Japanese wineberry is an excellent but relatively unknown bramble and much better than a blackberry. It has delicious small red berries, which the birds don't eat so quickly, as they wait for them to blacken – which of course they never do. *Aronia* 'Chokeberry Viking' is an ornamental with gorgeous autumn colouring to its leaves and the blackcurrant-like fruits make an excellent jam. The Kumoi or Nashi pear from Asia is superb: not a big tree, it is pretty in flower and leaf, has no major pest and disease problems and is self-fertile; the fruits are perfumed and succulent, resembling apples but more like a pear to eat. The ground cherry, *Physalis pubescens/pruinosa*, is a small annual, grown in the same way as outdoor tomatoes but needing no supports; the fruits are like small greeny Cape gooseberries in a similar paper case and are almost pineapple-flavoured. Although not rare, the josta berry should be more widely grown: it is like a giant thornless gooseberry with blackcurrant-flavoured berries. The old Worcesterberry (probably a native North American species) is similar, even tastier, but immensely thorny and quite unpickable unless trained.

Which tropical fruits from the supermarket can be grown in Britain?

Given the space of Kew Garden's Palm House, almost all of them could be grown, as the only real problem is the size that some of them have to reach before they fruit – avocados and date palms, for example. But you do not

Date palm
*Phoenix
dactylifera*)

Custard apples (*Annona reticulata*)

Passion
fruit flower
(*Passiflora
caerulea*)

Pineapple
(*Ananas
comosus*)

need an enormous stove-house. Many, if not all, tropical plants can be grown for years, even if they will never get a chance to fruit, and they are so interesting and educational in the process. And almost every fruit comes with a free packet of seeds inside to try!

Almost all of them will germinate, especially if given some warmth in a propagator. Many of them, like date palms grown from the stones, make really gorgeous house plants in only a few months, even if you cannot let them grow big or old enough to fruit. Pawpaws, tamarinds and custard apples are all easy and make impressive plants. With just a frost-free greenhouse or conservatory it's fairly simple to produce a tropical harvest. Guavas are surprisingly easy, and passion fruits can often be produced on plants sown the previous spring. Ginger and lemon grass are both very simple to grow from small pieces detached from the fresh product. And pineapples can be grown from the crown of a fruit: detach and dry it for a day or two, then peel the lower dried leaves to reveal vestigial roots ready for potting. Given a couple of years, a crown will be 1m (1yd) across, and will then throw an amazing flower like a red pine cone, with purplish sage-like flowers coming out of it. This swells into the fruit over several months and can do so while in only a bucket-sized container, as long as it is kept in a hot sunny place.

Very few tropical fruits are unhappy during England's summer – it is the cold dark days of winter that upset them. Under cover, although the temperature may be kept up, the light levels are low so their metabolism is under stress and they become prone to root rots and leaf moulds. Thus most of them are best started in early spring to get them as large as possible by the autumn. Then they can be prepared for winter by being kept only just moist enough for life to continue. Keeping the air dry and their compost barely moist enables the plants to withstand the low temperatures that even a heated greenhouse will reach rather too often. Where the temperature rarely drops below comfortable human levels, such as in a living room-conservatory, then the plants need more watering to prevent them drying out, but must not be left wet or they may be threatened by root rots. But don't be put off: every tropical fruit's seeds will be fun to sow and see grow for a while, and they don't cost you anything, do they?

I grew a banana from seed, but will it fruit?

First, congratulations on your achievement, as these are not one of the easiest plants to start from seed. They make spectacular house plants and can even be planted outside for the warmer part of the year. It may indeed one day flower, and even fruit. First there will appear an enormous sweet-corn-cob-like shoot, which will arch over and open in a series of 'hands' of blooms. These have vestigial bananas behind each small flower. Then, after the hands have come out all down the now-pendulous spike, the male flowers will appear at the end to fertilize the fruits. After these have ripened the whole 'tree' dies to be replaced by a new tree from a shoot – or several – coming from the base. Unfortunately, as you grew yours from seed it will be a seedy variety and these are not usually very tasty. The best sorts for fruiting are the 'Dwarf Cavendish' forms, as grown in the Canaries, and these are only grown from vegetative offsets, just like giant lupins or delphiniums.

VEGETABLES

Which of the gourmet vegetables are easiest to grow?

Without a doubt globe artichokes are tops; they can be grown from seed one year to start cropping the next, suffer little from pests and diseases, taste wonderful when really fresh, are expensive in the shops and are so beautiful in leaf that they can even be planted in the flower garden. Asparagus is more work, as the weed control is more difficult – you can heavily mulch artichokes and they choke out weeds themselves, but asparagus needs bare soil for warmth for the early crop, so mulching is counterproductive and the open fern encourages weeds to grow in the dappled shade underneath. Asparagus is also slow; it takes three years to get strong enough to crop, but if you're patient then grow asparagus, as it's so good when it's fresh.

Sweet and hot peppers are as easy as tomatoes if you have a greenhouse and can be even sweeter than shop-bought ones (or hotter), and there are a vast number of varieties to choose from. Sweetcorn is only really sweet when cooked within 20 minutes of picking, so it is essential for any gour-

Globe artichoke (*Cynara scolymus*)

met to grow and pick their own. It is easy to grow in a good summer but not so sweet or prolific in a cold, wet year.

The best varieties of new potatoes are another gourmet's must; my favourite is currently 'Dunluce', which also stores well, to make a really tasty chip. Extra-early new potatoes grown in pots indoors, started from before the New Year, crop before the end of March and are wonderful. For the less patient gourmet it is hard to beat weekly sowings of salad rocket for repeatedly fresh supplies of the leaves, which are much more succulent and tasty than those from older plants.

Which crops are best value for their work, cost and time?

Without doubt those that someone else grows for you as a gift – it is easier to befriend a gardener and then enjoy their munificence than it is to grow your own! Gardeners are always only too willing to give away their surplus: my point is that we all tend to grow too much. Therefore too often many of the crops and thus much of the work goes to waste, and that is the very worst value, regardless of the comparative work each may have taken.

I carefully watch what is not used and consciously sow less the next year, unless it is for trial purposes. So although I quite like parsnips, I know I will never want more than half a dozen good ones, so I do not sow a row, a half-row or a bed – I sow but two dozen seeds in eight spots, at three apiece. Each spot is covered by a plastic-bottle cloche, and when they emerge the triple or double seedlings are reduced to the best one and covered again; when they are bigger, the cloches are removed and the crop is assured, and with a one-third surplus built in. So do not grow rows of beet, Brussels sprouts or turnips unless you dearly love them; do not sow a 9m (30ft) row of runner beans unless you have a lot of carrier bags to get rid of – because you'll need them for all the beans you must keep picking. The moral is: do not make work; grow only what you really like.

Courgettes, hot peppers, sprouting broccoli, Jerusalem artichokes, shallots and garlic seem to give amazing returns for the effort. Luxuries such as asparagus, sweetcorn, French beans and salad crops are cost-efficient to grow yourself. Large seeds, such as peas and beans, cost a lot to buy and are easy to save yourself. Tomato, courgette and cucumber plants are all expensive to buy in for early crops, but get cheap later when everyone dumps their surplus plants. Onions are cheap seed compared to the value of a year-round supply, while garlic from home-grown offsets is even more so; garlic is probably the most economic crop in terms of time, work, ease and value. Peas need sowing and supporting, then picking and podding, which is time-consuming. Courgettes and sweetcorn are not too much work to grow, and little work on their way to the table. Growing most crops takes nothing compared to the time spent harvesting and preparing them, especially if you want to freeze them.

What is rotation, and do we have to do it?

No one ordains that you must rotate crops, but you'd be foolish not to. Rotation simply means moving the plants around so that different ones (and not more of the same) follow each other on the same site. This prevents a build-up of pests, weeds and diseases and helps soil fertility, as different crops have different needs and then leave different nutrients behind as their dead roots and leaves break down.

You do not have to slavishly follow the examples set out in books – not unless you want exactly the same amounts of the same crops as the authors. They have done worked examples, and there is a logic to what they do; a typical rotation is brassicas, roots, potatoes, legumes. This is because the brassicas can be conveniently followed by the root crops, after which the potatoes enjoy the broken soil caused by removing the roots, and at this stage organic material is most usefully incorporated, as the potatoes respond to it best and its lumpiness is bad for the root crops but is incorporated by the time they come round again. After the potatoes come the legumes – these like lime, which is bad for the potatoes, so it is added with the legumes and is then available for the brassicas but is ameliorated by the time the potatoes return. Legumes also like the depleted soil left by potatoes, as they make their own fertility, and make so much that they leave plenty for the brassicas, which come after them as the round starts once again.

You can adopt this or almost any other rotation, but you do not have to follow it in precisely the same allocations. You do not have to have a quarter of your vegetable plot full of potatoes and another of root crops if you don't want to. Roots usually includes onions and leeks, as well as carrots and parsnips, so when root crops return an alternative is planted. An alternative for potatoes is sweetcorn. You can make a better rotation that takes a greater number of years to rotate if you grow more different crops in smaller quantities. And even when the same family returns you may choose a different member. For example, when the brassicas come round again you can put in spring cauliflowers where the first time you had Brussels sprouts, and the next time it can be summer cabbages.

If you decide also to adopt companion planting, then the mixtures of plants make it seem harder to plan rotations. But I simply rotate the most sensitive crops and fit their companions around them, rotating them as well but with not so much time elapsing. So, for example, all the brassicas, onions, potatoes and carrots must be rotated as a priority and must not return until the latest possible date, while French beans, sweetcorn and courgettes are not quite so problematic. If an accurate set of records is kept it can be simple to arrange very complex and involved rotations, as it is all done on paper (or the computer screen) first. Because of my interest in the rotational aspects of companion planting, I developed a simple method for the complex task of record-keeping for my 40 experimental beds. This has evolved over nearly 20 years of collecting data, so when considering what to

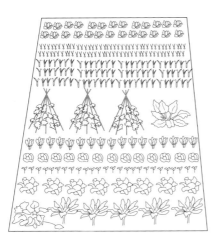
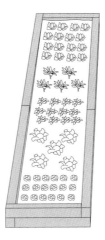

Rows

Raised beds

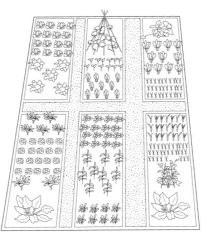

Fixed beds

grow where, I can choose a suitable bed and position, knowing exactly what grew on it over the preceding years.

You do not need to be this precise – just follow these simple rules; first, never plant the same crop again in the same place (this is a good idea for all sorts of gardening); second, try and keep the same plant or near-relations away from the same spot for as long as possible, and certainly for more than two or three years; third, when the same family is coming back, choose a different relation for the same site.

What is the difference between rows, fixed and raised beds?

These are differing methods of intensive crop cultivation that have evolved for historical reasons. Plants have always been arranged in some form or another since gardening began. Originally most cultivated crops were field crops, and little was grown by the individual for their personal use, save possibly a few herbs. The exceptions were the classical gardens and their monastic and royal descendants, but they concentrated on the herbal and ornamental and most foodstuffs still came from a field crop or were gathered from the wilds, though the rich have always had orchards and vineyards. Often when field or wild crops were adopted as household items they would be grown together with other sorts of plants, in the very mixed cottage garden. Field crops were almost invariably broad-cast, though some enlightened people have always advocated careful spacing and some, such as Jethro Tull, recognized the advantage that this gave to weed control.

The desire for greater yields and prize-winning produce made it necessary to grow crops more carefully. On the Continent they continued to grow many vegetables in small blocks – miniature fields on the Roman pattern – but in Britain we went for the row method. This may be a result of copying the strip pattern of farmland culture practised throughout the country or it may come from copying Tull, with his seed drill and horse-drawn multi-hoe. Whatever the historical reason, the row method involves spacing plants one distance apart in the row according to their vigour and required size, and spacing the rows apart according to the crop's height and how much it will compete with its neighbours. As in most schemes the rows move each year, the soil that is compacted in one year needs digging to be available in another.

With fixed beds the paths are fixed and never dug, as the beds are never walked on – only the paths. This means that you need not dig the beds every year simply to remove the compaction from treading. Most people find that beds about 1–1.2m (3–4ft) across is about right, as you can reach in from either side to do any work and this gives enough room to grow, space and rotate almost every conceivable crop. Beds made longer than 4.5m (15ft) or so tend to get walked across as a shortcut, defeating the object. Fixed beds and a card index make record-keeping concerning what went where and when very simple and greatly facilitate good rotation.

Raised beds are fixed beds with height. This may be to a great height, to avoid bending or for wheelchair access, in which case rigid sides are needed. For regular garden use, though, a gain of only about 30cm (12in) gives a lot of benefits, and some drawbacks. Beds that are raised tend to warm up more quickly, avoid some chilling frost damage and are better aerated and drained. However, they also dry out too quickly, while mulches slide and get scratched off by birds. And many people make their beds raised with wooden sides to hold them up; this uses a lot of materials and creates hiding places for numerous pests. I prefer beds to be raised only as far as they will naturally grade to and using only the soil itself for the sides. Likewise for the paths, though for sure footing sand or other loose mulches can be used, but choose those that can be incorporated and hoed, such as spent mushroom compost, as they inevitably get mixed in.

What is the cheapest way of extending the season of vegetables?

At the front end you can grow crops under glass or plastic with heat, though many are difficult to manage in the low light of winter. This is not cheap, but the value of these crops is high because of the season, so it pays off. Growing early crops under cover without heat cannot be achieved nearly so early, but will still beat outdoor crops by months. A greenhouse is expensive but lasts many years, while a walk-in polythene tunnel comes much bigger for the same price but needs recovering every fifth year. Low crop-covering plastic tunnels are very cheap, but not as effective as the bigger walk-in tunnels. Likewise cloches and coldframes are useful, but can only be used economically to bring on small amounts of crops for a few weeks' gain or to shelter a batch of early plants for putting out later. Without doubt recycled clear-plastic bottle cloches, with the bottom cut away and the cap off, make the cheapest way of getting individual plants weeks earlier. Of course another way of bringing the spring forward is to move to a south-facing slope, which increases the effective insolation. You can't slope a whole flat garden, but you can manage one bed, and a slope of only 15 degrees will effectively move the soil surface to Spain, from the point of view of sunlight per square foot.

Many crops can be grown in succession under cover from late summer in autumn sowings, though they rarely do as well as spring-sown ones. At the latter end of the season you can likewise cover many crops to keep them usable for longer, although this is harder, as they are now bigger in size than the seedlings of spring. Fortunately, many crops can be stored fresh. I find that covering roots and cabbages, leeks and so on, with loose straw and sheets of plastic keeps them fresh and usable for months, no matter how cold or bleak the winter.

Are there any good companion plants for all vegetables?

Not really – many are generally liked, but detested by some. *Alliums*, for example, get on well with many crops but not with beans. It's a bit like people with partners – it's hard to find just the right one; with neighbours it's easier to get on with more diverse people, as they're not so close. Likewise for vegetables; they do benefit from many plants that are nearby, but not too close. Thus almost all the aromatic herbs are generally beneficial, as their smells confuse pests, but many of them also suppress seeds from germinating if they are too close. Chamomile is thought to be good for healing sick plants. Dead and stinging nettles are reckoned to be good for other plants, but few gardeners want to encourage the latter in among their vegetables!

Which are the easiest herbs to grow for year-round use?

In many open gardens rosemary, thyme, lavender, sage and bay can often be available year-round. As long as you cover them on really frosty nights, their foliage will stay fairly succulent, although not as nice as in summer. For safety, though, some can be grown in pots under cover, and it is a good idea to propagate and replace all of these every few years anyway. With a cloche, coldframe or an unheated greenhouse you can easily have marjoram, chives, chervil, rocket, mint and parsley all year. Almost any herb can be grown year-round in a heated greenhouse, or even in pots on a sunny windowsill, but they will tend to be poor compared to the summer ones, especially light-lovers such as basil.

I want to eat more green saladings. Can you please suggest some?

Rocket is the quickest real crop, but mustard and cress are even faster. Much more rocket can be eaten if it is from recent sowings rather than from old plants, so sow successively every week or so. Chives are very easy to multiply, are available much of the year and can be eaten in greater quantity more easily than many other herbs. Chervil is not as much appreciated as it might be and it goes well in mixed salads. Sweet Cicely is even better. I like quite a bit of dill, tarragon, mint and garlic chives mixed in my salads, but they may be a bit strong for some tastes. For summer use all the different cut-and-come-again lettuces can be added and varied with endives and radicchio. In the winter lamb's lettuce, miner's lettuce ('Claytonia') and the curly kales can all be welcome. Indeed, most of the brassicas make tasty young leaves and after the head of, say, a cauliflower or cabbage has been cut, you can leave the stump to produce a load of fresh greens, which can be enjoyed raw while small and cooked when larger.

Which vegetables are easiest to keep in store for winter use?

Parsnips, leeks and Brussels sprouts keep fine in the ground and are thought to be improved by a frost or two. However, they are more harvestable if covered in loose straw and plastic before everything freezes solid. Cabbages, cauliflowers, beets, carrots and other roots all keep freshest covered in the same way. Alternatively, they can be kept in a root cellar, or the modern equivalent – a dead chest-freezer in a shed. There the temperature and humidity are constant and if the vegetables are put in when chill, they will stay fresh for months (part of the lid seal needs perforating to allow some ventilation). Onions, shallots and garlic are very easily kept for up to six months if they are really well dried in a hot, airy place and then kept cool and dry; hanging up in the roof of a dry garage or shed is a handy place.

1

2

4

3

1 Rocket (*Eruca sativa*)
2 Miner's lettuce (*Claytonia*)
3 Sweet Cicely (*Myrrhis odorata*)
4 Chervil (*Chaerophyllum bulbosum*)

Why can I grow cabbages but not cauliflowers?

Cabbages are trying to make an enormous terminal bud, which is a very difficult task for the poor thing as it wants to burst open and show its leaves, which are congested and blanched. A cauliflower is even more of a high achiever, trying to produce a head composed of thousands of succulent unopened flower buds. This is a much tougher task, so the cauliflower is more likely to grow badly. Any check to its growth, such as drying out, overcrowding, being planted out too late or with insufficient roots, or too little watering after planting out, will cause the cauliflower to bolt and produce a button head, whereas in the same position and with the same treatment a cabbage would probably just be a bit smaller. I suspect that your soil is poor and/or dry and you will grow better cauliflowers if you enrich it with lots of compost, water it well and plant the cauliflowers out when they are much smaller than you are used to doing.

Why can I grow good cauliflowers but not good carrots?

Cauliflowers revel in a rich, deep, moist, heavy soil. Carrots do best in a light, dry, sandy soil. Therefore I deduce that your soil is heavy and rich and probably moist. Your soil will be extremely productive of all sorts of crops, except carrots and similar roots, such as salsify and scorzonera, all of which like a different set of conditions. Alternatively, it is just possible that your carrot roots are being decimated by a pest such as carrot root fly, in which case growing them under a horticultural fleece or nylon-net curtain will stop the adult fly laying its eggs in the ground next to your seedling carrots. Slugs and cutworms will also eat the tops, so that carrots do not thrive, and in new gardens wireworms can eat away the roots.

How do I stop caterpillars eating all my cabbages?

There are three methods that work, other than hand-picking, and a couple of tricks that reduce the level of attacks. First, they can be killed organically either with a spray or dusting of Derris or by using the bacterial disease *Bacillus thuriengiensis*. This is a powder containing a disease of these sorts of caterpillars – it is naturally occurring and thought harmless to us and most of the ecology. Personally I prefer to use plastic-bottle cloches over the plants while they are small, and horticultural fleeces or nylon-net curtain for the bigger plants; if the adult can't lay its eggs, then there will be no caterpillars. Sometimes they lay on the fleece or net, but not if it is supported on sticks above the plants. Alternatively, it has been shown that mixing your cabbages with French bean plants, nasturtiums or *Shungi-ku*, the edible chrysanthemum, can reduce attacks by caterpillars. So will wormwood, but the cabbages do not like it either and will not prosper.

Why do my brassicas turn purple and die?

There are several reasons why brassicas may get purple colours: cold and phosphate deficiency will both cause it, but neither is likely to be fatal. Waterlogging in a heavy acid soil may rot the roots and cause the plant's demise. Indeed any damage to the roots, such as club root (see p. 289) could cause some coloration, but I suspect that the most likely reason is cabbage-root fly. This is a maggot that eats the stem at and just below ground level, and the plants often turn purple and then wither or fall over. There is no cure, but future attacks can be thwarted by putting a hand-sized piece of cardboard with a slit in it around the stem. This excludes the fly and precludes it laying its eggs in the soil by the stem, and thus no damage occurs.

Why are my root crops not coming up?

Many root crops are reluctant to germinate in cold, wet soil, so maybe you are sowing too early. Alternatively, sow under cloches that were set in place a week or so previously to pre-warm the soil. Sometimes heavy rain can make certain soils cap – that is, form a crust that small seedlings such as carrots cannot break through. Capping can be prevented with cloches, mulches, regular watering and by increasing the humus content of the soil. But it may be that your roots did come up and that something ate them before you noticed. Often pests such as cutworms and birds will decimate small seedlings. I have found the carrot fly-resistant carrots to be particularly tasty to something, probably slugs.

I have trouble growing turnips and swedes – why?

These do not do so well in the drier counties of Britain as they do in the wetter. In the drier ones they need considerable soil enrichment and/or careful watering if good yields are wanted. They are prone to bolt, if too dry or if sown too early, and turnips will often do best from late sowings. And although neither likes dry conditions they do like full sun. I find a little bonemeal improves them tremendously.

Why do my carrots have holes, and how do I stop these appearing?

Carrots are most prone to carrot-fly attacks (see pp. 142, 287), but these are easily prevented with horticultural fleece or nylon-net curtain, or even with a barrier around the carrots just 60cm (24in) high. However, slugs also do a lot of damage, and a plague of millipedes likewise, and even worse can be wireworms if it is a new piece of ground. All of these pests are best reduced in number by baiting them away from the carrot roots with bits of potato, or carrot, placed in tin cans hidden in shade close to the carrot seedlings, from before their roots start to swell.

Why do my French/runner beans never do well?

I suspect the most likely reason is that your garden is cold, shady or windy. French beans revel in warm places, but sulk in colder ones. In particular they are hard to germinate if the soil is cold and then the slow emergence and early poor growth may result in stunted plants. I suggest that you put cloches or clear plastic sheet over the soil for a week before sowing and afterwards until the plants are a hand's breadth high; support the plastic sheet on sticks so that it does not rest on the soil or seedlings, as it may damage them.

How do I stop the maggots in my peas?

The pea moth lays its eggs on the flowers, so although there are approved organic sprays that could be used, there is a danger to other insects that may be attracted to the flowers. Rotation and hygiene will keep the pest down in your garden, but it may come in from your neighbours. The earliest sowings nearly always escape the pea moth, which is a summer pest; likewise late sowings may also be free – but may suffer from mildew instead. I go for early sowings and the maggot has rarely bothered me, especially as I usually steam my peas in the pods and eat the peas in the manner of asparagus, drawing the pod outwards between my teeth.

Why do my potato plants all die back in July?

It is conceivable that in a warm, wet early season you might just be suffering from potato blight (see also pp. 277, 291), but that is pretty unlikely. You would know, as one day a few plants would be affected, then a day or so later the lot would be decimated and smelling, and the blackened foliage would be rotting down the stems. At this stage the tubers can often be saved if the stems are cut off at ground level and the crop not dug for a fortnight. If the plants are dying back indiscriminately and at random, then look closely at the stems and pull some up. If they are rotting at or below ground level, then it is blackleg disease, which comes in on the seed pota-toes; do not save your own seed, but otherwise the tubers are fine to eat. If, however, the plants are withering and are doing so uniformly, then it is probable that you have grown an early variety that is now maturing and ready for use. You might find the same with second earlies or main crops if you chitted them for too long before planting.

Why do my potatoes never keep well?

Several factors affect the storage of potatoes. Not all varieties store well, par-ticularly earlies. Digging the potatoes from wet soil in cold weather makes them prone to rotting, as does overfeeding the soil by using far too much fer-tilizer. Bruising the tubers will cause them to rot, as will slug holes. Frost damages the tubers, while warmth makes them sprout and shrivel. Some diseases, such as blight, can make the tubers rot, though they look good when harvested. I find it best to dig the tubers on a sunny, windy day, then I dry them in the sun for an hour or so and pack them in paper sacks to store in a cool, dark place. I also use dead chest-freezers, as these are rodent-proof and the constant temperature helps the potatoes to keep really well. In freez-ing weather I can put a bottle of hot water in each day to keep out the cold and, as the weather warms up in spring, I can similarly defrost a small bag of ice to keep the temperature down and prevent sprouting.

My onions rot in the ground and in store – why?

It could be white rot (see p. 288), but hopefully it is not, as there is little you can do about this. Onion smut causes the leaves to distort and twist,

eventually showing black spores, and the plant usually fails to mature; if it does mature, it rarely stores well. There is no cure – only rotation and hygiene as preventatives. Onion mildew covers the leaves with a greyish bloom that spreads from pale patches. It is worst in cool, damp weather, and the bulbs that survive usually fail to keep. I find that generous dressings of wood ashes during the early part of the season keep this at bay.

Onion fly can cause the total death of the plant by eating away the roots and bottom of the bulb, and spring-sown plants usually suffer worse from this than sets, which often escape. Fine net curtain or horticultural fleece will keep this pest off the crop. Another possible cause of onions not keeping is that you are not drying them off sufficiently, which is likely in Britain's poor summers, so try more careful drying and then suspend them in netting so that they keep aired.

AS I suddenly had this problem with onions grown from sets when I moved to Devon. I think the heavier soil and moist climate took me by surprise. The solution is almost certainly to grow from seed instead of sets, which is what I intend to do in future.

My sweetcorn is poor. How do I make it better?

Sweetcorn only does well out of doors in the warmer south and Midlands, and is difficult to grow in the north, except under cover – where it is usually too tall, so choose dwarf varieties. The biggest problem is that they need a long growing period and, if sown outdoors, do not ripen early enough while the sun is still hot. We cannot sow earlier as the seed rots in the cold soil. Sowing indoors in pots ensures plants, but if these are then kept too long before planting out they do badly, as they resent confinement and root disturbance and really need deeper bigger pots than we can easily give them.

I find that sowing some sweetcorn in pots and some *in situ* under individual plastic-bottle cloches works best from mid- to late April. I also sow in several small batches, a week or so apart, to try and catch the best time and this usually gives at least one really good batch! If your soil is poor or dry then you will get much better crops if you enrich it with loads of compost or well-rotted manure and keep it moist with regular irrigation, as sweetcorn is a hungry, thirsty feeder.

What unusual vegetables are worth growing?

It all depends what you call unusual – some people may find globe artichokes, aubergines and chilli peppers adventurous, and even garlic too foreign. Most of our regular vegetables are well known simply because they

Skirrett (*Sium sisarum*)

Asparagus peas (*Lotus tetragonolobus*)

Tomatillos (*Physalis ixocarpa*)

are all reliable, productive and reasonably tasty. Most lesser-known edible crops never catch on because they fail in one of these prerequisites. For example, Jerusalem artichokes are reliable (in fact bomb-proof), incredibly productive, but have never become widely popular as they are not that good to eat, and giving you wind does not help matters. Scurvy grass *(Cochlearia officinalis)* may be healthy-eating, reliable and productive, but I'd only try it again if suffering from scurvy! Almost all the plants listed in reference books as having edible leaves can be used to make a similar spinach to the true one, with variations in flavour and a lot more ease than trying to get true spinach not to bolt. 'Good King Henry' *(Chenopodium bonus-henricus)* and Turkish rocket *(Bunias orientalis)* are two of the better ones.

Some of the unimproved roots are tasty but need selection to give the yields. Skirret *(Sium sisarum)* and earth chestnuts *(Bunium bulbocas-tanum)* are both quite good fare, but give very little return for your efforts. Salsify and scorzonera are better-known, as they are more substantial crops resembling carrots, with different and interesting flavours. Asparagus peas *(Lotus tetragonolobus)* are very tasty little pods when small, thrive on poor soils and look decorative, so they should be more widely known. If you can grow indoor tomatoes, try tomatillos *(Physalis ixocarpa)*; these are grown just like tomatoes and even look like them, in a paper case. They are usually purple or green when ripe, add the authentic taste to salsa and are highly productive.

What do organic gardeners feed tomatoes with, if soluble fertilizers are not allowed?

The first principle in organic methods is not to use anything that harms life, especially in the soil. Soluble fertilizers used as granules, and in the concentrations normally employed, kill many forms of life. Indeed, if used a little more strongly they will kill the plants, too. I feed the soil with non-soluble fertilizers such as well-rotted manure, compost, green manures and ground rock-dust. In turn the soil feeds the plants. Thus I rarely apply feeds directly to the plants, though in effect I may do so when I enrich the soil specifically, such as when I add extra ground-rock phosphate dust before planting strawberries.

However, all this becomes altered if you wish to grow plants in pots. A pot is a confinement and plants can hardly be expected to do as well as they do in the freedom of the ground. Organic gardeners would thus usually prefer to grow crops directly in the ground, but for some more tender plants, and for house plants, this is not possible. You can give plants bigger containers of rich potting compost, and can often pot up to a larger container, or top-dress with more potting compost, but eventually this becomes too difficult. Therefore you are forced to apply some fertility with the water, which must therefore be soluble. As you wish only to help the plant, and not hinder it, any such feed must be made from very natural extracts and applied in an extremely diluted form. The commonest is probably comfrey tea: comfrey leaves packed and rotted under water in a bucket, then diluted down in a ratio of 50:1. This suits tomatoes and many other plants in pots. I add a small proportion of stinging nettles and borage to my comfrey tea, as this seems to improve it. An alternative acceptable to some people is a very well-diluted mixture of fish emulsion and seaweed solution – the plants love it. An unfortunately unacceptable option to some people is urinating into the watering can. This is powerful stuff – tomatoes grow lush and citrus plants thrive on it. Another old-fashioned 'tonic' was a bag of manure (usually sheep's or cow's) soaked in a butt of water.

Why do my tomato plants in bags look good initially but do badly?

First, tomato plants would prefer more space for their roots than most bags offer. Second, many people put too many plants in each bag; one on its own will often produce as much as – or more than – two or three plants jammed together, especially if they are not carefully watered and fed. And that is the problem: a bag only has so much fertility mixed in. In order that the bag should perform adequately, as generous an amount is used as possible without damaging the plants. However, because this fertility is usually chemical in origin and very soluble, it is mostly available rapidly and as soon as the plants go in. Thus initially the tomatoes have loads of fertility and grow lush and fast, but as they start to compete and the soluble fraction is used up, or washed out, the plants slow down. Because of the limited root run they cannot find their own food and now need extra provision and regular feeding is required. Finally, though just as importantly, the plants are unable to find their own water. When plants are small they do not need much water, but when they are big and carrying a crop they need a lot, and several competing with each other in a bag cannot get enough unless automatic irrigation is arranged or frequent waterings are made – a splash from a can when they wilt is simply not enough.

Can I grow any sorts of peppers in a cold greenhouse?

Provided you have a heated propagator, a very warm, light windowsill or you buy the young plants in, you can easily grow peppers. They do need starting off early, much like indoor tomatoes. They cannot go into the border of an unheated greenhouse until late May, and even if you heat it they will not thrive down there. For this reason they do much better if they are grown in large pots up on the staging for longer, before planting out. However, they certainly crop better once in the ground. On top of raised beds is probably the best compromise under cover. In very sheltered gardens they can be grown in coldframes or even in the open, but then they rarely crop that well. Your cold greenhouse will do nicely as long as it is bright, as they detest shade.

Aphids can be troublesome early on, but are soon cured with soft soap, but take care that slugs do not damage the fruits. Sweet peppers are good croppers and will need some support, unless you pick all the peppers young and green. Leaving them to ripen fully to deep red suppresses many more forming, so they produce most if picked green or half-ripened. Hot peppers get just as hot here as in the heat – they are very, very productive. It is possible, by diligently searching catalogues, to grow many dozens of different sorts.

How do I sterilize my greenhouse and pots organically?

If you really must, then a steam pressure-washer will do the job very quickly and effectively. However, I try and work it the other way and encourage loads of predators to over-winter, as well as the few pests. I find spiders and other such friends are useful and that, by working around them, I get free pest control. Likewise, I never wash my pots and have rarely experienced any problems.

Are there any good companion plants for the greenhouse?

French marigolds keep whitefly from visiting new greenhouses, though they will not drive them out once they get in. Basil seems to keep the aphids off tomatoes by getting them itself. Sweet tobacco does the same for whitefly, and broad beans for red spider mite. Many flowering plants seem to be convenient for attracting pollinators but, with limited space, it is best to stick to the herbs that you can also find a culinary use for.

How do I start gardening organically?

First, stop using soluble fertilizers, all herbicides, most fungicides and most insecticides. Anything that damages soil organisms, or kills any life in general, is not wanted, as the idea of organic culture is to foster all forms of life so that our plants stay healthy, living on the by-products that the micro-life creates. The interplay of many different larger organisms creates a self-regulating pest and disease control system.

Second, use wit and cunning to grow healthy plants and to outmanoeuvre the pests and diseases that cannot be controlled with natural checks and balances. But maximize the latter by growing a wider variety of plants and by making more diverse habitats in the garden. When the system lags, employ the least invasive measures that you can, such as nets or barriers, traps and sacrificial crops, so that you do not make holes in the ecosystem, but just fine-tune it.

Third, recycle all garden (and many household) wastes as compost. A gardener who squanders valuable waste is throwing away fertility. Anything that has ever lived is turned back into fertility by the composting process, which is essential to every organic garden.

Finally, consume carefully to save nature. Stop using peat from threatened sites; don't buy imported wild plants or mass bedding; choose materials from renewable sources, such as managed woodland; and avoid plastic whenever natural or longer-lasting alternatives exist.

How do I make good compost?

Composting is the accelerated rotting of once-living materials. It converts wastes into a rich soil that is pleasant to handle. Any pile of material will eventually break down to make a useful compost, but the best sort is carefully made. The important difference is that in proper composting the whole heap is cooked by the heat that is generated. In small heaps, made in layers over weeks, this heating never occurs and the product is in many ways inferior. If you only accumulate small amounts of waste at a time, don't worry – just keep getting them until you have loads. You can even accumulate them in your bin.

When you have at least as much waste as will fill your bin, then do a thorough mixing. Empty all the materials onto a sheet of plastic and mix them up. Add ground lime, wood ashes and any manure or urine you have to hand. If the mass is wet, add shredded paper or straw; if the mass is dry, then wet it. Then pack it all into the bin: it does not matter if it will not all go in at once, as it will soon settle. Do not pack it down, though, as air is essential in the process. When all the heap is stacked, cover the top with something insulating and waterproof. If you are really enthusiastic, turn it all over again in a fortnight. Leave the stack for several months, then take the sides away but leave a cover on it. Once it is fairly dry it is easily sieved, and the sieving spoil returned to inoculate the next heap. Some say that meat, fat and bones should not go into a compost heap as these attract vermin. I find this good advice if you only make a slowly decomposing heap, but in a hot heap these wastes soon compost. However, such wastes as meat and fat would be better fed to a pet or a chicken, as it represents high-grade protein and is rather under-utilized as composting material.

Anything that once lived goes into my compost heaps: feather pillows, woollen clothes, cotton undies, flat animal-road victims, vacuum-cleaner dust… But I am careful never to put anything in too thick a layer and try to keep it all mixed up and moist. The only things to leave out are obvious hazards, like plastic, glass and metal, and large bits of wood, though shred-ded prunings and the live roots of pernicious weeds are fine. The latter are killed by steeping them in water for a few months first. Masses of glossy evergreen leaves will not compost very easily and should be used as mulches under their parents. Lots of autumn leaves are best rotted down on their own to make leaf mould, though some can be mixed into a compost heap. I believe that diseased material and weed seeds can go into my heaps, as they heat up and 'cook' these problem items, but those who make cold heaps would do better to burn such materials.

Rather than making a small heap and little compost, it is a good idea to devote some time to collecting all sorts of wastes, such as a neighbour's household waste, shredded paper, hair, grass clippings, pet droppings (ham-ster, rabbit, and so on – not dog or cat) and of course weeds: you can offer to weed other people's gardens just to get their fertility! If you make more compost at a time the process works better, you get more fertility – and you help clean up the world.

What should I best do with the small amount of compost that I make?

This is a perfect plant food in a form readily available to plants, with no risk of overfeeding, as can be caused by chemical fertilizers. The vast num-ber of different organisms that have made compost go on to inoculate and colonize the soil, further aiding fertility and controlling pests such as eel-worm nematodes (minute wormlike creatures). So it does not need applying in bulk, but more as a catalyst. I suggest that you do as I do, and sieve the compost to make it pleasant and uniform to handle. The sieved compost is then mixed into the soil when putting out any plants and as a top-dressing around established ones. I also use it as a sowing compost for robust plants and as a potting compost for most.

Can I buy any truly organic fertilizers? If so, which are the best?

Eventually you should be able to produce all your own fertility by compost-ing wastes and growing green manures. Some seaweed solution is always useful, but is more of a 'vitamin pill' than a fertilizer, especially as it is applied as a foliar feed. Manures from conventional agriculture are tradi-tional and can be used in an organic garden, provided they are well com-posted for several months first, though many people prefer to avoid them for philosophical reasons. However, composted manures are at least being recycled and when delivered in, say, pelleted form are convenient for the city dweller with little access to animal wastes.

Of course many people also do not wish to use bone- or fishmeal, dried blood or hoof and horn, as these are animal death products, though they are allowed in limited amounts to the organic gardener. Much better are ground rock dusts, which are natural slow-release sources of potash, phosphate or calcium, plus lime, which is especially necessary to keep the soil sweet for vegetables and stone fruits. Calcified seaweed is a lime made from seaweed, which has trace elements in profusion and stimulates the soil's life as well as sweetening it. Probably the best all-round commercially available fertilizer is dried, ground seaweed meal, as this has almost everything (including nitrogen) in a safe but available form.

What is green manure?

Green manure is fertility that we grow our-selves. It usually occupies the soil over the winter or between crops, when otherwise the earth is doing little but leaching nutrients. The green manure may be dug or hoed in to incorporate it *in situ*, covered with light-

Limanthes douglassii

Phacelia tanacetifolia

excluding mulches to do the same thing, or the top growth may be taken away for composting, to be returned later. Hungarian grazing rye, clovers, tares and vetches are traditional farming green manures, but not well suited to the garden scale. I find that spinach, mustard (which must be used for only short periods if you have clubroot, as it is related to brassicas), lupins, *Phacelia tanacetifolia* and the poached egg plant *(Limnanthes douglassii)* are excellent – the latter pair especially good for insects, if left long enough to flower.

It is better with green manure to grow two short immature crops rather than one mature one, as the succulent young material is more use to the gardener on most soils than fibrous older growths. Incorporating young growths adds a more instant fertility, while adding old growths adds fibre and improves the soil texture. Of course you have to buy in the seed for the first year, but thereafter you can always grow your own – after all there should be plenty of plants to choose from.

How do I start on a weedy allotment without weedkillers?

Traditionally you skim off the topmost layer and stack it to rot down, then fork over the soil, removing weed roots as you go. This is best done from late autumn until early winter so that the soil can consolidate again before the spring. You never get all the roots, and hosts of weeds come from seed, so it is absolutely critical to hoe off the weeds as fast as they appear for the first six months or so. Hoe once a week, sharpen your hoe every 10 minutes and work forwards, taking care not to firm any weeds back into the soil. It is sometimes the case that people put a lot of effort and enthusiasm into the initial preparation, but then cannot keep up with the weeding, especially if they have filled the area with crops, which then obscure the weeds.

The first spring grow only widely spaced crops so that it is easier to hoe the weeds. Choosing transplanted crops will give you longer to get on top of the weeds before the plants go in. Tomatoes, brassicas, squashes, courgettes and sweetcorn are all good crops for the first year. Potatoes are reckoned to be good for the soil because of the cultivation required, but the tubers will be full of slug and wireworm holes. If you are not gifted with much free time, it may be easier to share your allotment with someone else until it is established and running, and then you could both take on a second plot. Alternatively, only bring half of your allotment under cultivation initially and put the other half down to grass and keep cutting it. Return the clippings, as this will improve its fertility and control the weeds. Indeed, if you can wait, then sowing it down to grass and cutting it weekly with a nylon-line trimmer or rough mower will get rid of most weeds in a year or so. There are very few weeds that survive regular close cutting and these are removed when the topmost layer is skimmed off. Certainly making a new bed is always easiest and most profitable where the area has been down to mown grass for a while.

Another control method that can be used is to mulch out the weeds. Although most established weeds thrive with a loose mulch, they are soon killed by the lack of light under a flimsy black plastic sheet. It must be totally light-proof, however; if it is not, then put down layers of newspaper or cardboard first to improve the blackout. All weeds that come up in the dark turn yellow and rot away, exhausting the roots, which also rot. However, this will not happen if the roots under the blackout are connected to leaves in the light somewhere else. In this case dig a narrow isolation trench about 30cm (12in) deep and hang the plastic sheet over the edge. Occasionally the weeds may push the plastic up and need flattening under an extra newspaper or three.

Where well-rotted manure and compost are available, they can be spread on the ground first, before the mulching layers are laid. It helps if they are used to smooth the surface, especially if only thin plastic is applied. Indeed, holes and hillocks should be levelled first and any stumps removed, although it is far easier to do this after the mulches have killed the weeds, so if it is very weedy then only roughly prepare the surface and cover any sharp projections with a wad of newspaper to prevent the plastic being punctured. Basically, if you can drive a rough, tough mower over the surface beforehand, that will do. The plastic light-exclusion method works best if applied just before the spring flush of growth, so it should be laid in late February or early March. It can be removed in autumn and the soil will be in amazing condition, the weeds will have disappeared, most of the cardboard will have rotted away and even many of the pests will have gone, as the larger creatures such as shrews will have eaten them.

Once the plastic is removed, the soil can be forked over and, as all the established weeds are gone, it will require only simple maintenance hoeing. But there is a bonus: you can cut holes in the plastic and plant out any of the crops listed above during May, when the weeds will already be almost gone. Thus you get some production that first season, while the plastic does the work. (By the way, I used to use old carpet instead of plastic, but the value of this has risen and any available second-hand carpet is now generally too threadbare, though totally synthetic carpets work well and are best used upside down.)

How do I get rid of ground elder/Japanese knotweed/bindweed/ bracken/bamboo/equisetum?

These are the most pernicious weeds and are troublesome to get rid of. Their main strength comes from their wide-ranging root systems. As fast as you kill off the bit in your garden, it is replaced and reinforced by more coming from the roots and leaves elsewhere. Even weedkillers usually fail to work on them, because of their spread and their ability to return. Total extirpation is possible, but only where the weed cannot regain access. Thus, if by chance the weed is growing in a border in the middle of a large lawn, with no roots joining it to more of the plant elsewhere, then it will be fairly simple to destroy and should never recur. However, in most gardens it will be coming back from under hedges and fences.

It is possible to stop most ordinary weeds' roots, and those of ground elder, by setting an unbroken plastic sheet barrier in a slit trench, but the other pernicious weeds have roots that dive too deeply for this to be practical in most cases. There is only one way to get rid of all weeds, and that is to remove every leaf from the whole plant every week from early March until the following October. If every leaf is removed every week, then the root systems become exhausted and die away. But if just one leaf survives unnoticed, then it will keep much of the root system alive to enable it to return. So it is no good working hard on your bit of the plant if your neighbours do not do likewise, and at the same time (or you do it for them with their permission).

It does not matter how you remove all the leaves – scissors, fingers, shears or trimmer – but every single leaf must go every week! You need only be methodical and persistent if you want to get rid of these weeds. The first months are the hardest, because after this fewer roots will survive to recover, but do not stop looking for the next few weeks or they will come back. The price of freedom from such weeds is eternal vigilance and diligent weeding.

BG These pernicious weeds are the bane of many gardeners' lives, as they have such extensive root systems compared to the amount of foliage. If you use glyphosate or Tumbleweed, you need to get a good rate of uptake to give reasonable results. The key to this is in the timing. Do not be tempted to rush out and zap them in early spring as soon as they appear; instead, wait until they are just about to flower, when they have developed a lot of foliage. In this way more chemical can be taken up by the plant. Use the highest concentration recommended on the bottle, but do not be tempted to go more concentrated than this, as it can have a detrimental effect. Equisetum is the most difficult of the three, due to its waxy layer and sparse foliage. In order to break this down you need to bruise it lightly before you spray it. Use a small roller, or a garden broom. This way you should get an 80–90 per cent kill the first time, but you will need to establish a programme to keep hitting it. Autumn kill can be effective, as all the sap is going back to the root system and the chemical goes down with it, hitting it where it hurts.

The problem of treating these weeds in borders is more difficult still. With bindweed you can put canes in your plants and let it scramble up and then, when it's head and shoulders above the rest of your treasures, you can stroke it sweetly with a brush full of the gel form of Tumbleweed. Or you can put a rubber glove on, with a tightish-fitting woollen glove over it, dip your fingers in the gel and stroke it onto the offending parts. For ground elder and equisetum these systems work, too. I also keep a small pint-sized spray mister full of solution ready to hand, and apply it to any perennial weeds that are not entwined with a garden plant.

Never plant any border until you have eradicated perennial weeds. They are so much easier to control if you can get at them properly without the hindrance of plants in your path.

What is a flame gun, and how do I use it for thermal weed control?

A flame gun is a giant gas or paraffin blow-torch. Some come with hoods and wheels, others with a wand. The idea is that you cook the weed leaves with the intense heat. You do not burn off the leaves, but simply pass the flame over them very quickly – they change colour and then the dying foliage exhausts the root systems. They work really well on flushes of weeds in empty beds, such as before asparagus emerges, and not only kill the weeds but also any weed seeds on the surface. Two or more hits, a week apart, may be needed for weeds that have got bigger than seedlings, and tough recidivists such as thistles may take up to half a dozen hits before expiring.

On the second or return trip the flame cooks any new leaves and sets fire to shrivelled ones. This wastes organic material that could have been more usefully employed in the compost heap, though the ashes remain. Thus a flame gun is not really a good idea for heavily weedy areas, with established weeds, but is ideal for keeping bare vegetable beds or gravel paths weed-free. It can also be used with cunning: if you flame-weed a seedbed, then sow it, you know for certain the minimum number of days it takes for that crop to germinate and emerge. You can then flame-weed the bed a day or two beforehand, catching any new or recovering weeds and leaving it totally free for the emerging seedlings.

Most flame guns are too big for garden use, and they are a serious fire risk as well, so take all due precautions. On a much smaller scale, a hobby blow-torch can be used in the same way to cook the weeds in a rockery or patio, avoiding valued plants. But I have found that there are several much safer alternatives: a steam iron, a steam wallpaper stripper or, best of all, a hot-air paint stripper. A quick cooking with any one of these once a week soon cleans up problem areas of all weeds.

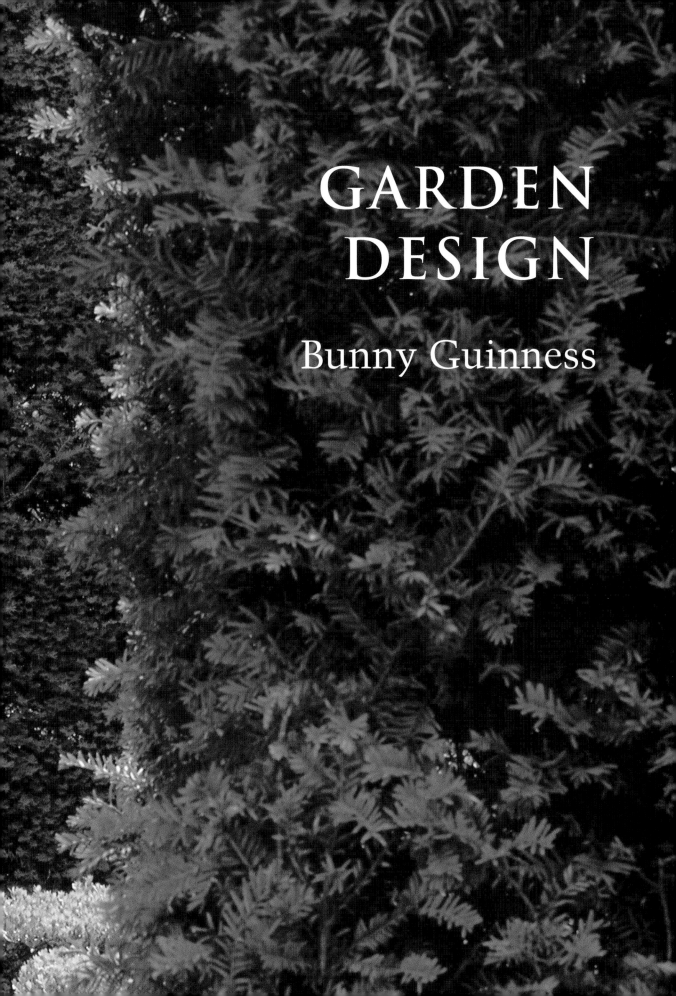

GARDEN DESIGN

Bunny Guinness

I have, as long as I can remember, been fascinated by outdoor spaces – and gardens in particular. They often have great potential and are an exciting challenge to create. They contribute so much to a home in terms of both function and aesthetics. They are dynamic, changing week by week and year by year as the seasons progress and the garden matures. I visit many gardens both for pleasure and to give advice and think that for many gardeners the design side is often the most perplexing. The scale of the outside makes it much more problematic than tackling, for instance the interior design of an internal room. The possibilities are seemingly endless with the vast array of materials, plants, colours and ornaments on offer today. In addition, exactly how you achieve what you want, tend it and maintain it, complicate the issue still further.

I firmly believe that good garden design is a logical and rational thought process, that the spaces are created as a result of solving problems and finding imaginative solutions. Common problems that crop up regularly are hiding neighbouring eyesores, making a space look bigger, concealing an unattractive elevation of the house and livening up a dark corner. Knowing what materials are available and how you achieve certain effects is an important part of producing exactly what you want, so I have included the details of suppliers and manufacturers where possible.

If you are in the process of making a great garden, I hope that some of the answers I have given here might be applicable to your space. They include the questions that I am most frequently asked. One of the most frequent remarks I hear from gardeners who are not totally satisfied with their plot is 'I know it's not right but I do not know what to do to get it right.' Hopefully the list of questions will help you to define and analyse the problems in your garden and also help you solve them.

SCREENING, BOUNDARIES, ARCHES AND PERGOLAS

I have a small back garden, which is overlooked on both sides by houses, and would like to have some privacy – how can you suggest I achieve this?

Lack of privacy is a common problem in many back gardens. Many people find that the use and enjoyment of their garden are severely curtailed if other properties overlook their private space. In addition, a lack of privacy often affects the appearance of the garden, as the views of other properties leak in. This was certainly the main problem in my back garden, and so it became the main influence on the overall design. Not only was the space totally overlooked, but a large, 1960s' flat-roofed extension, two storeys high, formed the dominant focal point of the garden.

My approach, in this case, was to plant a double line of hornbeams *(Carpinus betulus)* down the two long sides of the rectangular plot and returning at both ends, to leave a wide gap to frame an attractive, agricultural view. I planted transplants 45–60cm (18–24in) high and then started to pleach them when they reached about 1.8m (6ft) high. Now, some eight years on, they obliterate the vast majority of the building, frame the views and give us total privacy in the summer. In the winter months they heavily mask the extension, but do not give total privacy, but then I'm not so concerned about people watching my activities in the garden in the winter months anyway!

Pleached trees are particularly useful for screening in confined situations, as you cut them back annually, so preventing them becoming too tall and oppressive. They are effectively hedges on stilts; they have bare trunks at the base – usually to just below eye level – and then form a hedge above this. The point about restricting their height is also important as it determines their root spread. When you reduce the tops, the roots are affected too, compensating by dying back. In confined areas you do not want large trees too near buildings, especially if you are on a shrinkable clay soil, as the roots can affect the foundations. In a small garden having the bare trunks below eye level gives you useful space below the canopy. Because I planted a double row down each side, I have formed two shady walkways leading to a focal point at either end. A single row of tress would have sufficed in terms of privacy, though. A hedge on one side and a wall on the other form the boundary below eye level, but a climber-clad timber fence would work well, too.

There are many trees apart from hornbeam that can be pleached – the broad-leafed lime (Tilia platyphyllos) is commonly used, but it does tend to sucker, and clipping of the foliage has to be done with secateurs because of the size of the leaves. Whitebeam *(Sorbus)* and hawthorn *(Crataegus)* are useful choices, especially for smaller spaces, though only the hawthorn can

be cut with clippers. The thorns make it more difficult to work, but they are not usually present on young wood so do not cause too much of a problem.

When you are establishing the trees, plant them 1.5–2.5m (5–8ft) apart. Go for the closer spacing if you are impatient, but bear in mind that you will have more training and more work to do as a result. I planted my two rows 2.8m (9ft) apart – if I had put them much closer the shady alley between would have been too constricted.

In order to get that structured look, which is achieved by training the lateral branches to grow in one plane (see the diagrams), it is necessary to put up some framework. The simplest method is to use long bamboo canes, with which you join the lateral branches on two neighbouring trees at the same height from the ground. You can just put them in as your trees grow, so when your first lateral branches develop at about eye level, approximately 1.5m (5ft) up, you can link the corresponding laterals with a horizontal cane. As the trees grow and laterals develop higher up, you add further canes at about 30cm (12in) centres. I didn't use this method, but put in vertical metal (less obtrusive than timber) posts, which stand about 4m (13ft) high and are drilled at the top end to take wires at 30cm (12in) centres. This was necessary because my garden is extremely exposed and I didn't want to spend the rest of my life searching for canes blown away by the south-westerly gales.

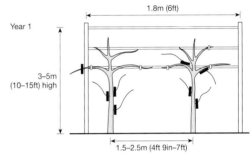

Year 1
1.8m (6ft)
3–5m (10–15ft) high
1.5–2.5m (4ft 9in–7ft)

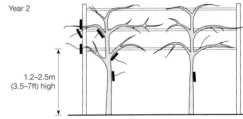

Year 2
1.2–2.5m (3.5–7ft) high

The training is easier than it looks, and once it is established can be maintained by clipping over in mid-June, once the first flush of new growth is over. This keeps it looking trim for the summer months, although some people prefer to do this during the winter. The main difficulty is the height that you are working at. One day I'll treat myself to a scaffold tower, but for now I use some tall stepladders.

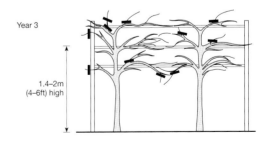

Year 3
1.4–2m (4–6ft) high

Year 1: Tie the laterals firmly to the horizontal canes or wires, remove all other branches.
Year 2: When the leader reaches the top of the framework bend and tie to one side. Train a suitable lateral in the opposite direction. Cut side shoots back to two or three buds and remove any wayward growth.
Year 3: Continue to cut back any new branches that grow away from the frame. Tie in well positioned shoots all over the framework and keep the top and bottom lines as horizontal as possible. This will encourage bushy growth to fill the framework.

Pleached trees hiding a two storey flat

If you are impatient, you can buy ready-formed mature pleached trees, and on several jobs my clients have asked for these 3m (10ft) high trees in huge containers. Invariably these are on jobs where the garden access is limited, resulting in heavy wrestling with awkwardly shaped trees as they are transported through the house – so be warned: it is not always easy!

There are alternatives to screening apart from pleached trees, of course. Trees that are suitable for small gardens can be appropriately positioned, but the problem is that they are usually very close to someone's house and so you may well need to prune them repeatedly to prevent problems with the foundations. Tall hedges may work, but they can look quite oppressive in a confined space. Trellis panels on top of existing fences are often used, but you are only allowed to have a fence 2m (6½ft) high on a boundary away from a road, unless you have planning permission. However, unless you are putting up an eyesore or restricting a neighbour's light, it is unlikely that this would be refused. Bear in mind that a fence would need to be seriously high to block a view from anything other than a single-storey dwelling, and this in itself could look strange. On one job we solved the problem by training horizontal wires to a height of 4m (13ft) on top of a wall, then planted vigorous climbers to provide the screening.

My house has an ugly extension. What can you suggest I do to soften or screen it?

The house is often the most important focal point of any garden. Because of this, I almost invariably start any design with a critical appraisal of the building. The garden layout can address the problems of the house – it should emphasize the good and hide the bad. The entrance area to a property is one of the most important spaces in the garden. As such, it should create a sense of arrival, be appropriate to the house and make the visitor feel welcome. Extensions – particularly those added in the 1950s and 1960s – often look out of kilter with the original building as the building style looks more modern and utilitarian. The windows are often larger and more numerous, while a flat roof or a shallow roof-pitch is frequently used over a single-storey structure.

Assuming that you wish to make the newer part of the building less obtrusive, there are several different approaches you can take. Often the additions are set back from the front of the building, leaving a space in front of the newer part, which can be planted up with some substantial planting, preferably at eye level or above. Small, standard trees can be particularly useful in this situation. Their more formal shape, with a mophead on a clear stem, ensures that both the canopy and the roots are kept to a restricted size, so minimizing problems of light restriction to the house and foundation damage from the roots. In this situation planting is often quite close

Partially screened extension

to the building, so these factors can be critical. Where the soil is a shrink-able clay, making building foundations more vulnerable, it is safer to put trees into large pots, which gives you scope for a lot of impact. A short row of standard, clipped Portugal laurel *(Prunus lusitanica)* in large terracotta pots is an attractive way to divert attention away from a utilitarian building behind. Other good trees grown as mophead standards are hawthorn *(Crataegus monogyna)*, bay trees *(Laurus nobilis)* and evergreen oak *(Quercus ilex)*. These last two take some time to form big specimens. If you are not keen on these more formal-looking types, then smaller trees kept with their canopy restricted by less formal pruning would be suitable. Some of the smaller whitebeams tolerate regular pruning well, as does quince *(Cydonia oblonga)*.

In the example in the photograph, the extension was set well back. This enabled a trellis fence to be attached to the original building, forming a planted screen in front of the extension, making it far less prominent. It also has the merit of forming a tiny, semi-private entrance courtyard, which was an hitherto open windswept space. Apart from the trellis screen, the paintwork on the windows was altered. Initially they were bright white, but anything painted white jumps out and demands attention. By painting them in a stone colour, the windows immediately receded into the stone wall. The fascia board to the flat roof was also given the same treatment.

Pleached trees in front of an unsightly addition are also extremely effec-tive at screening (see p. 161). An altogether less dramatic way would be to use climbers and large shrubs to camouflage what you can.

We have just moved and our garden is extremely exposed – it is rare that we have a day without the wind whistling through it. The garden is completely bare. Is there any way we can establish a windbreak so that we can enjoy the time spent there?

When you move into a new garden, windbreaks, if necessary, are one of the essential things that need to be sorted out immediately. Any outdoor space is much more enjoyable to use if it is sheltered – not just for you, the plants will respond accordingly too. The prevailing winds over most of Britain are the south-westerlies, but make sure that this is the case for your garden and then start planning how and where you are going to put up your shelter belts.

Solid walls, although instant, are not ideal shelter belts as the wind tends to form eddies and turbulence on the lee side of them. Hedges and trees are more efficient because, if they are well planned, they will lift and filter the wind. Generally speaking, a shelter belt will provide shelter for a distance of ten times its height. My own garden was extremely exposed to the south-west winds. Because the distance I wanted to shelter is fairly extensive and it would take a long time to establish trees to that height, I formed a series of gardens, all with hedges as boundaries, giving protection from the south-west winds. The most south-westerly boundary has a deep screen, which is made up of an external boundary hedge with dense tree planting on the inside.

In order to help your shelter-belt plants establish quickly, it is well worth putting up a fence to filter the wind. You can buy several different types of proprietary windbreak fencing, which are usually made from dark-grey plastic or a woven green fabric, rather like onion bags (see Suppliers Index). They come in rolls at a variety of heights, from 1m (3ft) to 3m (10ft), and you fix it to supporting posts. You often see such fencing around commercial plant nurseries, but it is not particularly easy on the eye. Another inexpensive screen would be to make up your own panels from 1.8 x 3.8cm (¾ x 1½in) roofing battens fixed to a timber frame, 1.8 x 1.8m (6 x 6ft): nail the battens on horizontally, leaving a gap of about 3.8cm(1½in) between each batten. I have seen this combined with shelter-belt planting on the inside. Trellis would be more attractive still, but slightly more expensive.

The general principle with the planting design of a shelter belt is to have lower shrubs at the outside, graduating in height to taller trees on the inside. This has the effect of lifting the wind up and over. The overall width needs to be about 3–4m (10–13ft) – more if you have the space. You should plant suitable shrubs that will tolerate exposure on the outside. These could either take the form of thicket planting or a mixed native hedge. Suitable plants would be hawthorn *(Crataegus monogyna)*, field maple *(Acer campestre)*, wayfaring tree *(Viburnum lantana)*, native privet *(Ligustrum vulgare)* and sea buckthorn *(Hippophae rhamnoides)*. For a hedge, plant them in a triple row if you have space, with 50cm (20in) between the rows and the same space between the plants in the rows. This will form a tough, fast-growing buffer for the outside edge. Mix up random groups of three to nine of each plant, and maintain it as a clipped hedge, as this stops the stems becoming bare at the bottom. The height could be maintained at about 1.2m (4ft). Inside this plant small pioneer trees, such as the goat willow *(Salix caprea)* and field maple *(Acer campestre).* Hawthorn would form the next layer in, and these should be planted at about 2m (6½ft) centres to form a good, dense screen. If you have room, an inner layer of large trees, again at the same centres, of suitable native trees, such as the wild cherry *(Prunus avium)* and the common silver birch *(Betula pendula),* will grow very fast, even in exposed areas, and tolerate a range of soils.

To make sure that the trees establish quickly, plant them bare-rooted, as transplants – about 45–60cm (18–24in) high. Use a translucent tree shelter (see Suppliers Index); do not stake the tree, as the wind helps to rock the plants and so develop a good fibrous root system, and keep it free of weed competition for the first three years at least. Plants with no grass or weed competition will grow about 60–70 per cent faster than those with competition.

The walls and fences around our small back garden are a complete mish-mash of timber fencing and rendered walls, punctuated with drainpipes and assorted windows. What can I do to make them look more uniform and attractive?

A small space always looks more coordinated if the colour scheme is restricted to a few colours. Consider choosing a coordinating colour for all the rendered surfaces; this could be a colour such as Biscuit from Farrow and Ball (see Suppliers Index), which is nearly the colour of Bath stone and is a good neutral but warm colour. Alternatively, an intense, strong colour, such as Book Room Red (also Farrow and Ball), a dark terracotta red, would make the space look more dramatic. If the timber fencing is not a particularly attractive style it can be made to recede, if it is painted with a very dark-green opaque stain. I often tend to mix these myself, as many ready-made ones are too light and eye-catching. I get the darkest green I can and then add black to it. If you are after a very dark greenish-blue colour, then add dark blue, too.

A simple way to unite the walls and fences is to make up trellis panels (see the diagrams) and paint them in a lighter or brighter colour in an opaque wood stain that goes well with both background colours. This makes them stand out and catch the eye, diverting attention from the disparate surfaces behind. A pale green (such as BS 12B21, which can be made up in Jotuns Demidekk), is one I have used repeatedly. Besides having an extremely comprehensive chart, Jotuns (see Suppliers Index) are able to make their wood stains (both translucent and opaque) up in the complete

Designs for
easy-to-make
trellis panels

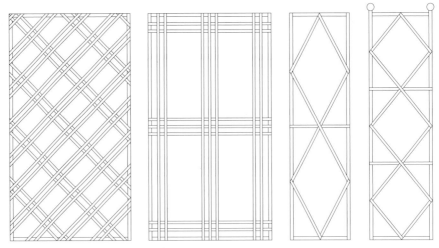

BS colour range. I find the colour schemes work best when I spend time with lots of trial pots, painting samples and tweaking colours accordingly, so that you can easily see which colours work best in that particular space.

For the drainpipes, try painting them in a dark lead colour – 'Down Pipe' (Farrow and Ball) is a good dark-grey colour for imitating lead on exterior ironwork and as such is useful for 'losing' plumbing against brickwork.

Having sorted out the hard aspects, the softer side (the planting) can then be used to pull everything together. Try using a climber that can be used on every aspect, to add uniformity. Then add additional ones, according to aspect, to spice it up a bit.

I would like to make a tunnel from metal arches to form a path through our orchard. Can you suggest how to make this look more interesting?

Metal tunnels work well in soft green spaces such as orchards, as metal can be used in light, thin sections that just define the arch shape, then rampant climbers can add impact. Timber can look too heavy and hard in this situation unless rustic, natural timbers are used, which give a completely different effect.

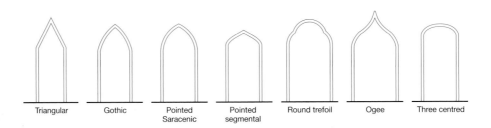

Triangular   Gothic   Pointed   Pointed   Round trefoil   Ogee   Three centred
                          Saracenic   segmental

Arch shapes

Many people buy arches ready-made, but I always prefer one-off designs as this gives you the scope to do something more interesting. It does not always cost more to do this, providing you are prepared to hunt around a bit and find someone who relishes doing something a little different. There are more and more craftsmen around today who are keen to make individual items, and there are many different styles of arches – the diagram illustrates only a few of them. If you have any existing arches on your house or surrounding buildings you could pick up on this shape and reflect it your arch. On one scheme I designed, the garden backed onto a church and we repeated the shape of the Gothic arches in a pergola.

When designing your arches, you should bear in mind the various thicknesses and shapes of metal bar that you can use. For smaller archways, up to about 1.4m (4¾ft) wide, a 1.5cm (⅝in) solid round steel bar is usually adequate. For larger spans the blacksmith or metal worker may advise using a heavier section. If you want larger structures, square-section hollow tubing might be more suitable. Sometimes I have used flat steel bars, usually bent so that you see the thin section as you look at them straight on.

When you have decided on the shape of your arch, you can decide how to connect them. In a fairly loose, informal area, such as orchards tend to be, it can be effective to connect several arches together with horizontal metal bars along the outside and then leave a gap before the next part of the tunnel starts. The metal bars connecting the arches can be quite widely spaced – they just allow the climbers to clamber up the sides and make the arches slightly more rigid. Finials on top of the arches are quite fun, and you could try something like a fleur-de-lis picked out in gold leaf, with one at each end of the tunnel. Transfer gold leaf is available by mail order from some art shops (see Suppliers Index). This is fantastic: it is real gold, beaten out to a very thin film, and then put onto a transfer backing paper for ease of use outside. You need to ask for a high-carat gold for outdoor situations, as the red and yellow golds oxidize more quickly. It is fairly easy to apply yourself and is surprisingly inexpensive, as a little goes a long way. It stays shiny for many, many years, unlike gold paints, which look dull after a few months. The remainder of the metal work would look good with a matt-black finish.

How do you make hazel arches for the vegetable garden, and where do you get the sticks from?

Hazel arches are fun and easy to make. Long hazel sticks are becoming more readily available (see Suppliers Index) as they are becoming popular for garden use. It is best to make sure that they have been cut during the dormant season – that is, between November and the end of February. If they are cut when the sap is not flowing, they will last longer. When you are ordering them tell the supplier what they are for. They need to be as long as possible, preferably just over 3m (10ft) long and about 2.5cm (1in) thick at the base. At the top they will be nice and whippy.

If you are making a tunnel about 1.2m (4ft) wide, the most basic way to do it is to push one stick into the ground to a depth of about 30cm (12in). This should be enough to hold it rigid, but it does depend on the soil type. Repeat on the other side with another stick and arch them over to meet each other. Then tie them together where they cross over at about 15cm (6in) intervals, with some natural-coloured string (you can dirty this down with soil if it looks too noticeable). The arch will need to be at a height of about 1.9m (6¼ft). If your sticks are not this long or you want a wider arch, you can create it using three pieces, one each side and one over the top. You then tie them together, as before, over the overlaps (see the diagram). In order to make a framework to take runner beans, sweetpeas, gourds and other climbing plants it will be necessary to make a series of arches and to link them together with horizontal sticks tied onto the arches. You can play around with the distances apart that you make the arches and the horizontals: 30cm (12in) for both forms a good rigid struc-ture, which is attractive and functional.

I have just bought some hazel archways. Can you suggest how to prolong their life?

As mentioned above, if the hazel is cut in the dormant season it will last longer. Depending on how wet the ground is, the sticks should last for about seven to eight years. The part of the hazel arch that rots quickest is that which is in the ground. To prevent this, fix the bases to independent 'grandad posts'. These posts, which you knock into the ground to a depth of about 50cm (20in). You can then nail or tie, above ground level, each end of the hazel arch to one of these. If the grandad posts rot before the arch disintegrates, they can be replaced.

For anyone making their own hazel or willow arches, another system is to get some simple metal arches made up in groups of two or more about 30cm (12in) apart. Ask for them to be joined by horizontal bars at about 30cm (12in) centres. Paint them with a gloss paint (having primed and undercoated them first) in the same colour as your coppiced material and then weave the coppice material in and out of the side ladders. The finished article looks like a solid hazel/willow tunnel, but lasts a lot longer.

OPTICAL ILLUSIONS

I have a tiny town courtyard surrounded by dark brick walls. It is north-facing. How can I make it appear larger?

Occasionally in these situations it is possible to create a two-storey garden, with a small raised platform in one part. This has the big advantage that the raised area will get more sunlight; it also creates a lot more interest and enables you to get much more into your garden. However, often in town gardens, unless it is a basement garden, the inclusion of a platform creates 'overlooking' problems for neighbouring properties. It would be necessary to check this factor out with your local planning department before proceeding. Access to the platform could be via a spiral staircase (concrete, stone or metal) or some simple timber steps. The design should be of a style to enhance the property – whether chunky and rustic or lightweight, modern

Mosaic mirror

and totally smothered in plants. If the creation of a double-decker garden could only be a fantasy for your situation, then a more down-to-earth approach might involve mirrors, trellis work and *trompe l'oeil*.

Mirrors are the most effective way to bring additional light into a space, but they need to be used with a bit of caution in order to avoid making it obvious that they are being employed. To this end, do not use large expanses of uncovered mirror. Better to fix some interesting trellis design to the walls and apply mirrors behind one or two key sections of it. For instance, you might cover the whole wall with a double lattice effect, but cut out two small arched gaps that would resemble 'windows', with mirrors fitted in them. Mirrors are far more convincing if they are not positioned so that they are opposite the main viewpoint, since then you see yourself reflected. Instead, position them at a slight angle, or at one side, so that they reflect some planting, paving or another feature. Alternatively, they can be positioned so that they are not perpendicular to the ground but at a slight angle, or battered.

You can plant climbers and shrubs adjacent to walls, adding texture and shadow to help break up an expanse of brick wall. The mirrors will bounce light into the space, making it look as though something is happening behind the wall. Another approach would be to add a false door, which would convey the impression that the space leads somewhere. The top half of the door could be mirror, which gives the effect that the garden leads into another garden. I used this detail in a tiny London garden and put the 'doors' on a side wall so that they didn't stand out too much.

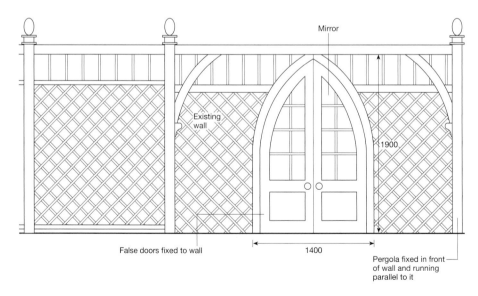

In a similar situation I created a short line of columns on either side of a walkway on one side of the garden. These terminated in a mirror against the boundary fence, to which I fixed two half-columns (which were reflected in the mirror to give the appearance of full columns). The line of columns was covered with a rampant, edible vine and, because of the shade it created, the mirror was incredibly convincing, making you believe that the path went on far beyond its real limits.

I tend to use acrylic mirror outside. It is fairly easy to cut with a Stanley knife or jigsaw, and you can screw through it for fixing trellis or timber over it. It usually comes in sheets 2.44 x 1.22m (8 x 4ft) in a thickness of 3mm (⅛in). It can be cut to size by the suppliers (see Suppliers Index). When you use acrylic mirror, mount it on some external-grade plywood, to stop the damp penetrating from behind, and put some battens or beading over the ends to help prevent the damp penetrating. Bear in mind that acrylic does contract and expand, so make the size of the screw holes slightly larger and fix it with mirror screws or use washers to allow for movement.

Choose the colour of the trellis so that it lightens the space, to compensate for the slightly oppressive bricks – perhaps a pale green. You could consider rendering a wall and painting it in a lighter colour before adding the trellis, if you don't consider it sacrilegious to cover your bricks. Occasionally I have done so, as although I love a lot of bricks, you can have too much of a good thing in small spaces!

Trompe l'oeil is another way to add interest in a small space, tricking the eye into believing that something else is happening (see over).

We have a blank, 2m (6½ft) high concrete block wall at the end of the garden, which is an eyesore. What can you suggest we do with it?

Concrete block walls are inexpensive to put up and can be treated in many different ways to produce a huge variety of effects. If you watch the creation of the show gardens at Chelsea Flower Show from the outset, you will see hundreds of blocks being employed for boundaries and buildings in many of the gardens. Two weeks down the line you rarely see two similar surfaces among them.

If the blockwork is rendered, you then have a neutral surface, free of joints. The render may be a rough one with an uneven finish, creating shadows on the surface, giving rise to extra depth and colour. Many of the buildings at Portmeirion in north Wales have this type of finish. There the walls are painted in an assortment of colours, but always the colour is darker at the bottom and slowly lightened with the addition of white as it progresses up the wall. This makes the buildings look taller – necessary because most of the buildings at Portmeirion are built at two-thirds of 'normal' height. Contrasting with a rough render is a stucco, or marmorino, which is a smooth, fine-textured plaster. These are more specialized finishes – best left to professionals.

You can add detail into the render. You could insert shells, a vertical sundial, interesting tiles or salvaged pieces of intriguing stonework, such as a gargoyle, arch or a window mullion – often available from a reclamation yard. You could form quoins in the render on the corners, to give the impression of a stone wall.

Another variant is to paint the wall with a finish. This may be stone blocking, which gives the effect of an ashlar wall, or you could paint on a *trompe l'oeil*. This is best applied to a wall that receives little direct sunlight, as the painted shadows, necessary to make the subject look real, will conflict with any real shadows on a sunny day. In order to make the subject look convincing, it is best not to include living things, such as birds and rose bushes in full bloom, as the viewer will quickly realize that it is all fakery. Keep the subject simple: an urn in an alcove, or a glimpse of a landscape through a partially open door. Try to position something in front of the wall, so that the viewer cannot get too close, perhaps by using some deep planting.

Do not forget the possibilities offered by coping. At the Chelsea Flower Show one year we made a rendered block wall look like part of a ruin by putting some well-weathered, rugged blocks of old stone on the top of the wall, stepping down the ends with smaller sections of stonework. We put

Trompe l'oeil surrounded by stone blocking painted on to a rendered concrete block wall

the odd weathered stone pinnacle on top and planted quite heavily in front of the wall. By placing the real stone pieces near eye level, we gave them greater prominence than the larger areas of render below eye level. You could substitute brick, slate or even timber for the stone coping, if that was more appropriate to your own set-up.

GARDEN BUILDINGS, FURNITURE, POTS AND ORNAMENTS

I would love to have a small thatched gazebo in my garden. Can you suggest ways to make my own thatch?

There are many different materials that are used to thatch buildings, but straw and reed are the ones most frequently used in Europe. These are fairly complicated to use if you want to finish up with a reasonably neat job, although I have known people who have done the basic thatching using a book from the library and then called in a thatcher to finish it off and do the more intricate top part. For those that are less DIY-orientated, a simpler way is to form the building with a pitched, marine plywood roof (covered with roofing felt) and then clad it with bundles of material, which completely conceal the plywood. If the roof is a simple pitched roof, bargeboards at either end will conceal the ply. You would not need to do this with a pyramid roof.

Suitable alternative thatching materials are sedge and willow, the former is sometimes available from thatchers. It comes in bundles, which you lay one bundle deep on the ply and then fix on with screws and wires. A thin metal rod can be positioned horizontally over the bundles, which is also fixed on with screws and wires. Thick rope, about 1.2cm (½in) in diameter, can be positioned over the metal rods to hide them. You will probably need about two to three rods per roofside, depending on the length of roof. The bundles will fold over the top and tuck under the top rod on the other side to hide the ridge. At the bottom edge of the roof the sedge can be trimmed off neatly with shears. Sedge has very sharp edges, so take care when working with it and wear gloves. It needs to be soaked in water for 24 hours before use, to make it pliable. It should last a good 10 years (if not longer) and is not particularly expensive.

Willow is again simply positioned on the roofing felt over the ply. When I have done this we have used 3m (10ft) long willow rods, which we laid about three to five deep, with the thicker end laid at the base of the roof. The rods were a maximum thickness of 1.5cm (⅝in). We attached the rods to the roof using galvanized staples fixed into the plywood, then wrapped wire around the willows in groups and secured the wire to the staples. At the top we bent the thinner end of the willow over the apex and fixed it down in a similar fashion. We let the base of the willow overhang the ply by about 15cm (6in) and trimmed them evenly at the ends. We covered the

Sedge
thatch
tree
house

wire with 1.2cm (½in) thick rope, laid horizontally, as with the sedge. It is best not to use freshly cut willow, but to leave it for about two weeks, as the high water content makes it shrink quite rapidly as it dries, which would leave large gaps. The willow was surprisingly heavy, so make sure that your roof can take the weight! The end result was attractive and, as it was used on a large treehouse, fitted appropriately into its surroundings.

I would love a small greenhouse, but the attractive ones cost a bomb and, as our garden is small, a utilitarian one would be too prominent. Any suggestions?

If you have any free-standing high walls in your garden, they can be ideal for positioning a greenhouse against. In my garden the only available wall was a north-facing one, but my main priority was for over-wintering tender plants, which happily tolerate the resulting lower light levels. The production of tomatoes, cucumbers and other crops in the summer is secondary to my ornamentals, so I willingly accept a slightly lower yield in return for a more attractive-looking greenhouse. It also has the advantage of not becoming too hot in high summer. If you do not have a convenient wall, consider altering part of your boundary fence to incorporate one. It could be a rendered block-work wall with an attractive colourwash finish, to minimize costs.

I think solid walls at the base of a greenhouse look more attractive than

Greenhouse

glass walls right to the ground. Again the construction could be blockwork faced with brick or stone (whichever suits your situation), or just rendered blockwork with a paint finish. For my greenhouse walls I tracked down some second-hand timber window frames, about 1.1m (3⅔ft) high, and fixed them on walls that are the same height as the staging, 78cm (31in). I formed the slope for the roof on top of the window frames with timber boarding and then made the roof from twin-wall polycarbonate roof sheeting. The back wall is too low to get a good, steep pitch – it is 3.2m (10½ft) high – so I put a shelf at either end of the greenhouse filled with terracotta pots, to hide the unattractive, shallow pitch. The door was salvaged, too. All the timber was painted with an opaque green stain. Needless to say, I now require more space and my next project is to build a greenhouse that is partially sunken into the ground, probably using sleepers to form the retaining wall and building the glazed area above with reclaimed windows. Sunken greenhouses require far less (if any) heating in the winter to keep them frost-free.

I love lots of plants outside in pots, but do not like the problems they create when I go away in the summer. How can I avoid the pitfalls, or do I have to forgo my summer holidays if I want decent containers?

Most keen gardeners have collections of plants in pots, which require fairly high maintenance, particularly during warmer spells. It is worth organizing the way in which you grow these treasures so that they do not dictate your lifestyle.

First, wherever possible, I buy only large, broad pots, 60cm (24in) tall or more, for the majority of my plants. These larger pots are more expensive and in some areas they would not be suitable, but they do greatly reduce the required frequency of watering. There are many plants that will tolerate neglect for two weeks – such as agaves, aloes, yuccas and house leeks, to name a few – and smaller pots can accommodate these happily.

Second, it is well worth adding a water-storing polymer to the compost, such as Broadleaf P4 (see Suppliers Index). In independent trials it was found that hanging baskets with this in their compost could be watered every third day, as opposed to every day. It was also found that this interval could be increased to once every fifth day if you spread a layer of gel onto the liner. Soaking the granules overnight in water and then pouring off the excess liquid the next day forms the gel. A 3cm (1¼in) thick layer should be spread on the liner that is directly underneath the compost. Once the roots reach the gel the extended watering interval of five days is quite adequate. If, in addition, you move your hanging baskets out of their sunny location and put them in a sheltered and shady spot, you will probably get away with extending this interval to 10 days. As hanging baskets have high water requirements compared to a larger pot, you can see the potential for extending your watering interval with the granules and gel. The gel layer, in this instance, can be spread on a piece of capillary matting or some old pan scourers, which are then placed on gravel or crocks in the base of the pot (these are obviously still necessary for drainage). As long as your pot will drain, the water-storing granules will not let the compost become waterlogged.

Another approach is to install a mini-irrigation system in each pot, such as the ones available by mail order from Tanker Irrigation (see Suppliers Index). These are rather like round, plastic cake tins, with a vertical tube that projects up to the surface of the soil. They are put in the base of the pot and covered with the compost. The container is then filled with water through the spout and a geo-textile membrane in the top of the container gradually allows the water to disperse through the compost. These allow you to increase your watering interval to two weeks in the summer, provided you do not have huge water-loving plants in small containers. Again resite your containers in a cool spot, water well before you leave and cover the top of the compost with some pebbles or mulch to reduce evaporation from the soil. Happy holidays!

We have a fallen oak tree in our garden. Should we chop it up for firewood or can we do something with it?

A large oak tree is quite an asset and there are many possibilities. I have seen fallen logs carved into a range of items; my favourite was in the form of a Hereford bull lying down, which incorporated a seat carved into his side. He had a ring through his nose, complete with a chain attached to an

adjacent tree. A junior school in Cambridge has a large carved dragon, which is used as a seat, a climbing frame and sculpture. I have a dragon in my garden. Its head and tail were carved from large logs using a chainsaw and its body is formed from mounded earth.

Oak is a hard wood to carve, and it is worth getting hold of a local sculptor, unless you have talents in that direction. The Crafts Council produces a register of makers for a wide range of external and internal crafts, including sculptors (see Suppliers Index). This is an excellent starting point for sourcing someone to transform your tree.

There are many uses, besides having it carved. Large sawn hardwood log-rounds make good sections for rustic paving; a wide, thick plank or two from the middle would make a wonderful top for a rustic table and benches – if the tree was not wide enough, two planks could be put back-to-back. The simplest way to do this is to involve a timber merchant who has a bandsaw and a saw bench. They usually have the necessary equipment to lift the tree, and can saw it up to your requirements. A large tree trunk set vertically in the ground also forms a good basis for a climbing frame for children, and you can put horizontal pieces of dowel into the trunk for foot supports.

Finally, if none of these ideas appeal, rather than burn a fabulous piece of hardwood – assuming that the timber is of reasonable quality – it is always worth getting a local timber merchant round to see if they are interested in buying it from you.

My husband has a ghastly old, home-made brick barbecue on the terrace, which is an eyesore, but he does cook the odd brilliant meal. Can I replace his 'faithful old friend' with something that looks good but also performs well?

I have seen a fair number of barbecue eyesores on my travels and they are usually hideous for two reasons: first, the materials are often cheap concrete bricks, which do not match up or look good with the house; second, they are often sited in the most prominent position on the patio or terrace and so are highly visible. Conversely, one of the best-looking barbecues I've seen was a converted stone trough that was built up on brick piers. It backed onto

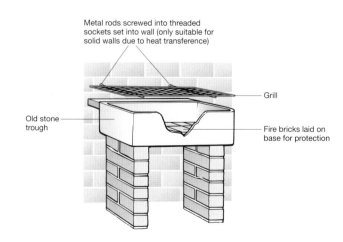

Metal rods screwed into threaded sockets set into wall (only suitable for solid walls due to heat transference)

Grill

Old stone trough

Fire bricks laid on base for protection

a wall, and a pair of horizontal metal bars could be screwed into the wall at different heights, supporting the metal grill (see the diagram). The trough was found in a salvage yard.

Another success story was a home-made brick affair, not too mammoth in size and slightly tucked away, in a dedicated cooking and eating area that was designed as such, although it was still accessible. If you go down this route, it is still feasible to leave room for planting fairly near the structure – within reason – as this will help blend it into the garden.

Many people have gone down the route of gas barbecues that can be wheeled away when not in use. In a small space, I think there is a lot of merit in this, especially if you select one that ensures a good outdoor barbecue flavour. Several manufacturers have lava rocks in their gas machines, which impart an excellent flavour to the food.

I would love a turf seat. Can you suggest how to make one?

Turf seats are nearly always 'one-offs', so they add a touch of individuality to a garden. The drawbacks are that they do need maintenance if you plant grass for the seat, which involves fairly constant clipping and watering in dry periods. You could avoid the clipping if you substituted chamomile (*Chamaemelum nobile* 'Treneague'). This is the non-flowering form that doesn't grow so tall and smells divine when you brush against or sit on it.

I have seen turf seats with the seat part retained with bricks, stone

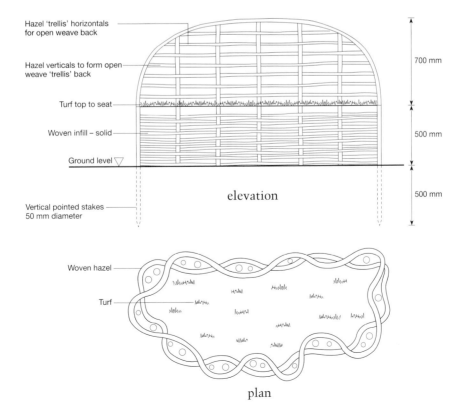

plan

walling and timber, all of which work well if executed in an attractive fashion. But an easier structure to make to retain the earth is of woven hazel (see the diagram). This is formed by banging posts into the ground around the perimeter at 30cm (12in) centres. These are inserted to a depth of 50cm (20in), and are 5cm (2in) in diameter and 1m (3¼ft) long, pressure-treated, pointed fencing stakes. Then 3m (10ft) long hazel rods are woven horizontally in between the fence posts, to form a solid weave. If you want to form a back to the seat, this can be made by fixing stout vertical lengths of hazel rod, about 1.2m (4ft) long, to each fence post along the back. Horizontal hazel rods can then be woven in between these at the density required.

To help retain the soil in the seat, put Mypex fabric (available from garden centres) around the inside of the woven hazel and nail it to the top of the insides of the posts. Soil is then used to fill in the seat. Make sure that you compact it down well, otherwise it will settle and leave a big gap. Then you can turf the top and water it in well.

I love the idea of sundials, but am not over-enamoured of the predictable ones that you see in most garden centres. Can you suggest how to make one?

Sundials are a fascinating way of telling the time by natural means. The simpler ones are vertical and attached to a wall or building, while horizontal ones are usually mounted on a column or plinth. The former can transform a bare wall by adding a useful and eye-catching item.

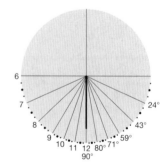

An unusual way to make a horizontal sundial is to make a large one on the ground. You could set the pattern out on the ground in a lawn area, ensuring that the 12 number points north. The numbers could be represented by paving stones set in the grass, with gilded metal Roman numerals fixed to the paving. A person standing in the appropriate place forms the gnomon (the object in the centre of the dial that forms the shadow – pronounced with a silent 'g').

Vertical sundials are also fun to make. One that I saw recently was made from a thin sheet of slate, which had the numbers picked out in gilded Roman numerals. Slate is available in a range of attractive greys, greens and blues; a thickness of a 5mm (¼in) would suffice. The numerals were gilded using high-carat, transfer gold leaf (see p. 169), while the gnomon was made from a piece of metal crafted by a blacksmith. This has to be fixed at an angle of 39° up from the vertical board, assuming that you are at about 51° latitude. In order for it to work correctly using the dial shown in the diagram, the wall should be facing due south, although it can be worked out for any orientation (providing the sun hits it). The British Sundial Society is a good starting point (see Suppliers Index). If you want to add more detail, an inscription such as *Tempus Fugit* ('Time flies') would be appropriate.

We want to add some lighting to our garden – could we have some guidance, please?

Lighting in the garden can be magical, highlighting the best features and making them spring to life. Being unaware of the light source will often make the scheme even more effective: the darkness and the shadows are just as important as the light. There are different types of lighting, the main ones being uplighting, downlighting, spotlighting, moonlighting, mirror lighting and backlighting.

Uplighters can be recessed into the ground, making it easy to conceal the light source. They can be used to great effect, dramatically highlighting trees, tall architectural shrubs or a structure such as a bust in a hedge, so that it stands out far more vividly than it would in natural light.

Downlighting needs to be positioned in a high source, such as a tree or climber-clad pergola, so that it produces pools of light and shadow. This

needs to be handled with care to hide the light source and make sure that the effect is subtle yet exciting.

Spotlighting is a common form of lighting, but you often see it handled in a brash way in hotel forecourts and municipal buildings. To avoid being too obvious, the narrow beam of light should be positioned a fair distance from the subject and arranged so that it illuminates only part of it – perhaps just one side of a figure – to add some drama.

Moonlighting is a very subtle, romantic way to light a garden. It needs to be hidden in a high tree and arranged so that it gently washes over the main areas of the garden, forming dappled shadows in the enchanting way that the full moon lights up a garden on a cloudless night.

Mirror lighting works in conjunction with sheets of water in pools and lakes. The hidden light source illuminates a key feature, such as a sculpture or unusual tree, which is then reflected in the water. Mirror lighting can be very subtle yet incredibly striking.

Backlighting is often used in conjunction with uplighters and down-lighters. If the light source is hidden behind a wall or some thick shrubs and planting, it has the effect of throwing the tree or feature into shadow. This highlights its form and accentuates the atmosphere.

In some gardens you will want to use a mixture of effects, so that different spaces have different moods. Apart from using these methods, you can also approach lighting in a simpler, low-key way. For my main entrance courtyard, which is surrounded on three sides by buildings, I use interior lighting to illuminate the exterior. If all the rooms are being used, the indoor lighting bounces out to the courtyard, making the house look warm and welcoming. In other areas I have used low-key alternatives, such as large glass lanterns and flares. Other options, such as nightlights and storm lanterns, are readily available in many different styles and can be hung up to light well-used spaces.

THE PAVED AREA, SURFACES AND DRIVEWAYS

We are about to resurface the drive and my husband wants gravel, but I dislike the way it gets picked up on shoes and dragged into the house, although we both agree that we prefer its appearance to the more practical brick pavers. Is there any way to lay gravel so that it does not move?

There are several different methods of stabilizing gravel – some more successful than others. Loose gravel does undoubtedly move, but some sizes and shapes of gravel are definitely more mobile than others. It is often laid too deeply, which makes it more prone to being kicked around. The base course of compacted hardcore should be well rolled and a thin layer of gravel laid as surface dressing, then rolled well in.

My local gravel is a golden colour, which comes in various sizes. The size that I favour for drives is 2.5cm (1in) 'down' angular gravel, laid to a depth of 2.5cm (1in). The 'down' indicates that the gravel has passed through a sieve of that size, but you will get smaller sizes, too; the angular shape means that the gravel interlocks. Additionally, to stop the gravel being kicked into the house, I tend to lay several bands of paving, which can take vehicular traffic if necessary, up to the doorways. These can be laid about 5mm (¼in) proud of the gravel to help retain it. Then, if gravel is picked up on shoes, it comes off onto the paving, which is easy to sweep.

The type of bound gravel that I like best is Breedon gravel. This is pale beige with a particle size of 1.5cm (⅝in), grading down to dust. A hardcore base is laid and then a depth of approximately 5cm (2in) is laid on top. It is rolled while being flooded with water over the roller; the water brings the fine particles to the surface and these set to form quite a hard surface on the top. It is accessible for wheelchairs, too.

Another system of binding gravel is to spray the blinded hardcore base with a black bitumen emulsion, then apply 9–12mm (⅜in –½in) granite gravel or other hard chippings and roll them in. This should be repeated, leaving a day between each coat, and applying smaller chippings of 6–9mm (¼in –⅜in) the second time. If there is a lot of traffic and if a lot of manoeuvring is done, the chippings do wear loose and need to be swept off regularly. The surface can be reapplied as necessary. I have also used this method to cover concrete and tarmac.

Resin-bonded gravel is the most expensive system, but it does stabilize the gravel totally. The chippings, which are usually fairly small (7mm or ¼in), are mixed with a clear or suitably coloured hardener and then laid on top of a concrete or tarmacadam base. You can do this yourself or use a specialist firm (see Suppliers Index).

We have a lovely front garden, which leads up to a red-brick thatched cottage. Unfortunately, I can't see the front garden from the house as our cars block the view. When you approach the house all you can see is tarmac and cars. How can I sort out the car parking?

It sounds as though you have potentially a stunning entrance area leading up to a highly attractive property, and the last thing you want to do is fill it with cars and tarmac. Without seeing the layout it is difficult to tell you exactly what to do. But in this situation, which crops up regularly, it is best to draw up a scale plan of the whole area in question. A scale of 1:100 would probably do (you will probably find that you acquired a fairly accurate conveyancing plan to a fairly small scale, such as 1:1250, when you

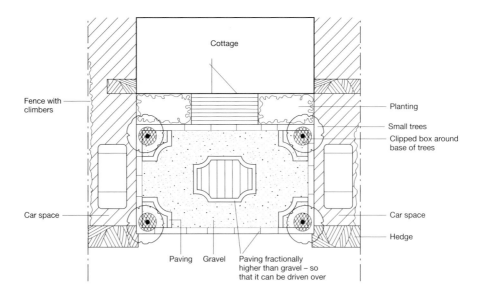

Fence with climbers

Car space

Planting

Small trees

Clipped box around base of trees

Car space

Hedge

Cottage

Paving   Gravel   Paving fractionally higher than gravel – so that it can be driven over

purchased the property and this could be enlarged). Plot on the scale plan any trees, large shrubs or other features that you could not live without and then see how you could rework the driveway and parking into the layout.

The average parking bay is 2.4 x 5m (8 x 16½ ft) and you must decide how much parking it is essential to squeeze in. The turning area is fairly critical to the scheme of things. Drives that are shaped like a hammer-head (which is one of the most economical shapes that you can turn a car in) make the space look as though it has been tailor-made for the car. Add some tarmac as a surface and it definitely becomes a car park. Instead, try designing the hard surface so that it looks like a well-balanced forecourt or courtyard that is in scale with the house (see the diagram). It might be possible to tuck the car parking off to the sides, screened by some hedging. In the diagram, the area of hard surface is quite large, although it is not just one surface, but gravel in conjunction with paved areas. These paved areas should be set fractionally higher than the paving, to help stop the gravel drifting over it, but should be laid so that they can be driven over. Gravel is an adaptable surface, blending equally well in front of a chocolate-box cottage and a stately home. By mixing it with paving slabs, stone setts, bricks or other unit paving, the area no longer shrieks that it is a car park but becomes instead a multi-use, attractive space that is very much part of the garden. As your cottage is brick, matching paving brick would pull the two elements together.

When you have arrived at a solution on paper, get some traffic cones and put them on the ground to define the hard space. Check whether you have made the turning spaces large enough and that the arrangement looks in scale with the cottage. Generally people make the hard area too small, causing the space to look mean in proportion to the house. People's car sizes and driving abilities vary greatly and this will have a huge bearing on what spaces work for you. Live with the cones for a week or two to make sure that your solution really does work.

Our eating area is in an extremely sunny spot. I would like to have some sort of shade, which would make it more pleasant to use in the hottest parts of the summer. Can you suggest alternatives to those big umbrellas?

Awnings and pergolas are the first items that spring to mind. The option you choose will probably be influenced by the style of your house. In many situations I prefer awnings, because you can put them up when needed and they can be used to add a splash of fresh colour. If the site is very windy, large awnings can be quite vulnerable and it would probably be a good idea to get advice from a specialist (see Suppliers Index). Awnings need not be made from fabric; I have seen them made from reeds, bamboo canes and hazel twigs. In all instances they were laid on a light timber framework. They do not usually need to project much more than 2.5m (8ft), but this is enough to shade part of a table, which is often exactly what is wanted. All these materials (particularly bamboo and hazel) would look fine with either modern or old buildings.

As far as fabrics are concerned, I have made – or seen made – awnings from heavy-duty canvas, dustsheets and ordinary heavy cotton. All of these can be livened up by edging them with a coloured bias binding. They can waterproofed, if required, by painting them with a silicon-based liquid that is used for waterproofing tents (available from most camping shops); but it is usually better to take them down during damp and windy weather. You can either design a timber or metal frame to attach them to or fix one side to the house and the opposite side to removable tall poles. Small concrete post-holders with additional guy ropes can anchor the poles. Another form is a metal trellis-type awning fixed to the building at a slight angle and covered with a rampant vine. This method can look very elegant, and could be easily made by a local blacksmith.

Pergolas, usually made from timber or metal, and sometimes also employing heavy ropes, are effective shade-giving structures. A horizontal trellis laid on top creates a fair amount of shade, but the addition of climbers (perhaps sweet-smelling roses, honeysuckle or clematis) obviously gives more shadow still. The main drawback is that pergolas tend to drip for some time after showers or in the early morning, which can make the area unpleasant to use.

Pergolas covered with climbers provide wonderful shade

JC Bunny has given you a patio that you can use on the hottest day, but I enjoy having my siesta horizontal, so I would plant two semi-mature white-stemmed birch *(Betula utilis* var. *jacquemontii)* on the sunny side of the patio about 3m (10ft) apart and swing a hammock between them. They will cast dappled shade on both you and the patio.

Put up strong supporting wires and grow grapevines over them. You get shade in summer, but the leaves drop and make it light in winter. And you get wonderful grapes hanging down in front of you: try 'Boskoop Glory'.

I would like to make a paved area like a draughtboard with paving slabs and a neat, flat-growing plant. What plant would you recommend to fit the bill?

An effective way to soften large areas of paving is to intersperse them with areas of low-growing planting. It is quite usual to see paving broken up randomly with a mix of different low-growing plants, but by using strong patterns (like a chequerboard) and one type of ground-hugging plant, the effect has a more dynamic and dramatic look. Perhaps one of the simplest plants to use is grass, but a fine-growing type, not a rye grass. This should be established so that it is marginally higher than the paving slab, by about 6mm (¼in), so that the mower can run over the top without damaging the blades. The grass will tend to creep out beyond the squares over a period of time, making the shapes less dramatically defined, but occasional edging up with an edging spade soon sorts this out.

Other suitable plants are pearlwort *(Sagina glabra)*, which is covered with small green flowers and is sometimes considered to be a weed, though in this instance it is a useful, functional plant. There is a golden form of this, *S. g.* 'Aurea'. It also grows a mere 1cm (½in) high and is ideal if you like something very bright. In cold winters it can tend to die back in patches, so it is worth bringing in a few plants in the autumn and dividing them up, ready to plug any gaps. *Thymus serpyllum* 'Minimus' is a very close-creeping thyme, which has pretty mauve-pink flowers in summer and, of the ground-hugging plants, would probably be my first choice.

When you are establishing your mats of plants, it is worth planting them into compost or sterilized soil, as they are best planted at close centres, perhaps 10cm (4in) apart, to get them to knit together quickly, and it helps to prevent any weeds creeping in and spoiling the effect.

ORNAMENTAL WATER

We have an informal pond in a sunny spot, which is about 12sq m (14sq yd) by 2m (8ft) deep, which we put in last summer. Ever since then the water has resembled thick pea soup. How can we get the water to clear naturally?

When a new pond is filled up it is quite normal for the water to go green and murky initially, until you get the correct balance of plants in the water. This can take three weeks or as long as three months, but it is definitely worth persevering and not resorting to chemicals or mechanical filters. In very small, shallow pools, which rapidly heat up on sunny days, these may be necessary, but not in one your size.

The green colour is formed by the abundance of algal growth. This is triggered by sunshine and nitrates. Ideally you should aim to have about one-third of the water in shade, provided by free-floating aquatic plants such as floating water hyacinth (*Eichhornia crassipes* 'Majorin') and floating water soldier *(Stratiotes aloides)* and by floating leaf-rooted plants, such as water lilies. Pondside trees could also provide shade, but the mass of debris from leaf fall can be detrimental to the water quality.

Your aim is to produce a rich soup of tiny aquatic animals feeding on rotting vegetation, on minute green plants and on each other. To do this you need to establish a good framework of aquatic plants. There are several different categories of these, apart from the two already mentioned. Submerged rooted plants such as hornwort *(Ceratophyllum demersum)*, spiked water milfoil *(Myriophyllum spicatum)* and curly pondweed *(Potamogeton crispus)* are often referred to as oxygenators. They do just that, as well as providing food and shelter for tiny pond creatures. These plants are often sold in bundles, which can just be weighted down and thrown into the water. A safer approach is to anchor them into some soil on the bottom of the pool with a brick. It is recommended that you have three plants per square metre (square yard) of surface water area.

The emergent plants and marginal plants are two other categories of aquatic planting that create a habitat for wildlife and help maintain the quality of the water. Emergent plants, such as flowering rush *(Butomus umbellatus)*, bogbean *(Menyanthes trifoliata)* and arrowhead *(Sagittaria sagittifolia)*, tolerate a depth of 3–40cm (1¼–16in). Marginal-plant favourites, including marsh marigold *(Caltha palustris)*, yellow flag *(Iris pseudacorus)* and water-forget-me-not *(Myosotis scorpioides)*, like the shallow edges, with a depth of 0–25cm (0–10in). Add good quantities of several (or all) of these categories of plants and some water snails, and if you can resist it, leave out fish, as they eat the frogspawn and newt tadpoles as well as upping the nitrate content.

You will find that you need to regulate the vegetation, and that the oxygenators will spread like a thick green carpet all over the pond and will need reducing to about half their volume every so often. Some plants will become too dominant and will need to be thinned out. But these are pleasant tasks on a sunny day.

Sometimes during long hot spells in the summer, even in established ponds, algal growth (often in the form of blanket weed) just explodes, creating your 'pea soup' effect. This may be exacerbated because you are continually topping up the pond with tap water, which may well be high in nutrients such as nitrates. The algal growth can then lock up the oxygen, which the pond life needs. It also can reduce the light levels too much. You can rake the blanket weed out, but you will probably find that if you leave it be, the snail population will increase and will slowly get on top of the problem for you. Another approach, which I use, is to add a couple of biscuits of barley straw, wrapped up in old hay net, and submerge them in the pond. The rotting straw releases algal inhibitors that work on a wide range of algae. The common one least affected is *Spirogyra*. In trials 90 per cent reported partial or total success, but it can take between one and three months, so don't lose heart and rush off for some chemicals before giving it a chance!

One final approach, if none of the above answers your problem: by circulating the water, perhaps with a fountain, you increase the oxygen levels. This helps to improve the water quality, so if you like the idea of some artificially moving water, you could try this solution.

 Shade is important. If you are able to construct a wooden bridge over part of the pond, this will cast shade at all times, helping to reduce the soup effect. It is also nice to be able to look down on the water. The bridge will offer fish somewhere to hide from herons.

We have just put in a formal pond and want to add lots of aquatic plants. Should we plant them in containers or just plant them into soil on the bottom?

There are opposing schools of thought on this subject. Your second system of planting the aquatics on the base of the pond is the way I planted my formal pond initially, but I have now reverted to using containers. By planting the aquatics in perforated baskets, the plants are kept in check, are easy to divide and repot and you can put them exactly where you want them. But bear in mind that it will take longer to get a lush, well-established-looking pond. To this end I would use large perforated containers, so that you can establish generous clumps of plants. I think it is trickier to get clear water by restricting the planting this way, as the natural balance is more difficult to get right, generally due to the lower volume of planting. In addition, to avoid looking at plant pots on the bottom of the pool in the winter, it is necessary to hide them with pebbles.

If I were making an informal pool I would choose a modified version of planting in soil directly on the pond bottom. The problem with covering all the pond base with soil, as I did initially, is that the plants quickly colonize the whole pool. My water lilies became very crowded, and it was quite a performance lifting them all out and splitting them up. Other plants have to be regularly thinned, too. If your water is more than 1.5m (5ft) deep, then these deep areas will naturally remain free of plants (with the exception of a few water lilies), so rapid colonization may not be a problem to you. If, instead of covering the whole of the pool base with soil, you just form built-in planters on the ledges around the edges, the marginal and emergent plants can establish themselves in large, more natural-looking drifts in specific, planned zones.

These built-in planters can be formed by putting underlay on top of the liner, then laying low brick 'walls' about 15–23cm (6–9in) deep on the cushioning underlay. Then fill these up with soil. Do not be mean when you are forming these planters – you may well want to cover an area one-third the size of the pool, or more. Water lilies can be planted in containers made in the same way, but instead of drifts, circular or square-shaped brick containers, about 50–100cm (20–36in) across, would be more suitable, as they can be positioned towards the middle of the pool rather than squashed up against the sides.

If you do select this method, do not use a soil with a high clay content, especially if you are adding fish. This is because clay contains very fine particles that easily get disturbed by the movement of fish, creating almost permanently cloudy water. A good medium to use is a sandy loam.

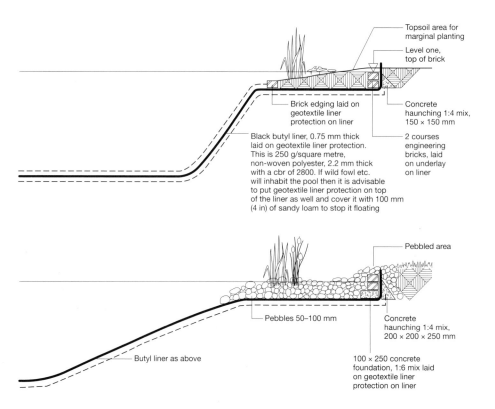

Pond edges designed to disguise the pond liner

We want to make an informal wildlife pool, but are worried that the liner will show. Can you suggest how to build it without creating this problem?

If you are trying to make your pool look well established, it is a real give-away if a large expanse of black liner is visible! The diagrams show how you can detail it to prevent this happening. The only place where the liner is at the surface is where it comes up vertically at the edge, and it can be snipped off just above soil level. As soon as the grass and aquatic plants grow, this will be lost in the vegetation. By building in a ledge planter, which is covered in soil, you can totally hide the liner in the shallower areas, where it is usually most visible. In order to make the marginal and emergent planting around the edge look natural, it is a good idea to vary the width of the shelf.

We have a piped stream, which is covered, running through our garden. I would like to open it up and make it look more natural. How do I go about it?

The first step is to contact your local office of the Environment Agency (see Suppliers Index). One of their main aims is to conserve open water courses. To this end they encourage and promote the removal of culverts in order to restore a more natural river environment. They are helpful and can advise on any potential problems. They have a lot of experience in reworking and planting up channels to achieve natural-looking streams and water bodies.

The diagram illustrates a possible plan for part of the 'stream' and a couple of sections through it. It is well worth following the channel immediately upstream and downstream and observing where it flows naturally in an uncovered state. This will give you an idea of the shape of its meanders and the natural profile of the banks. Over time it is likely that your section will gradually end up looking fairly similar to this, although it could take hundreds of years! Having said this, it does make the course more interesting if you can implement some gentle curves, which then leave you with the opportunity to exploit the various profiles with different types of plants.

Having decided what you want, you now have to arrange how to go about the work. It will probably require the use of a mechanical digger to break out and remove the existing channel and then carve out the proposed new route. Again the Environment Agency will be able to advise on this aspect. On one scheme we did exactly this, but we did leave a couple of sections of channel, which served as bridges. The old pipes were of historical interest and so it seemed fitting to leave some small lengths.

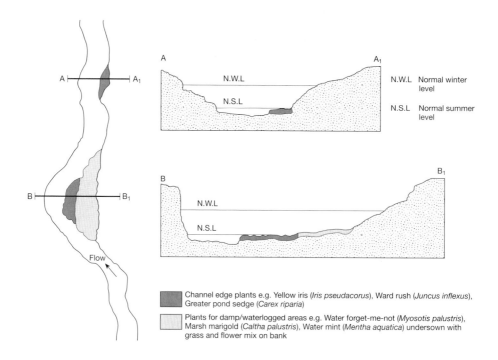

A   A₁   N.W.L   Normal winter level

N.S.L   Normal summer level

Channel edge plants e.g. Yellow iris (*Iris pseudacorus*), Ward rush (*Juncus inflexus*), Greater pond sedge (*Carex riparia*)

Plants for damp/waterlogged areas e.g. Water forget-me-not (*Myosotis palustris*), Marsh marigold (*Caltha palustris*), Water mint (*Mentha aquatica*) undersown with grass and flower mix on bank

My koi carp are being plundered by local herons; apart from resorting to a twelve-bore, have you any aesthetically pleasing ideas?

The diagram shows a small metal post, made by a local blacksmith – one of my clients put these around his pool at about 1m (3¼ft) centres, with thin wires running between the posts, as shown. His pool is literally heaving with vast, plump koi in a range of flashy colours. Before he erected the fence (which, incidentally, is painted a smart dark green) he regularly lost his fish to herons. The paving slabs around the pool were drilled to take the posts, which do not look too conspicuous and are almost elegant; they are certainly the best-looking of all the fences for this purpose that I have seen. This method is particularly effective, as herons prefer to walk down to the water rather than make hovering attacks. And the pool edges are quite deep near the sides, about 60cm (24in), which discourages them from wading in.

Another system that I have used was a metal grid fixed under the coping, which was set 5cm (2in) below the water level, so that it was hardly visible. The water lilies and other plants grew through the grid, thus hiding it almost totally in

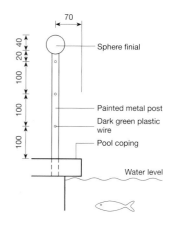

Sphere finial

Painted metal post

Dark green plastic wire

Pool coping

Water level

the summer. I inserted it to stop the children falling in, but it also kept the heron out. Its disadvantage was that it took quite an effort to lift it up to thin out the plants; in all other respects it is fine. Ideally, you should put it in when you build the pond; otherwise it is quite a palaver to lift up the coping in order to get the grid fixed underneath.

Some people swear by artificial herons, which supposedly scare off real ones, although they seem a bit hit and miss to me and have a tendency to look like the feathered equivalent of a garden gnome.

BF

I find a low log wall only 30–60cm (12–24in) high, made from cheap rotten logs, very effective. The heron does not land on water but on land, and wades in, so is not happy at having to scale a wee wall. The wall is also a good habitat for all sorts of creatures and, once grown through, is pleasing and naturalistic in the right setting.

CHILDREN IN THE GARDEN

We have just put in a climbing frame for the children, and we are worried that they might fall and hurt themselves. We are wondering about putting a safety surface in – what do you think of the various types available?

Many parents just leave grass as a safety surface under play equipment and, as long as the soil is fairly moist, this is quite an absorbent surface and often looks appropriate in a garden situation. But when there are periods of prolonged drought it can become extremely hard, with shock-absorption characteristics not dissimilar from concrete. Unfortunately, this is often when the play equipment is in constant use, such as during the summer holidays. Having said that, children who play on equipment with safety surfaces underneath do tend to get lulled into a false sense of security. They use the equipment in a more carefree fashion, whereas when they play on tarmac or concrete they tend to take this into account and exercise more caution.

In a private garden the most suitable surfaces are play bark, sand and, surprisingly, gravel. The diagram illustrates how these could be laid. These can all be laid so that they are flush with the ground, which generally looks better. The exception to this would be if the area does not drain or has a high water table. With bark particularly, this would cause it to rot down quickly. I have shown sand raised to illustrate how you could retain any of the surfaces.

I visited the garden of a young hazel coppicer the other day and he had retained his bark safety surface with a 30cm (12in) high woven hazel fence. It looked particularly appropriate in his woodland glade, surrounded by

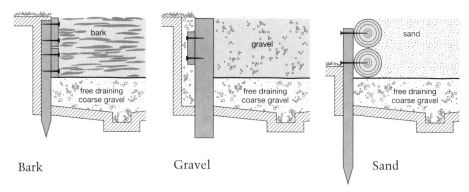

Bark   Gravel   Sand

Sections through safety surfaces

many other beautifully woven fences, gates and arches. (You could use the
same principle as the woven turf seat, see p. 181) Bark is particularly suitable: the recommended depth is 30cm (12in), but 20cm (8in) is certainly
better than nothing. There are two grades: a particle size of 8–25mm ($\frac{1}{3}$–1in)
and one of 1–5cm ($\frac{1}{2}$–2in). The former is probably more user-friendly to
toddlers, but the larger one will take longer to break down. Make sure it is
a good granular bark, which usually comes from pine trees, and avoid the
stringy elastic bark from spruce. Ensure that it has no additives, coarse angular
fragments or fine dust. It does get moved around and heavily compacted in
popular places, so you will need to rake it regularly to loosen it up and maintain an even depth. It is available as 'Playbark 10–50' (see Suppliers Index).

   Sand is popular with children, but unfortunately also with cats. So,
unless you can cover it or instil in your children an awareness of the problems, and therefore some rudimentary hygiene (a good thing to do anyway!),
most people tend to avoid it. But the time when children start playing more
independently of their parents' watchful eyes is usually the time when they
are starting to perform dare-devil feats on the equipment. By then they have
hopefully understood the problems with cat mess, and so the risks (see p. 240)
are hugely reduced, so do not discard this option lightly. The sand should
have a partical size of 0.25–1.5mm (less than $\frac{1}{16}$in across) and rounded, so
that air spaces remain between the particles when under compression. If
they are angular, they interlock under pressure and form a hard, non-shock-
absorbing surface. It should also be white or non-staining, laid to a depth of
30cm (12in) and will need raking regularly, as it becomes displaced easily.
(See also p. 202 for details on play sand.)

   Gravel is not popular, but it looks and performs well. Do consider using
it for older children, though, as its shock-absorption qualities are good,
although they may suffer from grazed knees. But in a way this may encourage them to exercise a higher level of caution in their play, which may in
itself be welcome. As with sand, the particles must be rounded, to prevent
interlocking, so that under compression they keep the cushioning air spaces
between them. The ideal particle size is 3–12mm ($\frac{1}{8}$–$\frac{1}{2}$in), and the

depth should be 30cm (12in). Again, raking will be necessary to keep a constant depth.

We have four exuberant children under six, and both my husband and I are keen gardeners. Can you recommend how we can cater for all the family's needs in our garden, which is 15 x 50m (50 x 164ft)?

My approach to this common conflict in a garden is to try and create, with your children's help, a honeypot zone that is definitely their part of the garden. Even in a small garden you can usually identify an area that will absorb the children's activities in such a way that it does not impinge too much on the remainder of the garden. Children will often spend far more time using the garden than adults, so you really need to exploit the space so that they maximize the fun they can get from it.

My own children are now 11 and 12. Without doubt, their all-time favourite is an all-weather trampoline, which is 4.2m (14ft) in diameter. It is used practically every day of the year, unless it pours with rain all day, and is great exercise, terrific fun – and we grown-ups use it too. It does not look hideous because I have sunk it so that it is flush with the ground and have formed a mounded grass amphitheatre around it to screen it. I had to ask for a dark khaki-green plastic edging for it, as opposed to the standard brilliant blue. Not only does the sinking reduce its impact dramatically, but it also makes it safer. Trampolining is a sociable activity, which children can do together, and they make up endless games and routines on it. It is particularly successful because several children or just one can use it. Even in a smallish town garden it can be hidden, so don't worry that it will be an eyesore. Trampolines provide more long-term entertainment for a wider age range than any other equipment I am aware of (see Suppliers Index).

We also have a large live-in treehouse in the children's 'patch'. This too is popular and fun as basic guest accommodation when numbers swell in the summer holidays. It has a sunken firepit nearby, where the children light campfires, cook weird and wonderful food and terrify themselves with ghost stories after dark.

The cable runway or flying fox is also fairly high up the list of success stories. It is a rope slung between two trees with a pulley attached so that the children can swing across the orchard on it. One from TP Toys is available from large department stores and is not too obtrusive in a small space. Swings are always popular, but my children no longer use theirs, so it was removed last summer. It was a double swing, so that two could play together on it, rather than it becoming a source of friction.

Apart from providing an area for them, it is definitely worth encouraging children to garden. Give them a say in what they would like elsewhere and get them to help with the fun parts of gardening, such as growing seeds, watering plants, propagating simple shrubs, feeding the birds and picking vegetables. This way they can participate in the garden's development and well-being, and then they are less likely to abuse it with footballs, bikes and cricket bats.

I would like to make a small maze that will look interesting and can also be a play feature for the children. The area I have in mind is about 5 x 5m (16½ x 16½ft). What can you come up with?

Mazes provide outdoor puzzles that fascinate all ages. They have a long history and a wide geographical distribution. In the diagram I have illustrated a simple maze, which is a small version of one I designed for a school. The paths are paving slabs flush with the grass, but they could equally take the form of gravel, brick or pebbles surrounded by shallow rills of water. Alternatively, dwarf hedges and paths can be used. If you want to capture the secretive element that the tall hedges in the grand mazes of stately homes create, you could form one using a network of willow tunnels, which could be made in a similar fashion to a willow house (see p. 204). This would fill out in a matter of months, but its rapid growth inevitably means a lot of pruning and weaving in to prevent it becoming a huge, untidy mass of willow shoots. I have not shown a complicated path network, but examples of these are available in specialist books on the subject.

Another simple maze would be a turf maze – there are about eight intact ancient turf mazes in England today, which are definitely worth visiting. These mazes usually have their paths defined by banks of earth upon which

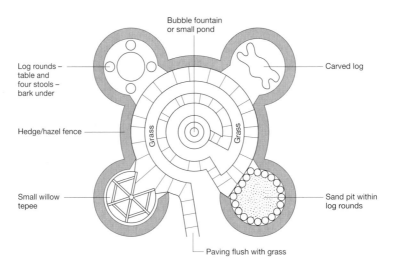

Bubble fountain
or small pond

Log rounds –
table and
four stools –
bark under

Carved log

Hedge/hazel fence

Grass

Grass

Small willow
tepee

Sand pit within
log rounds

Paving flush with grass

Plan of a small maze

grass is growing and so these low banks provide many possibilities for children's play. An alternative central feature such as a sandpit, or a small weeping tree with a bench around its trunk and an archway at the beginning, could be added to increase its interest.

Our 10-year-old son is desperate for a treehouse. We have a large old Bramley apple tree, but its canopy is not spreading enough to house a platform. Is there any way round this?

If you look closely, you will notice that very few treehouses are entirely supported by the tree. Old apple trees do make good homes for treehouses, as they are tolerant of having their branches pruned or removed to accommodate the structure (as is often necessary). Also, their growth rate is slow, so new growth is unlikely to distort the house over the next few years. If the tree is old, you must check that it is safe, and that it is unlikely to blow down or shed any limbs. It is worth removing all dead wood as well.

In the diagram you can see various different ways in which the building can be supported. By far the most usual methods are to provide extra or total support. If the latter system is used, the treehouse is free-standing but tucked into the canopy. I have designed several houses in this way, using four to six vertical posts. This means that it is not putting any load on the tree; but you must take into account that, if you rest the structure on a limb, this limb will grow and put a pressure on the house. It may be better to leave room for growth and totally support the building.

To make the posts less visible, they can be covered with ivy (*Hedera*), old man's beard *(Clematis vitalba)* or other rampant, shade-tolerant climbers. On one occasion, when I designed a treehouse for the Chelsea Flower Show,

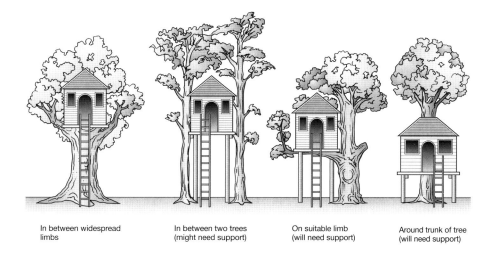

In between widespread limbs

In between two trees (might need support)

On suitable limb (will need support)

Around trunk of tree (will need support)

Possible ways to fit a tree house into a tree

we brought in a semi-mature, misshapen beech tree. To fit in the house we removed a limb and then used this limb to support the building.

My children want a den-making area at the end of the garden. How do you think we should go about this, bearing in mind that they would like it as soon as possible?

The sort of space that is most conducive to good den-making needs to be tucked away from general day-to-day activity. A piece of woodland that is fairly robust, and that will not suffer from high use by numbers of energetic children hell-bent on having a good time, is probably the ideal. Assuming you are starting off with the opposite – a flat, close-mown lawn – the first priority is to establish some shelter and fast-growing cover.

If you can start off by contouring the land, this does provide more potential. It is easiest with the use of a small mechanical digger – it is possible to hire ones that will fit through a gap 84cm (33in) wide. In the diagram a pit has been dug and the excavated earth used to form a low mound to surround it. In this case the depression has been retained by vertical logs, sunk into the ground. Two large-diameter concrete pipes have been positioned in the mound to form an additional access point.

The fastest-growing, most resilient shrubs are the willows. They grow well even on free-draining soils; I have often grown them in hardcore on reclamation sites. There are different types: *Salix alba* var. *vitellina*, the golden willow, has bright eggyolk-yellow shoots; *Salix alba* 'Britzensis', the scarlet willow, has brilliant scarlet-orange shoots; *Salix daphnoides*, the violet willow, has attractive violet-purple shoots that are partially covered in a whitish bloom; *Salix elaeagnos*, the hoary willow, is more elegant than the others but does not feature highly-coloured stems, and has long grey-green leaves similar to those of rosemary. It is slightly less robust than the others and may be better on the outside of the mound. All these willows can be established from cuttings taken in the dormant season and pushed straight into the ground in their final position. There is no need to use rooting compound, for they will just get on with it themselves – and rapidly too – without any artificial means. Potentially they will grow to be vast, although you don't want tall trees, but coppiced shrubs to provide a dense screen about 2–3m (6½–9¾ft) high. To do this (which also encourages the development of the newest, brightest-coloured stems), cut them back to 15cm (6in) every other year or so, in the spring. Do not cut all the bushes at the same time, but stagger it, so that you continually have some higher plants for cover. Plant them at 50–100cm (20–39in) centres, depending on your impatience and how much you enjoy cutting things back.

Other good den-making plants are the taller, more vigorous bamboos, such as *Sinarundinaria nitida*, but these need to be well established before you let children into them. Hazel *(Corylus avellana)* is a wonderful choice;

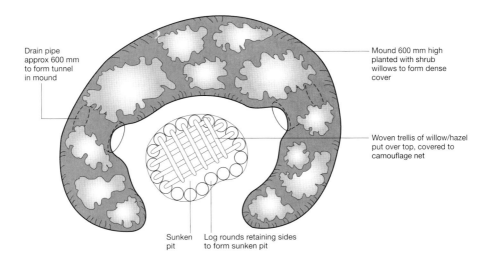

Drain pipe
approx 600 mm
to form tunnel
in mound

Mound 600 mm high
planted with shrub
willows to form dense
cover

Woven trellis of willow/hazel
put over top, covered to
camouflage net

Sunken
pit

Log rounds retaining sides
to form sunken pit

Plan of den-making area

it is not as rapid as willow, but put some in anyway and gradually remove the willows as the hazel coppice gets going. A few evergreens are also useful – the Portuguese laurel *(Prunus lusitanica)* grows fairly fast and forms a thick screen. Ground cover in the form of ivy, dotted with foxgloves, honesty and comfrey, adds to the woodland feel. One last thing: if you want the shrubs to establish fast, keep weeds out as they compete for water.

My husband has just made a big wooden sandpit for our twins. We have a heap of sand left over from building the new playroom – can we fill it with that?

Sand is an extremely variable material, and because playpit sand is classified as a toy, it has to satisfy certain criteria in order to be sold as such. The most obvious difference between builder's sand and playpit sand is colour. Playpit sand should be non-staining, and is generally white. The staining element is formed from brown and black specks and, if you examine a handful of sand closely, it should be difficult to notice these darker specks.

Another difference is the particle size and shape. Playpit sand is composed of uniform, rounded grains and when they are squeezed together they don't interlock. This is important because if a child gets some in his or her eye, tears will break down the sand and wash the particles out, whereas if it comprises angular, interlocked particles, they stay bound together, forming an abrasive group. The size of the particles – larger than caster sugar, but smaller than granulated – is important as it affects sand's moulding characteristics. It should hold together to form an impressive sandcastle, whereas builder's sand often forms a sludgy mess! Silver sand is often recommended for playpits, but a lot of silver sand will stain and it doesn't always have rounded grains, so it can be abrasive.

Another criterion for playpit sand is that it should be free-flowing. It is dangerous if it can be used to form tunnels, which may collapse, burying children. For this reason it is advised not to have sand to a depth greater than 30cm (12in). Playpit sand must also be non-toxic, and as such is tested regularly to make sure that it doesn't contain any heavy metals or other harmful substances. It will not harm the lawn or borders if it is 'accidentally' spilt.

Public play areas and sandpits with high use tend to replace the sand annually, but it is not always necessary to do this. It is worth drying it out regularly, however, as bacteria and other bugs can breed in sand that is continually kept in a wet state.

You can buy sand in small, convenient sacks of various sizes, or order it from suppliers in large sacks or loose loads for a huge sandpit (see Suppliers Index). A large sandpit is a real bonus in a family garden. It encourages children of all ages to play together, creating large, exciting projects and helping their social skills, as well as learning basic physical concepts such as volume, density and gravity.

THE WILDER GARDEN

Our family is in the process of creating a wildlife garden. What is the best way to establish a small area of wildflower meadow?

The most successful wildflower meadows are grown on poor soils, because the vigour of the grass is restricted, allowing the wildflowers to colonize the turf. If you are starting off with a lush lawn,, you will get a better result by removing the turf and topsoil, perhaps to a depth of 7.5–10cm (3–4in) and beginning again. Make sure that the area drains well and prepare the seedbed, just as you would for a normal lawn. You can sow your seeds either in late August or mid-April, but it's best to leave a three-week fallow period before this, to allow all the weed seeds to germinate first, enabling you to kill them off.

Sow the grass seed (using one that does not contain rye grass) at about one-fifth of the recommended rate. After this oversow with the wildflowers. I recommend starting with easy-to-germinate, easy-to-grow plants suitable for a spring-flowering meadow, which tolerate a range of conditions. These include moon daisy *(Chrysanthemum leucanthemum)*, meadow clary *(Salvia pratensis)*, red campion *(Silene dioica)*, salad burnet *(Poterium sanguisorba)*, meadow buttercup *(Ranunculus acris)* and yellow rattle *(Rhinanthus minor)*. The yellow rattle is semi-parasitic on grasses and so helps to slow them down. It produces seedpods in which the seeds rattle. When all the seed has been sown, cover it gently by pulling the back of the rake over it, and maybe put up some bird-scarers.

If you would like some instant impact you could add some plants that have been grown in containers. Both cowslips *(Primula veris)* and primroses *(Primula vulgaris)* establish quite well like this, provided they get the necessary watering. I find that plants in 1 litre pots establish better than the smaller sizes. During the first year you will probably get few flowers, most of the plants' energy being spent on making roots and leaves. You should cut the grass carefully with a mower, with the blades set no lower than 5cm (2in), when the grass gets to a height of 7.5cm (3in).

If your soil is not that fertile and the grasses are the slower-growing, finer ones, then you will be able to achieve quite a good result leaving the present sward predominantly intact. You may want to remove just patches of grass, about 30 x 30cm (12 x 12in), by spraying or lifting the turf. Then you could treat these areas exactly as above (without taking off the topsoil), letting the remainder of the lawn grow long until you cut the rest.

For annual maintenance after the first year, you should cut after flowering has finished and the seed has been set. A strimmer or scythe is fine; or a sturdy rotary mower with wheels, which can have its blades set high, is the option that I use, but it is a beefy machine. The mowings should be removed to keep the fertility of the area down. Any pernicious weeds such as nettles and docks are best hand-weeded out; otherwise they will tend to take over. As the area develops and hopefully the flowers spread, providing that your conditions are suitable, you will find that other wildflowers come in naturally. You can add additional ones that take your fancy, and weed out any that become too dominant for your liking.

We want to make a growing willow house to go at the bottom of the garden. How do we do this, and how easy is it to maintain?

Willow houses are fun to make, and a basic one such as that shown in the diagram is fairly easy. To start with you need some willow cuttings, preferably about 3m (9¾ft) long. Many types will work, but the basket-making willow *(Salix viminalis)* is ideal, as is the almond-leafed willow *(Salix triandra)*. A couple to avoid are goat willow *(Salix caprea)*, as it does not sprout so well, and crack willow *(Salix fragilis)*, which does just that – cracks when you try and bend it. Some suppliers now sell long cuttings in bundles, and they are very reasonably priced (see Suppliers Index).

The best time to make the house is in the dormant season. First, mark out the footprint of the 'building' – the one in the diagram is about 3.2m (10½ft) wide by however deep you want to make it. Make sure that the soil on the outline, where you are going to push in the cuttings, is not compacted and is clean, so that it is not too difficult to push the cuttings in and they will not suffer from weed competition. Then push in the cuttings (thickest end into the ground) all around the perimeter at about 20cm (8in) centres, leaving a gap for the doorway. Take the front two willows, one

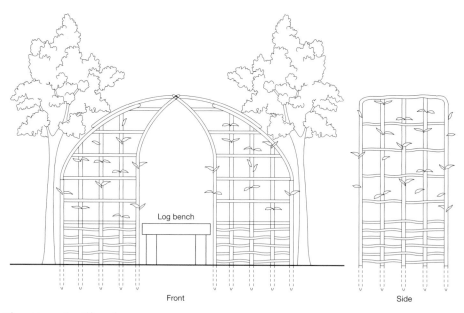

Elevation of willow house

from each side, and join them together by introducing a middle cutting, which will overlap both the side cuttings. Bind them in place. Work your way along the sides, continuing until you get to the end, then commence work on the front. Form the archway for the door by bringing the two willows together that are on either side of the doorway and join them together at the top. Tie the remaining ones for the front to the top and cut off the excess willow. Repeat this for the back.

To make the willow more rigid, weave the horizontals in place. Denser weaving at the base usually gives way to a more open weave at the top, but this is only a suggestion – there are many possible permutations. This horizontal willow will die, as it is not anchored in the ground, but it should still last for several years. Do not use the thick ends for weaving as they are usually difficult to manipulate. Willow is easier to bend if it is soaked overnight prior to weaving, so if you have a problem with it try doing this. Bark chippings are ideal for the floor.

The following spring water the willows in dry periods, to hasten their establishment. When the growth commences, you will find that new shoots grow rapidly, which you can then weave in. By the end of the first season you will probably have to cut a lot of growth back to keep it looking fairly tidy. The next year and subsequent years involve more of the same: weaving in and cutting back. The main cut-back is best carried out in spring.

I would like to establish a native hedge at the bottom of the garden to form a natural-type boundary with the fields beyond. How do I go about this?

The plants that you choose for your native hedge will depend on your soil type, and on how you want your hedge to perform. My soil is very free-draining and quite alkaline. In my garden I have therefore used a mix of hawthorn *(Crataegus monogyna)*, native privet *(Ligustrum vulgare)*, guelder rose *(Viburnum opulus)*, wayfaring tree *(Viburnum lantana)*, dogrose *(Rosa canina)* and field maple *(Acer campestre)*. The guelder rose apparently becomes particularly rampant in moist conditions, but on my dry patch it seems very happy too. Holly *(Ilex aquifolium)* would have been a good addition too, but it is much slower than all the rest and you would have to make sure that it did not become smothered before it had a chance to make its presence felt. Spindle *(Euonymus europaeus)*, sea buckthorn *(Hippophae rhamnoides)*, alder buckthorn *(Rhamnus frangula)* and common buckthorn *(Rhamnus cathartica)* could all be included. All of the plants listed are robust plants and will survive in most conditions. If you examine local hedgerows you can see what thrives best in your area and be guided by that. For moister soils I would include common dogwood *(Cornus sanguinea)*, too.

If you want to create a dense and eventually stock-proof fence, whatever soil you are on, then put in a large proportion of hawthorn – in the region of 70 per cent. Even if the hedge does not need to be stock-proof, I tend to plant about 50 per cent hawthorn as it is an excellent, inexpensive filler that will form a good stout backbone. Choose about six other favourites and plant about 5 per cent of each of these to fill the hedge. Plant the shrubs in random groups of variable numbers, to give a good mix to the hedge, but thread the dogrose throughout the hedge, planting it singly so that it laces through the other shrubs.

Plant bare-root plants (except in the case of holly and privet), about 45–60cm (1½–2ft) high, in the dormant season. Bare-root plants will establish better than container-grown ones and are less expensive. Plant in a double staggered row with 50cm (20in) between the rows and the same distance between the plants in the rows. Weed control is particularly important in the first three or four years as the competition for moisture can slow down growth spectacularly. If you plant into clean soil – preferably soil that you have left fallow and kept continually free of weeds for two months or so prior to planting – then you are off to a good start. Add a mulch of bark, well-rotted manure, compost or something similar and then its weeding demands on you will be greatly reduced. I do not put rabbit-proof guards on hedges: if the rabbits do nibble the plants over the winter, the plants sprout back, forming much bushier plants. I recommend that even if you do not have rabbit problems you cut all the plants back after planting to about 15cm (6in), which will promote this good, bushy growth.

With all these recommendations there can't be much space left but, if a gap should appear, plant a couple of scramblers, such as traveller's joy, also called old man's beard *(Clematis vitalba)*, and hops *(Humulus lupulus)*.

They are both native to the British Isles and are often seen scrambling through hedges. Traveller's joy has green-white flowers in late summer and autumn, followed by silky seedheads that last throughout the winter. Female hop flowers are green-yellow in late summer and supply the fruit clusters so necessary for making good beer.

I wonder why Bunny didn't mention hops? It must be because of one or other part of her name!

There is a housing estate at the end of our largish garden and I would like to block it out with a tiny bit of woodland. The space is about 10m (32ft) deep and the same width. How can I create this rapidly?

A small bit of woodland screen is a more successful way of hiding an eyesore than the ubiquitous, fast-growing evergreen hedge, which appears to flag up the fact that there is something nasty lurking behind it. I have seen an effective deciduous screen that is only 3m (9¾ft) wide. In the winter, although the view beyond is not obliterated, it is broken up.

The simplest and most economical way to establish woodland is to plant small, bare-rooted trees, 45–90cm (18–36in) tall at close centres, about 1.5–2m (5–6½ft) apart. I am sure that you are in a hurry to block out the view, but small plants will establish faster than their larger counterparts, so that in three to four years' time they will have overtaken them. They also ultimately form a more natural-shaped tree. Put in some quick achievers: I find the wild cherry *(Prunus avium)* a very fast tree. It is tolerant of a wide range of conditions: clay soils, light poor soils and exposed conditions. It does grow to become fairly large, so if this worries you omit it and plant a tree that you can coppice when it grows too big, such as hazel *(Corylus avellana)*, sweet chestnut *(Castanea sativa)*, ash *(Fraxinus excelsior)*, willow *(Salix)* and birch *(Betula)*. You should coppice (cut back the trunks to just above ground level) a few trees each year, to maintain your cover while at the same time not letting any trees get too vast. Apart from cherry, other fast-growing, attractive trees are field maple *(Acer campestre)*, alder *(Alnus glutinosa)* and birch *(Betula pendula)*. Which you choose will depend on what grows well in your area and which trees you like.

In a small area it is better to stick to one dominant tree and then maybe add one or two small groups of another type, so that it forms a cohesive block. Position them so that they look as though they have regenerated naturally, with random spacings. Two trees may be just 1m (3¼ft) apart – others up to 3m (10ft) apart. You are not aiming to produce perfect specimens; you are hoping to get woodland with character, so some may have slightly bent trunks or lopsided canopies. Do not bother to stake them – this is unnecessary and even detrimental at this size – but do remove all grass and weed competition in an area of 1m (3¼ft) diameter around the base of each trunk; the lack of grass competition will speed up their growth by 60–70 per cent. A good way to do this is to use tree spats; these are mats usually made from woven polypropylene, felt or polythene, which cover the soil and are put on at planting time (see Suppliers Index). You can make your own from black polythene, and bury the edges in the ground or fix them down with pegs to keep them in place. Protect the trees and promote their growth rate by using see-through, clear polypropylene or plastic tree shelters for the first three to five years.

Add some native, woodland-edge shrubs and maybe a native hedge at the end (see p. 205). Hazel, field maple, native privet, the guelder rose and the wayfaring tree all make an attractive shrub layer that will add substance, particularly in the short term before the trees look like proper woodland. Form one or two mown paths through the area. The trees will eventually block out the light so killing the grass, then you can plant ivy and other ground-cover plants replace it. I would keep all the ground under the trees bare initially, by using herbicide, and then as the light is shaded out by the trees' canopies I would plant bluebells *(Hyacinthoides non-scripta)*, fox-gloves *(Digitalis)*, red campion *(Silene dioica)*, periwinkle *(Vinca)* and other woodland favourites.

My mother-in-law has a large garden and is now finding it a bit of a strain. She is keen, but finds it a little too much. Can you suggest ways to reduce the maintenance?

When the maintenance of a garden becomes too much, you need to work out which elements are taking up the majority of time, which elements you could afford/find someone else to do and then see what steps you can take to simplify the work or even eradicate some of it altogether. Another factor is identifying which elements you enjoy doing.

Usually the mowing of grass is the most time-consuming part of a garden. Make sure that the machine being used is the most efficient one for the job and that it is large enough. Lawns that have fiddly, small parts to cut using a different machine could be redesigned to remove these. Mowing margins adjacent to borders eradicate the need to edge up with hand-shears. These are usually made from bricks, paving slabs or other hard material and are set fractionally (5mm or ¼in) below the turf so that the mower can run over the edge without damaging the blades. It is well worth adding these wherever feasible, as they keep the lawn edge looking crisp and smart. Mowing margins can also be employed where grass runs up to a wall, steps or hedge; an alternative is a narrow, bare earth strip parallel to the obstacle at the same level as the turf. This can be maintained with a herbicide such as glyphosate.

If you are trying to cut down on work, there is little point in putting fer-

tilizer on the lawn, which undoubtedly boosts its growth. Try leaving areas of the lawn longer, and consider turning some of it into a wildflower meadow (see p. 202). If longer areas are outlined with a nice, crisply mown edge it does help prevent that over-wild, out-of-control look that is evident in spring-flowering meadows just before they are cut in mid-summer.

Hedge cutting is another task that is quite hard work and monotonous, but is within the capabilities of most people, so it is a good job to delegate.

Borders can be time-consuming, especially if they have tall herbaceous plants that require staking and/or splitting, annuals, bedding plants and tender perennials that are moved in and out. On top of this there is also the weeding. Gardeners do all this because they enjoy it, but if it does become too much, then the planting could be rationalized so that the areas are composed of more trouble-free plants, such as potentillas, herbaceous geraniums, peonies, shrub roses and many of the viburnums. Applying a thick, 5cm (2in) mulch every two years or so of a coarse-grade (3–5cm (1–2in)) bark in the spring to suppress the annual weeds will certainly help. The finer bark mulches do not prevent weed seeds germinating in them, although they tend to look better. A better solution still is to plant the plants through a fabric such as Mypex (available from garden centres) and then put the mulch on top of this. This is only possible to put in when you are establishing the border and is not ideal for herbaceous plants that spread outwards.

STRUCTURAL DESIGN WITH PLANTS

I would like to grow a hedge house. How can I do this, and what plants would you suggest?

Hedge houses make a change from the more common type of garden building, such as pavilions or gazebos. They are much admired, but are not that common, as people assume that they take ages to form and so discard the idea. I have just planted one and, in order to create immediate impact, I have made a trellis framework, which is attractive enough to stand on its own. In 10 years' time the hedge will have grown up the trellis and trained along the wires at the top to form a green roof. A hedge arbour could be tackled in the same way, giving you a unique, green enclosure for a favourite seat.

My favourite hedge houses are grown from yew *(Taxus baccata)*. These take quite a time to grow up and form an enclosure over the top. Bearing in mind that it is reckoned that a yew plant grows at the rate of a boy (from birth to maturity it takes about 14 years to achieve a height of about 1.8m/6ft for both), you do need a little patience! But I find that you can greatly speed things up if you water the plants in dry periods. Although yew hates wet ground, it does respond extremely well to irrigation. A stretch of

Mowing margin

hedging edging my vegetable plot gets far more water than other stretches and is now beautifully thick and has reached a height of 1.4m (4¾ft) after only five years, and was planted at just 30cm (1ft) high.

Other good plants for a hedge house are beech *(Fagus sylvatica)*, horn-beam *(Carpinus betulus)* or, for the impatient person, *Cotoneaster lacteus*, but this would need more than one cut a year to keep it looking like a house, rather than a bush. The fastest choice would probably be ivy *(Hedera)*, but you would definitely need a trellis framework for this.

To form the hedge house, position your plants along the perimeters of the 'house'-to-be, not forgetting that the 'walls' are eventually going to be a thickness of up to 1m (3¼ft), so do not be too mean on size. I tend to put in double, staggered rows of plants about 50cm (20in) apart between the rows, with the same distance between the plants in the rows. Leave a good 1.3m (4⅓ft) gap for the entrance, and to form windows at the sides (if required) stop the hedge at the required height for the opening, and train the plants on either side back over to form the top. For the roof, train horizontal wires across at 30cm (12in) centres and then train lateral shoots along them.

If you want instant impact, try forming a trellis framework, such as the one in the diagram. This can be made from 5 x 5cm (2 x 2in) vertical posts, with the same-size timber used to form the main horizontals. The horizontal and vertical members can be joined with halving joints. Trellis made to any pattern can be formed from 1.8 x 3.8cm (¾ x 1½in) tanalized roofing battens. Added extras, such as simple finials in the form of timber balls sitting on a post capping, or an arch cut from marine ply, makes the structure more inter-esting. The timber can be painted with an opaque timber stain, in a dark green to make it quite low-key or an Oxford blue to make more of a statement.

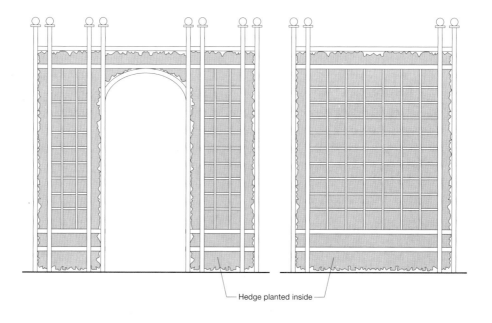

Hedge planted inside

Elevation of hedge house

We have an established yew hedge in our garden, which is a big asset, but we would like to make it a more interesting boundary. What can you suggest?

Hedges are frequently used to form the structural bones of the garden and, as such, they form part of the garden's architecture. When they become mature there is an opportunity to add some embellishment. In the diagram you can see just a few possibilities. The first one has been allowed to develop into a lumpy style, bulging along the sides as well as at the tops. The garden designed by Arne Maynard at the Chelsea Flower Show had box hedges shaped in this way. They had become partially neglected in a Dutch nursery and were then clipped back into a more informal shape by another grower who took the nursery over. But you do occasionally see hedges clipped specifically in this way.

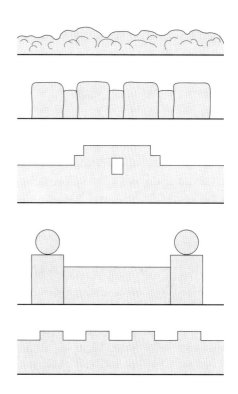

The second example has a strong, formal rhythm. The lower sections are also narrower, which gives a good three-dimensional effect. A window or archway cut through a hedge adds interest (see the third example), although ideally you need something eye-catching on the other side. By raising the hedge up to the window, you give it more importance. Green piers with oversized balls (see the fourth example) are simple and classical and will look well in a traditional or modern garden. The final example involves green crenellations, which again are traditional and stylish. Medieval buttresses coming out from the hedge at right-angles would blend well with the shaped top; they are a useful way to divide up long stretches of border into smaller chunks. These would have to be planted as an addition in your case.

I would like to plant a mini-parterre, but I am bored with dwarf box and am also concerned about disease. What other plants can you suggest that would form a suitable low hedge?

First, although it is right to be concerned about the disease of box, it is worth knowing a bit about it before you totally condemn it.

Cylindrocladium blight is a fungal disease that affects the foliage but does not usually kill the plant. It needs lots of moisture on the foliage to thrive and so the drier areas of the country do not usually have a problem. The dwarf edging box (*Buxus sempervirens* 'Suffruticosa') is far more prone to this disease than the ordinary *B. sempervirens*, because it has denser, compact foliage, which keeps wetter for longer. The later is also good for parterres and is quite happy to be maintained at a low height, but does require a bit more attention to keep it looking neat, as it grows more vigorously. So rather than abandoning box altogether, consider using it for part of your parterre, rather than all.

The best dwarf hedging plant, if you want that tight-clipped look, is probably dwarf myrtle (*Myrtus communis* subsp. *tarentina*). The down side of this is that it is not totally hardy. If you decide to use it, I would make sure that the soil is free-draining by adding grit if necessary. I would plant it in the spring in a sheltered position and cover it with a couple of layers of fleece in cold spells during its first few winters. I would also keep my fingers crossed for a few mild winters until it had got really established!

I used *Hebe odora* on one scheme where the client hated box; it has small crowded leaves, giving it a good bushy appearance. It formed a small, stout hedge rapidly, but needs to be cut back annually in late spring. This is a hardy hebe and has white flowers in the summer. Wall germander (*Teucrium chamaedrys*) is another plant that I have used in this situation. It looks less formal than a box, but forms an attractive hedge with pink flowers from mid- to late summer. Again, trim it over in late spring. One client favoured strong colours, particularly yellows and purples, so I planted one area with the dwarf purple berberis (*Berberis thunbergii* 'Atropurpurea Nana') as a hedge. I was rather apprehensive, but it did form a great small hedge, and the client loved it. By surrounding it with interesting greens, you could tone it down a bit. Unlike the others, it is deciduous.

Lavender, santolina and ruta are all regularly used for dwarf hedges. They tend to get leggy and unattractive if not clipped hard back annually (see p. 225) in spring, but against this they quickly make a strong and attractive statement and, if clipped tightly, will look presentable for about seven years. Of all the lavenders to choose from, I think I would go for *Lavandula angustifolia* 'Hidcote', which is a good compact form. Do not forget, though, that although lavender does look stunning for about four months in the summer, it can then look pretty unremarkable (particularly on moist soils) for the rest of the year. On dry soils it can be quite passable for all 12 months. My last suggestion is yew *(Taxus baccata):* too big and vigorous, you might say, but my uncle is trying it out at the moment. He is using it as a low hedge in his rose garden and it has now been in for about four years and looks wonderful. It does need two cuts a year, however, to keep it looking tidy.

We have an orchard that we would like to make more ornamental and less utilitarian. Can you suggest how we could do this?

One of my favourite orchards is in John Stefanidis' garden, Cock Crow. He injected style by planting hebes *(Hebe rakaiensis)* around the bottoms of all the apple trees. They form big, fat domes, which look great, winter and summer. Hebes love sun, and so the fruit trees are kept well pruned to allow the sun to filter through. To keep that wonderfully uniform, well-shaped blob of green so consistent throughout the orchard, the hebes would need to be replaced every six or eight years, I would think, but they are extremely easy to propagate from cuttings. I have seen the same effect in other gardens using box and lavender, but they didn't look so lush.

The fruit trees themselves can be trained into a range of interesting shapes. It is well worth visiting Hatton Fruit Gardens at East Malling, near Maidstone in Kent, where they have trees trained in a vast range of fascinating shapes. They have apple trees trained into goblets, *bateau*-trained pears, winged pyramids, tabletop trees and arches, to name a few.

An informal orchard with a spring-flowering meadow below, interspersed with a few mown paths, takes a lot of beating. Straightforward fruit trees, especially if they are grown on one of the larger rootstocks, have great charm of their own. If you want added value, send some climbing roses or clematis up through their canopies.

If you want to formalize your paths a little, you could add a metal archway (see p. 168), which is visually light to look at, so the tracery of the climbing plant is the most noticeable element. A rustic timber arch may work well in the scheme of things, too.

We want to make a small knot garden in the gravel forecourt in front of our house. What is the best way to do this, and how do you minimize weeding?

Geometric patterns formed with low hedging, growing through gravel, are an unusual method of making a gravel forecourt look more like a garden than a driveway. It can appear traditional or modern, and will fit in with many styles of housing, both grand and cottage. At Stapleford Park in Leicestershire, I was asked to think of a scheme to stop cars parking right outside the grand frontage, as they cluttered up the look of the building. I designed a knot garden, with box hedging growing straight out of the gravel. In this case the patternwork formed a compass on one side and letters representing the four hunts that met there on the other, worked into a fairly elaborate pattern. As the drive got a high volume of cars, I protected the planting from wheels with a line of stone balls in front of it.

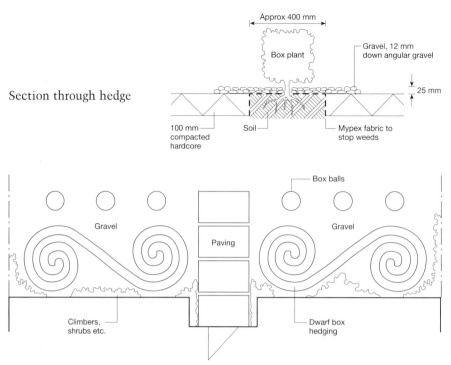

Section through hedge

Approx 400 mm

Box plant

Gravel, 12 mm down angular gravel

25 mm

100 mm compacted hardcore

Soil

Mypex fabric to stop weeds

Box balls

Gravel

Gravel

Paving

Climbers, shrubs etc.

Dwarf box hedging

Plan of small knot garden

For most properties this would be a little too grand. Shapes such as figures of eight, scrolls, circles and ellipses are simpler. They form architecturally shaped hedges, which combine both with the building and the garden. It is worth studying some highly ornate parterres and knot gardens, and you will see that many elements are used again and again. Find a simple one that you like and adapt it to your own space. I have used zigzags, intertwining hedges that resemble a twisted rope and serpentines; sometimes I mix them with solid geometric shapes as well.

Once you have drawn up your design on paper to an appropriate scale, perhaps 1:50, you need to transfer it onto the ground. I find the easiest way is to enlarge complicated bits such as scrolls on a photocopier to life size (1:1) and then transfer these onto hardboard and cut them out with a jigsaw to form a template. To minimise weeding, use a membrane such as Mypex, laid over the soil and under the gravel as shown in the diagram.

I am an inveterate plant buyer, so all my borders are planted with one plant of many different kinds. Unfortunately the overall effect is rather dire. How can I sort them out so that the plants work together, but I still have scope for my habit?

A lot of gardeners who adore plants have this problem. Often referred to as 'plantsman's gardens', such gardens are stacked full of wonderful treasures that have been acquired over many years. The borders have just been filled as plants have been accumulated, rather than designed as such. In truth, I think most gardeners are guilty of this to some degree, even those coming strictly from the 'designer' as opposed to the 'plant' end. A new, stunning plant is difficult to resist, but you tend to buy one rather than a clump of six – maybe because of cost, maybe because you are not quite sure where you are going to put it anyway.

But rather like being an alcoholic, a plantoholic who realizes the problem and wants to cure it is halfway there. When I'm designing a garden I tend to divide it up in some way to form different spaces, each with a different character, feel or style. One area may be tiny (a planted alcove around a seat), others larger (a sunny courtyard filled with tropical-type plants, for instance). The important point is that the character of the space is empha-sized by choosing plants that reinforce it. The planted alcove could be cottagey, with a rustic seat stuffed full of delphiniums, peonies, pinks and aquilegias; or it could be architectural, with a carved stone seat surrounded by two carefully placed clumps of bear's breeches *(Acanthus mollis).* To this end I like to have a clear idea in my mind of the mood I am trying to create and then I can choose plants to harmonize with the architectural detailing and the overall style.

Even in the tiniest gardens groupings or drifts of several plants of the same sort, and repeated clumps of the same plant in the same part of the garden, give a garden more unity and impact than one plant of each type. Even if your general planting in a border is still a little bitty, repeated clumps of a bold plant throughout that border would start to pull it togeth-er. Conversely, to keep the integrity of one space, I tend not to use the same plant in different areas of the garden, as it tends to water down its impact. If I only buy one plant, I try and propagate it to bulk up the numbers before putting them out in their final position. Well, final position may be optimistic; they might well get shunted around a bit before being allowed to settle down. But plants do not always conform to the textbook, and trial and error may be an important part in getting the best results.

Colour coordination also helps pull disparate plants together, and it does help to create unity in planting schemes if you confine yourself to a limited palette. Colours evoke certain characters or moods: greens are extremely restful; blue evokes feelings of mystery, complexity and depth; while red engenders excitement and passion. You can choose your scheme to rein-force your overall mood.

Another method of pulling planting together is to use low-growing hedging, such as box, either all along the front of the border or through the border in bold patterns, such as zigzags, swags or crenellations. Repeated strong topiary shapes in the border, such as cones, cubes and spirals, can work too, but not usually as strongly.

I want to create a new border from an existing area of lawn.
What is the quickest and most effective way of doing this? The
lawn has been down for 12 years and the soil is deep and loamy.

The soil under a long-established lawn usually has a good structure. If you
were to lift the turf and dig it over, you would be surprised at the number of
weed seeds that would burst into life. As soon as a new layer of soil is
exposed to light, previously dormant seeds are stimulated into growth. To
minimize future weeding I mark out the intended border area using spray
marker or string and canes, then spray off the grass sward using glyphosate.
It usually takes a week or two for the grass to die. Glyphosate is not always
recommended for use in winter, although I find it works well, but the grass
is slower to die. Then I plant through the dead sward without doing any
cultivation – the worms have done that all for you and I do not believe that
digging improves the structure. However, it does bring different soil to the
surface, which will then produce masses of germinating weeds triggered by
the change in light levels. It does not take long for the dead grass to rot
away, but you can always hide it by adding a 5cm (2in) layer of bark mulch
or something similar. If I am planting roses and other hungry feeders, I usually add well-rotted manure to the surface around each plant, then let the
worms and rain take the food down to the plants' roots.

PLANTING AND PLANTING TECHNIQUES

We have an old drive running down the edge of our garden. It is
made from compacted hardcore and I would like to plant it up,
but I cannot get a digger in to do it for me. Is there any way you
can establish planting in hardcore? And what (if any) plants will
tolerate this situation?

The first problem you will have will be a physical one of pickaxing or levering out with a crowbar small planting pits so that you can physically get
the plants in. At this early stage it is necessary to make sure that the pits
do drain (more work with the crowbar may be necessary), as stagnant water
is a killer.

Hardcore tends to have a high pH value – that is, it is often limy, so you
need plants that are tolerant of this. The sort of plants I would use to
reclaim blast-furnace slag (also with a high pH) would colonize your drive
quite happily. These include plants such as the goat willow *(Salix caprea)*
and the attractive willows with coloured stems, such as *Salix alba*
'Britzensis', *S.a.* 'Chermesina', *S. daphnoides* and *S. elaeagnos*. These need
to be pruned back hard every two years or so, in spring to keep the coloured
stems. Although people associate willows with wet conditions, they toler-

ate drought well, too.

You often see buddleias thriving in almost invisible crevices on stone buildings – indicative of the conditions they will survive in. *Buddleia davidii* is tolerant of a high lime content and is a great pioneer plant. *Buddleia* 'Lochinch' is my favourite buddleia, with grey young stems and leaves, scented violet-blue flowers and, last but not least, a good, bushy compact habit. Another good plant for reclamation work is the tree lupin *(Lupinus arboreus)*. This yellow-flowered shrub is pretty well evergreen, grows extremely fast and will reach a height of about 2m (6½ft). It is particularly useful because it is nitrogen-fixing and is easy to grow from seed. *Native privet* (Ligustrum vulgare) and *Hippophae rhamnoides* are other good starters.

AS

The plant that instantly springs to mind is the winter iris *(Iris unguicularis)*, which makes clumps of tough, narrow leaves joined, in winter, by lovely blue and yellow flowers. They would be welcome at any time of year, but doubly so in the darkest months. This iris seems happiest in the most inhospitable places and, strangely, often will not flower if treated to a patch of decent soil. At our last house we had an old drive down the side, but it was wearing away at the edges. Here, there was just enough wear to hack out small holes against the side of the house. We stuffed some small roots of iris in these holes and they grew to magnificent clumps, which flowered really well every winter. The only task was to clean off some of the dead leaves to make them more presentable.

We are designing a small, ornamental potager, which we want to fill with vegetables and flowers. It is highly visible from the house. What are the most attractive vegetables, and which ornamental plants would you put with them?

I find all vegetables attractive to look at, especially when neatly contained in a well-tended plot. The blocks or rows of contrasting foliage are very easy on the eye. There are now many vegetables that are grown more to look good than to taste good. When I grow them, I invariably leave them in well past their sell-by date, because they look too good to pull and eat. If you do, you tend to find that they are not great to eat.

One vegetable I would put in this category is red-stemmed chard. This is the most colourful vegetable in the garden, with its scarlet midribs set against dark-green crumpled leaves. It is good value – if sown in late spring it will look good until it starts to bolt the following spring. The ornamental kale 'Peacock Tails', with its purple and crimson leaves that develop more intense colour in the colder weather, is another example, as is the squash 'Sunburst'. This is a golden-yellow pattypan squash with a scalloped edge.

The Beetroot 'Bull's Blood' has stunning glossy, dark-purple leaves, but the roots do not develop as well as the less eye-catching varieties. I love to grow and admire all these now and again, but I certainly don't get fat on them.

There are bags of vegetables that are pleasing to look at and taste wonderful. Globe artichokes are my all-time favourites. They are easy-to-grow, weed-suppressing giants that look amazing and taste divine. The tastiest cultivars are 'Vert de Laon' and 'Camus de Bretagne'. Another eye-catching culinary favourite is the purple Brussels sprout, 'Rubine'. This is not supposed to make you flatulent, as the green ones do, but I have yet to carry out proper trials in this respect. The runner bean 'Painted Lady' has red and white flowers that can be shown off to the full on hazel wigwams. Sea kale (*Crambe maritima*) is an easy-to-grow perennial; it likes free-draining soil and needs blanching with sea-kale forcers (another comely addition to the garden). The blanched stems are ready in April, but you need to establish and grow the root for two years before your first cutting. It has huge, handsome blue-green leaves and clouds of white blossom and is similar to *Crambe cordifolia*. Golden-fruited courgettes and purple cauliflowers must be squeezed in to the 'look good, taste good' category, too.

As to the addition of ornamental flowers, I think I would limit them to useful types such as nasturtiums, which seem to keep pests away from peas, beans and soft fruit. They are colourful, the leaves and flowers are edible and the seeds when young can be pickled to use like capers. I love marigolds (*Calendula officinalis*), which attract hoverflies to gobble up aphids, and the tangerine sage (*Salvia dorisiana*), a half-hardy perennial with striking red flowers. The leaves are tangerine-scented and can be used in fruit salads.

We have a small roof garden, on which I would like to establish some substantial plants. What is the best way to achieve this?

Whenever I work on roof-garden schemes I find that it is necessary to know what loading the roof will take. Then you can exploit it to the full. Otherwise you tend to take a half-hearted approach, which will not give you the desired impact. An engineer should be able to tell you your roof's loading capacity and then spell this out in terms of soil depth, pot weights and numbers that you can use.

A problem with many of these elevated gardens is the wind speed – the eddying and buffeting you can get in tall blocks does affect the plants' growth and your enjoyment of the space. If this is the case, I would put up around the perimeter a dense trellis, hazel hurdles or some other boundary fence to filter the wind. These could form the support for a good backbone of climbers to form a fairly quick wall of green and would in turn help to provide shelter for your other plants. In places, or in addition to fencing, vertical canvas screens or curtains can be designed to form excellent temporary windbreaks and are a functional way of adding colour and style. Perspex or glass screens are invisible to birds, which fly into them, so I tend to avoid these.

Assuming that you are limited to planting in pots or troughs, consider some sort of irrigation (see p. 179). The high level of exposure to the wind and sun and the limited amount of compost can be compensated for if water is freely available. If you have areas with large troughs, these could be fitted with seephose, which can either be controlled manually or fitted with automatic controls. You can make these yourselves using pressure-compensating drippers fitted on polythene pipe or get in a specialist firm (see Suppliers Index).

The containers themselves need to be as large and light as possible. Timber troughs, made from either tanalized softwood or hardwood (heavier but more durable), are inexpensive and quite simple to make. And there is a huge range of woodstains, both translucent and opaque, with which you can create inspirational colour schemes. Galvanized iron sheet is available in various sheet thicknesses and can be used to form shiny, contemporary-style planters. Plasterer's baths in galvanized iron – either with rounded or square ends in a range of sizes – make extremely economical, usefully sized, attractive planting troughs (see Suppliers Index). Do not forget to drill holes in the base. Plastic pots can be vastly improved by painting them with a masonry paint. The late David Hicks chose simple, bold styles and painted them with a stone-coloured finish, and the effect was convincing. They are available in huge sizes, easily capable of taking a small tree.

When you fill containers, put a lightweight free-draining layer in the base, such as Leca, to a depth of 15–20cm (6–8in). Leca stands for lightweight expanded clay aggregate; it looks rather like pebbles and is sterile, non-toxic and inert. It is often sold in garden centres under the name Hydroleca. Then put a membrane such as capillary matting over this, before adding the compost. The matting stops the compost mixing with the drainage material. The use of mulches and the addition of water-storing polymer granules (see p. 178) apply here, too.

As for choosing your plant material, starting with the most substantial, there is a range of trees that will thrive in containers. Choose ones that like exposure and tolerate dry conditions, such as *Sorbus cashmiriana*, holly *(Ilex aquifolium)* and hawthorn *(Crataegus monogyna)*. This last can be attractively shaped and clipped. Snowy mespilus *(Amelanchier lamarckii)* looks wonderful grown as a multi-stem large shrub or small tree. Many cotoneasters, such as *Cotoneaster* 'Cornubia' and *C. frigidus*, would thrive in this situation. The larger trees may become unstable if they are grown in lightweight pots, so you may well have to tie them in position or anchor them down somehow. You may also have to reduce the canopy on a regular basis, but the restricted roots will not let the top develop to its 'natural' size.

Many substantial shrubs can be grown. As for all plants, choose ones that like dry conditions and exposure. Ones that I've used include pyracanthas, senecio, potentillas, phormiums, cotoneasters, viburnums, buxus and hebes. Climbing plants that perform well in this situation are ivies (*Hedera*), *Hydrangea petiolaris*, *Lonicera japonica* 'Halliana' and *Solanum crispum* 'Glasnevin'. Do not forget herbaceous plants, and grasses too: *Verbena bonariensis*, *Stipa gigantea*, *Acanthus mollis* and *Miscanthus sinensis*, to name but a few. There are many other suitable plants besides these, so if you have a favourite, give it a go. Feed the plants regularly: slow-release fertilizer granules mixed in the top layer of compost once a year in spring is a simple way, or regular liquid feeds during the growing season.

Last but not least, a small, shallow pool, if the loading allows, can look wonderful and can help the humidity in a potentially dry and dusty space. Then you have scope for aquatics, which contribute a luscious feel to a potentially arid-looking spot.

We have formed a steep bank at the edge of our driveway. Can you suggest a soft way to retain the earth? It is too steep to mow grass there. The bank is about 70cm (28in) high and fairly fertile.

If you use 'green' retaining walls or banks, instead of the more usual brick or stone walls, these create a far softer and more organic appearance. In areas such as driveways, which have a tendency to look sterile, these can dramatically change the end result and are often far less expensive.

A Dutch landscape architect friend of mine, who is a big fan of willow, uses it extensively to retain banks and walkways adjacent to rivers. He has used willow to retain a bank in his garden. The slope is almost vertical. In the diagram you can see how he formed it. You can use soil-stabilizing netting to help keep the soil in place, before the willow gets going (see Suppliers Index). This is recommended for slopes up to 1:1. First, he pushed in vertical willow cuttings (he used *Salix viminalis*) along the base of the bank, and then he pushed the tops into the bank top. These were positioned at about 10cm (4in) centres. Then he wove horizontals along through the uprights at about the same centres. The thick ends were pushed into the bank at staggered centres, so that they would grow too. This should be done in the dormant season, using cuttings about 1.2cm (½in) thick. As the willow wall grows, you can weave the new shoots in, and when it gets thick some cutting back will need to be done,

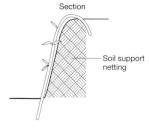

Section

Soil support netting

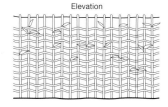

Elevation

If necessary, stabilize the soil with soil support netting. Push the willow cuttings into the ground along the base of the bank at approx 100 mm (4 in) intervals. Then push the tops of the cuttings into the top of the bank. Next, weave horizontal willow cuttings at approx 100 mm (4 in) intervals through the upright willows and push both ends into the bank. Stagger these ends along the length of the bank.

too. This can be done at any time of the year.

An alternative way is to build a turf wall using standard-sized turves (30 x 90cm/12 x 36in) folded-inside out (so that the grass is on the inside). The turves are folded once, so you get a unit about 30 x 40cm (12 x 16in). Then they are laid side-by-side along the ground at the base of the wall-to-be, with the 40cm (16in) length running along the length of the 'wall'. The next layer is laid on top of this so that the joints are staggered. Instead of making the wall vertical, it is best to batter it with a slight angle, which will depend on how much space you have. You carry on like this until you reach the top. Then you plant the face of the wall with a vigorous colonizer that likes dry conditions. Bugle *(Ajuga)*, periwinkle *(Vinca major)* and ivy *(Hedera)* are ideal. The plants should be well-soaked first and watered well in (awkward but possible), then kept moist until they are established. I tend to put them it at close centres, such as 30cm (12in), so that they quickly form a dense cover. It is a good idea to spray the turf with glyphosate at least six hours before you build the wall, otherwise some grasses will manage to grow back through at the edges.

If your bank is not exceptionally steep and the natural angle of repose of your soil is quite steep, you may well get away with just planting through the soil-stabilizing netting. Use the quick-colonizing plants, and as long as you can keep them moist while they become established, and you plant them densely, they should soon cover the netting.

I want to make some stone steps with plants growing in the risers. Can you suggest which plants to use, and how to make the steps?

Steps with trim, green bands of plants to form the risers combine the soft element of the plants with the hard element of the paving, producing an unusual and pleasing detail.

The diagram overleaf shows a general principle that you can use for constructing the steps. The treads need to be fairly wide, as they have a deeper overhang than normal (10cm/4in) and might topple off otherwise. It is important to bed these slabs down really well, and not to use them until the mortar has set firm. Allow 24 hours at least. The planting pockets are rather restricted and must have drainage, so they must be continued down onto the hardcore at regular intervals. Form them by alternating the smaller pockets with deeper pockets going down to the hardcore. Initially the concrete will look unattractive; you could paint it with a dark stone-coloured masonry paint. My favourite plant, which will survive in these potentially dry pockets, is box *(Buxus sempervirens)*. Plant it at 15cm (6in) centres, as a bushy liner with the stems as close in to the concrete as possible. It should be clipped to form solid, uniform stripes, and kept flush with the riser. Another common plants to use would be ivy *(Hedera)*; *Hedera helix* 'Cristata' is a most attractive form with margins that are twisted and crumpled.

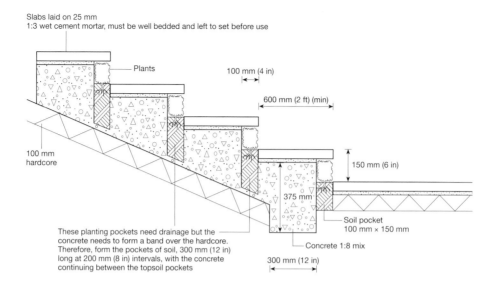

Slabs laid on 25 mm
1:3 wet cement mortar, must be well bedded and left to set before use

Plants

100 mm (4 in)

600 mm (2 ft) (min)

100 mm
hardcore

150 mm (6 in)

375 mm

Soil pocket
100 mm × 150 mm

These planting pockets need drainage but the
concrete needs to form a band over the hardcore.
Therefore, form the pockets of soil, 300 mm (12 in)
long at 200 mm (8 in) intervals, with the concrete
continuing between the topsoil pockets

Concrete 1:8 mix

300 mm (12 in)

Section through planted steps

HERBS

I love using lots of herbs in cooking. Can you suggest how to grow them so that they look attractive in the garden, as I find they can look a bit drab in their long off-season.

I mix certain herbs in with my vegetables, these being the ones that I use in copious quantities. Current favourites are parsley, both the moss-curled (*Petroselinum crispum* 'Moss Curled') and the French or Italian parsley (*P. c.* 'Italicum'), plus coriander (*Coriander sativum* 'Cilantro', which is better for leaf production and does not bolt as fast as the plain *sativum*), chives (*Allium schoenoprasum*), salad rocket (*Eruca sativa*) and lovage (*Levisticum officinale*). Apart from the chives, they all have long off-seasons or (as in the case of salad rocket and coriander) grow rapidly and then bolt, so need running replacements.

My vegetable garden is ornamental, so to keep up appearances I have eight herb blocks, which are geometrically arranged within the geometric design of the vegetable patch. These herb squares are edged by low box hedging and are designed so that a small cloche fits snugly inside the hedging. In this way I extend the picking season. Equally I could have used circles, ellipses, diamonds, triangles or other shapes, edged with a different dwarf hedge (see p. 211 for ideas), and incorporated these into my ornamental garden. These shapes might, for instance, form unusual full stops at the ends of borders.

Elsewhere I plant herbs in large, attractive tubs. In the winter the tubs are bare, but create impact in their own right, so this does not concern me. This applies to tansy (*Tanacetum vulgare* var. *crispum*) – I rub my dog with this and it is meant to prevent fleas – various mints *(Mentha),* dill *(Anethum graveolens)* and horseradish *(Armoracia rusticana).* The variegated form of this last herb is a stunner and excels in an ornamental border, as do many other culinary herbs, such as the sages, oregano, marjoram, bay, fennel and red orache. But fennel and orache are promiscuous and I sometimes feel like ditching them altogether.

My sage, lavender and cotton lavender all get very woody and unattractive. Which varieties look good for longest, and what is the best way to manage their lifespan?

There is a wide range of lavenders to choose from, but first I think you should question whether you have the right conditions to give them a sporting chance. On heavy soils in wet areas they do not perform as well as on a free-draining soil in drier parts of the country. My mother has a nursery in the West Country and says that she regularly has people coming in saying forlornly that most of their lavender has pegged out. This is simply because it hates damp. To avoid disappointment, when you plant them you can take this into account, find a sunny, well-drained spot and if necessary add a lot of grit. Close planting centres will also help to keep the soil drier, and of course will give you quicker results. Lavender is a fast-growing plant with a short lifespan, and to keep it looking good you should reckon on replacing it every seven years or so – maybe sooner. It also tends to suffer from shab, where the plant wilts, discolours and dies back stem by stem and then sometimes dies altogether. It is a fungus, *Phommopsis lavandulae,* that invades the plant via pruning wounds. You should cut back the infected parts and just keep your fingers crossed.

Having been so negative about what must be one of the best-loved plants in the country, I will concentrate on lavender's plus points. It look goods when it bursts into growth in late spring, right through until its flowers go over in midsummer. And in my garden, where it is planted in hardcore with about 5cm (2in) of topsoil on top, it looks pretty good for the rest of the year, but on wet soils it has a tendency to look drab until it perks up again the following spring. To maximize its appearance it does need cutting back hard every spring, but it does not break freely if you cut back into old wood. Dead-heading after flowering neatens the show. I have used lavender in a herb garden clipped into round balls, mixed with many other clipped spheres of various diameters using various plants – rosemary, cotton lavender, olive, box, bay and yew – and they formed a comely group. As far as hardiness is concerned, the dwarf lavenders tend to be less reliable than the English lavender *(Lavandula spica).* A good bet is *Lavandula angustifolia*

'Hidcote', which is a compact form with violet flowers; it has an AGM (Award of Garden Merit) and is a popular, readily available cultivar.

Cotton lavender *(Santolina chamaecyparissus)*, like lavender, appreciates sharp drainage, sun and cutting back hard both in spring and on initial planting, to encourage bushy growth. It looks well throughout the year, except after its annual haircut. The dead flowers can also be removed. Every two or three years, as the plant becomes more open and leggy, you can cut back into old wood. The older plants may not respond well to this treatment but the younger ones will benefit from it. Replace (like lavender and sage this is easy from cuttings) when it starts to look a bit decrepit. My favourite form is *S. c.* 'Lemon Queen', which has lovely, pale lemon-yellow flowers and is a good compact form.

Sage *(Salvia officinalis)* needs to be cut back every year, in spring to a framework of woody stems, otherwise it becomes sprawling and unattractive. If you neglect to do this and then cut back to near ground level into old wood, you may well get away with it, provided the bush is not too elderly. But I would advise taking some cuttings first, just in case. As to my favourites, I like the plain green form, though many find it boring, and the purple and golden forms (*S. o.* 'Purpurascens' and *S. o.* 'Icterina'). The tri-coloured form (*S. o.* 'Tricolor') does not survive for long with me in the Midlands, despite my free-draining soil.

I would like to grow a year-round supply of a few favourite herbs. Can you suggest how to do this without a heated greenhouse?

I grow my favourite herbs as mentioned above (see p. 224) in the vegetable garden, with protection from a cloche in winter and early spring. But I adore basil and find that, unless the summer is a hot one, it really is far better off inside. I got fed up with my windowsills in the kitchen being crammed full of collections of rather disgusting-looking saucers, so I got my local metal-worker to make-to-measure five shallow galvanized iron trays, which fit snugly, one on each of my kitchen windowsills. They were reasonably priced and not only do they look a hundred times better, but I can now cram in far more pots.

I buy ready-grown pots of basil from my supermarket – a tiny pot of about 20 plants grown cheek by jowl costs about 55p, and so is comparable with a pack of seeds. Immediately I repot them, about 4cm (1½ in) apart, in good potting compost; cut them back, as they arrive drawn up and leggy and tend to collapse; water them in well and liquid-feed them every fortnight or so. To water them I totally immerse the pots in water once a week for an hour or so. They are then regularly picked at and supply me with copious foliage for several months. When the poor things become exhausted they are discarded and I start again. The same applies to coriander, except that it is better to grow this from seed, as then you can be sure of getting the variety that doesn't flower so fast, *Coriandrum sativum* 'Cilantro'. I find that it needs replacing much more frequently than basil, and needs more regular watering to help stop it bolting.

We love mint – what is a simple way to contain it in the garden so that it doesn't romp everywhere, and which types do you recommend?

I grow my mint in a large pot, but it does need a lot of watering to keep a good lush supply going in dry summer periods. An easier method is to contain it by planting it in an old bucket or large black plant container. The bottom can be removed with a Stanley knife and then you can sink it into the ground, with about 2.5cm (1in) rising proud of the soil, to make sure that it doesn't sneak out over the top. Vita Sackville-West recommended growing herbs in an old cartwheel, and using the several divisions for various herbs. The names of the herbs were painted around the rim in the appropriate part. The real spreaders, such as mint, she suggested, could then be planted in old tins with their bottoms cut out, in a semi-circle around the outside edge.

As to varieties of mint, for flavour I like the Moroccan mint (*Mentha spicata* 'Moroccan'), which has an excellent spearmint flavour and grows to 40cm (16in); it has the advantage of not suffering from mint rust, too. I also grow pineapple mint (*Mentha suaveolens* 'Variegata'), which has striking leaves and can be added to vegetables, salads (especially good with tomatoes) and fruit salads. There are many other mints, including ginger mint, chocolate peppermint and a curly mint – none of which I've yet tried, but which for a mint aficionado would be a must. Send off for a comprehensive catalogue from a good herb nursery and that will really expand your horizons (see Suppliers Index).

Bottomless buckets were traditional but are in short supply nowadays. I have found that the drums of washing machines work extremely well when the holes are too small for mint roots to get out of.

I have a galvanized plasterer's bath, measuring 1.5m (5ft) long x 50cm (20in) wide. Could you suggest some useful culinary herbs to fill it and give me a good variety of flavours?

A lot of this is purely down to personal taste, and the beauty of it is that it is quite flexible: you can discard plants as they lose condition with age or as you get bored with them. In the diagram the centrepiece is a standard bay tree. If you find this too predictable, you could get one with a plaited, barley-sugar or corkscrew stem, or even make one, as shown in the diagram.

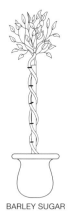

PLAITED   CORKSCREW   BARLEY SUGAR

Different ways to
form standards

Other good herbs for standards are lavender, rosemary and olive. The hardi-
est olive for outside is *Olea europaea* 'Aglandau' (see Suppliers Index).

Around the edge I have made a hedge of two different parsleys, assuming
that you will need a fair quantity of this. The rosemary tripods on either
side, together with the bay, add some height. The former are made by planting three rooted, non-bushy cuttings at 10cm (4in) centres in the shape of a
triangle. Then loosely twist the
stems around each other, with just
enough twist to combine them
together. Tie them with some wire
at the top. You can stop them at a
height of about 60cm (24in), and
then clip them to give a bushy pyramid shape. I use *Rosmarinus officinalis* 'Miss Jessop's Upright'.

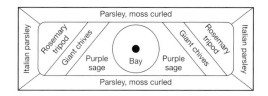

The two bands of chives would make more of a statement if the giant
chive were used. *Allium schoenoprasum* var. *sibiricum* tastes good and has
lots of large, attractive pink flowers. As with all chives, if you cut it back
after flowering you will get a second crop of flowers. Regular cutting also
promotes good leaf production. Chives prefer moister ground than many
herbs, so they are better not located around the edge of the container. I have
shown a block of purple sage (*Salvia officinalis* 'Purpurascens') in the centre
– another attractive but tasty plant. This is potentially large for the situation and would need regular clipping back to prevent it swamping the other
occupants. Other possible candidates for this spot are numerous: perhaps
golden marjoram (*Origanum* 'Aureum Crispum'), which has attractive,
golden curled leaves, or some thyme. *Thymus* x *citriodorus* 'Silver Queen'
is a reliable, almost evergreen plant with handsome, dark-silver variegated
leaves. It produces lilac-pink flowers in the summer. From a culinary point
of view it is excellent, too.

The only space for my herb garden is against a 1.8m (6ft) high north-facing wall. Would it be out of the question to put my herbs here? The potential space is 4m (13ft) wide.

In one large garden in the East Midlands on which I have been working there is a huge herb garden, which is about 36m (39 yd) long and 5m (16ft) wide and is situated behind a north-facing wall that is 3m (10ft) high. I do not know who put it there, but it was undoubtedly a long while back. A huge range of herbs is grown, and all of them look healthy, but obviously the ones that tolerate shade most are tucked up near the base of the wall. These include angelica *(Angelica archangelica)*, tansy *(Tanacetum vulgare)*, mint *(Mentha spicata)*, horseradish *(Armoracia rusticana)*, lovage *(Levisticum officinale)*, meadowsweet *(Filipendula ulmaria)* and bistort *(Polygonum bistorta)*. The fact that the wall creates a dry niche obviously does not worry these herbs unduly. The less shade-tolerant plants are sited in the sunnier part. Having said this, the garden is situated on extremely free-draining limestone in Lincolnshire. It is a very sunny but dry part of the county, and this no doubt means that the garden warms up quickly in the spring, which is definitely a contributory factor to the plants' success. If your soil is not free-draining, warm it up by adding grit, or consider making it into a raised bed. The latter course of action would also mean that the plants would get that bit of extra sunlight.

LAWNS

My lawn suffers from moss. What should I do about it?

Moss is one of the most common lawn problems, so you are not alone. It is generally a symptom of run-down turf. You can either try removing the causes and let the moss slowly disappear or, if you have large patches, you may prefer to eradicate it with a moss-killer based on a dichlorophen product or by applying Lawn Sand. The problem with the latter approach is that you will get bare patches, which will rapidly be colonized by other weeds. So reseed or turf the bare areas immediately after the moss has disappeared.

There are several factors that cause moss to thrive in lawns. One is that the grass is being cut too low, and cushion mosses can be an indicator of this. They have small, vertical stems close together that form dense cushions. Ideally you should mow regularly but not too closely. A utility lawn should be cut at about 2.5–3cm (1–1½ in) in the summer, and a smart lawn at about 1.2–1.8cm (½–¾ in). The cuttings should be removed, except when it is very dry – cut growth left on the surface can help reduce water loss.

Another factor is that the soil is too acidic. Even in areas with strongly alkaline soils, areas down to grass for many years will become acidic in the top few centimetres, so on naturally acidic soils this can be a prime cause. An easy way to find out is to do a pH test, making sure that you take your sample from soil that is directly under the surface of the turf. Take several samples, as the home-testing kits can be tricky to get an accurate reading with. If the result is below 5.5, then apply 47g of ground limestone per square metre (2oz per square yard) in the autumn or winter. Only do this if you are convinced that your lawn is too acidic – the fine grasses that make up a good-quality lawn will deteriorate if you make the lawn too alkaline.

Wet weather and poor drainage will also facilitate moss growth, particularly of the trailing mosses. These have feathery greenish-golden stems that lie on the surface. Spring and autumn are the main periods when the problem develops, usually combined with another factor, such as shade or compaction. Waterlogged patches will nearly always become mossy. Spiking, sorting out any drainage problems and the removal of any surface thatch by raking will benefit the lawn by providing better aeration. If shade is a factor, consider reducing or raising the canopies of any nearby trees. Alternatively, moss will often monopolize shady areas under trees – you might consider this an asset and encourage the moss in these places by removing the grass. It seems to develop much more rapidly on earth sprayed regularly with contact herbicides to remove annual weeds.

If your grass is in tip-top condition, then moss is unlikely to get a foothold. Feed it in spring or early summer, and water well before it shows signs of stress from drought. This will help prevent the growth of the upright mosses, which tend to be invasive on poor, acid, free-draining soils and usually take hold in the autumn after a dry summer.

BF

The answer to controlling moss and weeds in a lawn, without using chemicals, is to make the conditions favourable for the grass and less so for the weeds and moss. First, stop using moss killers or herbicides, as both can kill worms, and fewer worms means poorer drainage and aeration and even more problems. Do all the conventional jobs such as scarifying and then oversow with strong-growing grasses, which like lime and do not like acid conditions. Now spread lime at a handful per square metre (square yard) each and every winter. In spring feed the soil to feed the grass, not with quick-acting soluble fertilizers but with gentler organic ones. Raise the height of cut of your mower, but cut just as often. Soon the lush grass will choke out the moss and weeds.

We have just moved house and the lawn has been neglected for six months. Should we lay some new turf, or could we renovate it?

A lawn neglected for six months over the dormant period will not get in nearly such a poor state as a lawn neglected for six months during the growing season. In the former case, I would have thought it fairly straightforward to get it back into good heart. In the latter case, it will obviously take more effort. It is worth examining the lawn, and if it is made up predominantly of moss, pearlwort, dandelions, brambles, coarse grasses and other pernicious weeds and there are only a few sprigs left of lawn grass, then I would start again. I would kill off the weeds, cultivate it to easy running levels, prepare a fine seedbed and sow more seed. I always prefer seeding rather than turfing, as you generally get a better result and it is less expensive. However, I admit that you have to be patient and prepared to wait for about nine months before it is ready for normal use, as opposed to a few weeks.

Renovating a lawn is a satisfying job. First, I would cut down the vegetation to about 5cm (2in). You may well have to scythe it or use a strimmer on it first, then remove the vegetation and cut it with a rotary mower. The cut lawn will no doubt be a khaki colour, but it does not take long to green up, especially if you do this in spring – the best time. Raking the lawn and brushing the surface so that all the dead vegetation is removed allows air and light to get to the surface, and makes it look considerably better, too. Then, as the lawn recovers over the next few weeks, gradually reduce the height of the blades until the desired height is reached (see p. 229).

Next you need to identify the problems. Likely ones are moss (see p. 229), weeds, bare patches, undulations, moles and fairy rings (see p. 233).

For the weed problem I would use a selective weedkiller. This is best applied in spring or autumn. The newer hormone weedkillers (dicamba, dichlorprop, fenoprop and mecoprop) are effective against a wide range of weeds. If you do not want to take this approach or it is the wrong time of year, then mowing will have the effect of slowly killing a fair few weeds anyway.

The humps and hollows are best removed by carefully stripping back the turf in that area using a spade or edging iron and then either filling with soil or removing soil as necessary. Check that it is level, then firm down the turf again. Fill in any cracks with sifted soil and water in well. Bare patches can either be reseeded or returfed. For the latter, cut out a patch to a rectangular shape and then cut a turf to fit.

A good feed and water will make an amazing difference. Using a mechanical distributor does help to give an even result, and it is worth considering hiring or buying one. A fertilizer containing both quick-acting and slow-acting nitrogen would be best in the spring or summer. Once autumn comes, though, it is better to use a fertilizer with phosphates, potash and possibly some slow-acting nitrogen.

We have just moved into a new house and the lawn has been turfed by the contractors. There are huge cracks between the turves – what should we do?

This is a common problem with newly laid turf, due to lack of water when it is laid in dry weather. It is exacerbated when turves are not butted up closely enough. Additionally, sandy soil should be brushed into the cracks after laying, although many contractors do not bother to do this and in damp conditions they may well get away with it.

It is important to water the lawn really thoroughly before you repair it. When the turves have swollen back to their correct size, then you can brush a top-dressing into all the cracks and gaps. A pukka dressing should be made from sand, loam and peat. The peat helps to make it more acidic, while the sand makes it easier to brush in and helps drainage. When ordering the sand, make sure that it is lime-free and not too gritty (a silver sand would do). The peat could be substituted with a weed-free garden compost. A suitable mix would be one part peat, four parts soil or loam and two parts sand.

How can I minimize the time spent maintaining my lawn? I do not want a bowling-green finish.

The time spent on lawn maintenance will be dramatically affected by its design. Small, narrow verges of grass edging a shrub bed mean bringing out a small machine and lots of edges to cut. If you have to have these, make sure the verges are wide enough for your main mower to cut them. A mowing margin around borders walls and fences (see p. 207) reduces the time spent edging up and keeps the lawn looking much trimmer. It is expensive to put in and if you have a very informal lawn you might think it inappropriate. However, on one job I laid railway sleepers cut in half lengthways, with the top edge remaining 5mm (¼in) below the top of the turf. They look quite discreet and formed a good edge, but would not be much good for curves. Imported hardwood sleepers are available by mail order (see Suppliers Index) and are reasonably priced. Banks with a gradient in excess of 1:3 are awkward and may well be better off planted, using a strimmer.

Getting the most efficient mower for the job makes a big difference; select the widest cut that you can use quickly and comfortably. For a utility lawn, a rotary mower (either ride-on or walk-behind) or a hover would be suitable choices, but whatever you choose they should be capable of collecting the cuttings.

During spring, grass cutting becomes frenetic. High growth rates may well involve cutting the lawn twice a week, and in warm wet periods it is difficult actually to get at the lawn because of incessant showers. Spring is a busy time in the garden generally and the weeds are growing like crazy. If you can reduce the lawn area by making some of it into a flower meadow (see p. 202) or just by letting it grow longer and adding some bulbs (see p. 235), then you can leave the first cut until the beginning of July. At this point it does start to look tatty, but any wildflowers will have set seed. This system will reduce your mowing input dramatically.

Unfortunately, when you do wade in and cut this longer grass, it is quite a task. I use a strimmer or scythe and then remove the cuttings. Then I follow straight on with a rotary mower with the blades set high. A further cut could be done at the end of August just before the autumn bulbs spring into bloom. Then a final cut can be carried out in late October, after the autumn bulbs have finished, but before the daffodils get too far advanced. You could omit the last two cuts, but the sward tends to get tussocky and the choicer spring bulbs get a better chance if the competition is not too vigorous.

Certain areas of the garden may well be suited to this more romantic or unkempt style. Even so, I think they are improved by having a crisp mown boundary around the edges, and mown paths through them to differentiate the spaces.

An ingenious way to cut back on lawn care is to have a large shallow pool instead – it is perfectly flat, green all summer and needs no cutting at all.

We have numerous fairy rings in the lawn. How can I eradicate them?

There are several different types of fairy ring. If the grass is not discoloured at all and you just see the toadstools, then it is not necessary to take any action. If the ring is the type that produces a darker green colour at the outer edge, then eradicating it is difficult and the best method is to keep the grass well fertilized to mask this green band.

The third type of fairy ring is altogether more serious. Its characteristics are two dark-green bands with a balding, mossy or bare-earth ring between them. The size varies; it is caused by the fungus *Marasmius oreades*. The unsightly bare circle is caused by the presence of the mycelium, or vegetative fungal body, which repels water and causes the grass roots to suffer from drought. Eradicating these can only really be done by hard work. Dig out the topsoil to a depth of 30cm (12in) and make the trench extend 30cm (12 in) on either side of the inner and outer edges of the ring. Dispose of all the soil and turf, replace with new topsoil and reseed.

My lawn is plagued by moles. What is the best way to get rid of them?

Some people would be flattered to have moles; they tend to favour good soils where there is a high worm count. Having said that, I would be the first to admit that moles are a pest, leaving unsightly heaps all over the lawn. Sometimes the runs collapse, leaving an uneven surface. In several

European countries it is illegal to kill moles, but in England it is permitted.

Sonic mole repellers are the most popular method today, bearing in mind that mole smokes are now banned. These have a high success rate, but do work better on soils with high conductivity, such as clay loams, than on very peaty soils. They are battery-operated (batteries usually last for four to six months) and will repel moles for a radius of 15m (50ft). They are simple to operate: you just push them into the ground, leaving a section proud, and they pulse every 15 seconds or so. Moles tend to come into the garden from neighbouring pasture, so you can position the repellers accordingly. The Sonic Mole-Chaser has a good track record and is available at garden centres (see Suppliers Index).

Another method, requiring more skill, involves claw mole traps. There is an art to using them successfully, and for some reason they are less successful on lawns with good deep topsoil. You need to dig carefully down the small hole under a new heap and establish that it has a tunnel going in two directions. Some heaps have just one tunnel running to them, and these seem to be used far less frequently. When you set the trap, make sure that your hands are not squeaky clean and smelling of soap, for it's far better if they have a good earthy odour. Then get some longish grass and wrap it loosely around the base of the trap. Carefully put it down the hole, with the trap set so that it is aligned across the mole run. The grass helps to mask the smell of the trap and seems to increase the success rate dramatically. Cover the trap with an upturned bucket to prevent light getting into the hole.

If neither of the above methods appeals, you can call in your local authority, who will gas the moles with a toxic gas called Phostoxin, which is not available to the general public. They will charge a nominal sum for the treatment of moles.

I would like to terrace my steeply sloping garden with a series of formal sloping banks. What is the maximum gradient I could mow with my rotary mower? If I decided to plant them up instead, what would be the maximum slope for planting?

The normal maximum slope recommended for hover and two-stroke rotary mowers is 1:3. Having said that, most manufacturers of four-stroke rotary mowers say that the maximum for these types of engines is 15°, which works out at 1:3.7. The reason is that on steeper slopes the oil goes to one side and does not lubricate the engine properly. The machine still works, but you will not be doing it any good. If you decided to plant, the maximum slope for planting on most soils is 1:1. Few soils would have a natural angle of repose this steep, so it might be necessary to use a soil-stabilizing mat, such as Tensar (see Suppliers Index). This is recommended for slopes up to 1:1. It is a polyethylene woven mat, and you lay it over the slope, burying the top and bottom to anchor it and peg it in position. You cut small slits into the mat to plant through and then brush soil into the mat. As an alternative, grass can be seeded into it.

BULBS

I love tulips in borders, but do not have time to lift and replant them each year. I have free-draining soil, so could I get away with leaving them in? Which ones are best for this, and what plants do they grow well with?

I leave my tulips in and having a free-draining soil, like you, they survive for three to four years before finally giving up the ghost, and then I plant some more. They require a good baking in the summer in order to survive. The flowers produced in subsequent years are much smaller and the stems shorter – not surprising if you think that you plant a 1.2cm (½in) bulb initially, and the next year two or three far smaller bulbs are produced. The degree of success that you achieve has something to do with the planting depth, though this is far less important than having a free-draining soil. Normally you would plant a tulip at 10–12.5cm (4–5in) deep, but for leaving in, try planting at a depth of 17.5–20cm (7–8in). The other reason why tulips are often less vigorous when left in is that slugs have a good opportunity to munch their way through them. More serious, though, is the increased risk that you run of encouraging tulip fire fungus. The tulips will look as though they have been treated to a light session with a flame-gun. Initially this disease can get hold by attacking the plant when hail or storms have damaged it. Then it can develop so that it is present in the soil, and you have to keep your beds free of tulips for four or five years before you can replant them.

As to the type of tulips, the species and hybrids of known species are more successful when grown this way. They are closer to the wild types, which grow like this anyway. *Tulipa fosteriana* 'Purissima', a good sturdy milky white tulip, is one that I regularly grow, as is *Tulipa* 'Queen of Night,' a good, intense dark purple. Other good tulips for this are the Darwin hybrids, such as 'Apeldoorn' and 'Gudoshnik', which are inexpensive as they are easy and cheap to produce – another good indicator that they would thrive for a few years if used in this way.

What bulbs are useful to naturalize in grassy areas, bearing in mind that I want as long a period as possible with bulbs in flower?

There are several criteria that need to be fulfilled when you select bulbs for grassy areas. They need to look appropriate, be able to withstand the competition from the grass – either holding their own or able to bulk up and spread – and they need to stand up to being left in the ground over the winter. In addition the grass needs to be suitably managed. Close-cut lawn will not suit many bulbs – most need longer grass, perhaps in a semi-wild situation.

The common snowdrop will grow in grass; the main problem is that it dislikes being dried off, so it is better to plant it in the green. The flowers arrive in late winter, making you think that perhaps spring is on the way. *Galanthus nivalis* 'Gravetye Giant' is more robust, and grows up to 9cm (3½in) high. The winter aconite *(Eranthis hyemalis)* is a tuber that also dislikes being dried off. It looks wonderful in huge drifts and is worth the extra trouble. Crocuses are a useful bulb. I like *Crocus tommasinianus,* which does particularly well in turf. It likes full sun and blooms in late February to early March, so is a good bulb to choose if you want to resume your mowing early in the year. There are hordes of bulbs (in the loose sense of the word) that perform in spring. The Siberian squill *(Scilla siberica)* flowers in late March, holds its own in turf, but does not increase. The anemones are beauties, especially *Anemone blanda,* which has white, blue, pink or magenta flowers. They like well-drained soil in sun or light shade. *Anemone apennina* also does well in this situation, as does glory of the snow *(Chionodoxa luciliae),* with its starry blue flowers centred with white. Another blue flower is the grape hyacinth *(Muscari armeniacum),* which likes a sunny spot.

A spring bulb that never fails to cause a stir is the snakeshead fritillary *(Fritillaria meleagris),* which has an incredibly beautiful, purple and white chequered cap. There are also plain white varieties. It is inexpensive to buy, but on dry soil will die out after two or three years, so stocks need regular topping up. Ideally it likes a damp meadow. Star of Bethlehem *(Ornithogalum umbellatum)* is extremely easy to please, though. It will be a bit invasive in the border, so is ideally suited to growing in grass. The summer snowflake *(Leucojum aestivum)* really flowers in mid-spring, between March and April. It works well with daffodils and has white flowers that are chocolate-scented.

Daffodils are the most predictable

Snakeshead fritillary *(Fritillaria meleagris)*

choice for naturalizing in turf. My favourites are the smaller, less brash types, such as the Lent lily or wild daffodil *(Narcissus pseudonarcissus)*. It has a small, pale-yellow flower and grows to a height of 35cm (14in). It occurs naturally in damp woodland and grassland. Another good, smaller daffodil is *Narcissus* Tête-à-Tête, which grows to 23cm (9in) and flowers freely in mid-spring. It is more golden than the wild one. Another common choice is the Spanish bluebell *(Hyacinthoides hispanica),* which comes into flower towards the end of spring. It is used in gardens much more than the English bluebell *(H. non-scriptus),* although is a coarser, less graceful plant. But it competes well with grass and comes into flower when many of the other earlier spring bulbs have faded.

The Dutch irises are very happy growing in long grass. The Dutch ones start flowering in late spring and are followed by the English types *(Iris latifolia)* in mid-summer. They come in blue, violet, yellow or white and stand about 45cm (18in) high. As you might expect, they like well-drained soil and full sun.

Tulips can compete with long grass, providing the soil is free-drained and you choose the best ones. *Tulipa sylvestris* is a good choice: the flowers are yellow or cream and it grows 45cm (18in) high. For other tulips that are worth trying but not as effective as *sylvestris* see page 235. However, they will probably need topping up every few years. Another more unusual but excellent plant for long grass is *Gladiolus communis* subsp. *byzantinus.* This has bright magenta flowers and likes a sunny position with good drainage. The flowers arrive in late spring to early summer (May–June) and you must plant the corms in autumn.

Camassia esculenta is an unusual but stunning plant to naturalize. In a border on my free-draining soil it is not too happy and needs replacing after two or three years, but on a moist soil it will easily naturalize in grass, holding its own well.

The autumn crocus *(Colchicum speciosum)* flowers from mid-September until nearly the end of October, and the flowers are followed by the leaves later on in winter. It is easier and cheaper to grow than *Colchicum autumnale,* which is less able to compete with turf, but may well just hold its own.

A lot of my daffodils were blind this year, even though I knotted them after flowering. Why was this?

Some people find that their daffodils give them a good show the first year after planting, that it is not so good the next year and even worse the third year. The most common reason for this is not planting them deeply enough. This has the effect of the bulbs not having enough moisture in the all-important period during flowering and the period after flowering, but before the foliage dies down. The top 7.5cm (3in) of soil dries out far more than the 7.5cm (3in) below this. The large yellow trumpet daffodils, with a bulb size of about 13cm (5in), need planting with a depth of soil of at least 20cm (8in) over their noses, or 25cm (10in) if you are on a dry soil. The smaller types, such as the wild daffodil *(Narcissus pseudonarcissus)*, which has a bulb the size of a marble, needs to be planted with twice its own depth beneath the top of the soil.

The weather can have an effect, too; extreme dryness during the critical period during and after flowering when the bulbs are building up reserves for the following year spoils the show; crowding and lack of feed in established clumps will also greatly affect their performance. Splitting them up or applying a liquid feed every 14 days after flowering until they die down will solve this.

The other reason for blind daffodils (though this is less common) is narcissus bulb fly. The fly is rather like a bluebottle and lays eggs in the little hole in the top of the bulb. The maggots then damage the bulbs. Because growers now routinely carry out hot-water treatment on bulbs, it is unusual to buy infected bulbs. To prevent this occurring you can brush soil over the bulbs as they die down, making them less vulnerable to the fly. As for knotting the foliage after flowering, this is not considered to be conducive to good flowering, as you want the leaves to produce as many nutrients as possible to feed the bulbs, so they need to pick up the sun.

I have a woodland walk that is full of hollies, pulmonaria, hostas and lily of the valley growing in huge drifts. Can you suggest bulbs that would add colour but would blend in a woodland setting? The soil is a good neutral loam.

Several bulbs mentioned above would enjoy woodland conditions, including anemone, muscari, narcissus and scilla. But from that list I would tend to use the anemones and the native daffodil, although that's purely down to personal preference for this situation. Another favourite that springs to mind and invariably arouses people's attention in my garden is *Erythronium* 'Pagoda'. I like it not just because it is vigorous and spreads quickly, but also because of its tall (up to 35cm/14in) sulphur-yellow, starry flowers and its glossy, mottled bronze and green leaves. It seems to do well in sunny, dry places, though all the books recommend moister soil and partial shade. It flowers in April, and the flowers last for several weeks.

If you want to make a strong statement add some crown imperial *(Fritillaria imperialis)*. These fabulous plants look good in generous clumps in light woodland shade and would stand out well in front of your hollies. They comes in various colours, including 'Maxima Lutea', 'Aurora' and 'Rubra', which are yellow, deep orange and red. For a plant that looks so exotic you would expect it to be difficult, but this tall, dramatic plant (it is

90cm/3ft high) is surprisingly easy to grow. It flowers in mid-spring.

At the opposite end of the scale are the small, hardy cyclamen. These charming plants look magnificent in large drifts. There are varieties for winter, spring, summer and autumn, so you can take your pick. *Cyclamen neapolitanum* is highly popular, with marbled leaves and white, pink or red flowers in early autumn. *C. coum* is almost as easy to grow, but the attractive round leaves are usually all green.

Another more discreet but still eye-catching plant is *Corydalis flexuosa*, whose clear-blue tubular blooms grow to 30cm (12in) and fit in superbly in a woodland setting. Its delicate ferny foliage contributes its fair share. These are in fact tubers, and grow best in partial shade.

Last but not least, my all-time favourite is the native bluebell *(Hyacinthoides non-scriptus)*, an almost essential ingredient of woodland. This is certainly not exotic, but it reinforces the woodland character and can be planted in generous clumps.

It is now late November and I wanted to get some tulips and daffodils in this autumn – have I missed the boat?

Tulips can be planted a good while after autumn, with no problems at all. In fact as long as they are stored in a cool place, you can get away with planting them up until Christmas. If you leave it much after this, then a high proportion of them will probably shrivel up, but any decent-looking ones could at a pinch be planted up until about early spring, they will probably perform as well as those planted earlier and will flower only fractionally later.

Daffodils are also tolerant if you plant them late. They will still perform well as long as they are planted before Christmas, though they might flower a little later. Alternatively, they could be left until spring and planted in the green, although you can usually only get the smaller varieties in this way.

I am turfing a new lawn. What is a good way to achieve a naturalized effect with bulbs?

If you can plant your bulbs before you lay the turf you will save yourself some work. As a rule of thumb, most bulbs should be covered with soil to twice their own depth. So a 7cm (2¾in) deep bulb will need a hole 21cm (8¼in) deep, in order that 14cm (5½in) of soil can cover it.

You can also achieve fairly natural-looking drifts by gently scattering the bulbs over the seedbed and then planting them where they land. Plant them with a trowel, making sure you reduce the depth required by the thickness of the turf you are about to lay. Do not forget to leave gaps for mown paths through your bulbs, so that you can admire them at closer quarters.

PROBLEMS

The neighbour's cats invade our garden, digging holes in my new seedbed. What is an effective method of deterrent?

As much as I love cats, they are often a nuisance in the garden. As you mention, they mess up seedbeds, and tomcats will also spray on plants, scorching their foliage. They also damage trees by sharpening their claws on the bark. And weeding is less fun when you come across handfuls of cat droppings. This can be more serious if you are pregnant, as cats can pick up a tiny parasite *(Toxoplasma gondii)* and then excrete their eggs. While these are not harmful to healthy adults and children, if a pregnant woman picks them up for the first time, it is possible that the infection may damage the sight and brain of the foetus and/or cause epilepsy. To prevent this you should wear gloves when gardening and wash your hands afterwards. However, cats are effective at catching young rabbits, so to me they are an asset – but only just.

There are several different methods of repulsion that you can try. The first is a battery-operated device which, when switched on, is capable of picking up movement with an infra-red detector. When a cat comes into its range, it emits ultrasonic, high-pitched frequencies that scare off the culprits. It is not audible to humans. The usually range is about 10m (33ft) over an arc of 70°, and the batteries last for about four to six months, depending on its use. In some instances owners use them around their bird tables, to prevent their own and neighbouring cats invading them. They definitely work in most cases, but one or two cats may seem to detect the noise but remain undeterred. Such devices work better in fairly open gardens, for the ultrasound can be upset by shrubs and fences. One known as 'The Garden Pest Chaser' is available by mail order and from garden centres.

Another method is chemical control. A wide range of products exists, based on a variety of different chemicals, including pepper powder, essential oils and methyl nonyl ketone. These are aimed at deterring the cat without causing it any damage. The problem is that the protection is short term and that all cat faeces have to be removed first.

I have an ugly oil tank – how can you suggest that I screen it?

I think the key to hiding fuel tanks is to get them in the right place initially. Builders tend to put them in the most convenient place, rather than the most unobtrusive site. This may well involve biting the bullet and, when your tank is flickering on the empty mark, deciding to lift it and resite it in a more out-of-the-way place. I had to do this – ours was the main focal point as you came up the drive – and I certainly do not regret doing so now.

I saw an inspirational approach in Ian Hamilton-Finlay's garden. His tank was painted army camouflage-style – most impressive, but so well done that it was a little too eye-catching. If you have a metal tank, as he did, paint colour is a major factor. I tend to go for a dark, sludgy greenish-black, even if it is against a wall. Then I put climbers or shrubs and trees around it, depending on the space available. It is worth erecting a trellis and painting it in the same dark colour, but you should allow air to circulate around the tank (to stop the corrosion), so do not fix it to the tank.

Plastic tanks come in a range of shapes: round, beehive, square and rectangular. The standard colour is green, but a rather too bright green that tends to jump out at you. One or two firms do make blackish-green tanks, but you have to search around a bit for them. It is usually worth putting a trellis screen around these too, otherwise you see an odd-shaped lump covered with climbers, which rather gives the game away.

Good evergreen screening climbers include *Clematis armandii*, which is recommended for warm, sunny positions, although I have seen it thriving in several shady Midlands gardens. The ivies are an obvious choice, but I prefer the non-variegated types for this situation – you do not want to attract undue attention to what you are doing. The Persian ivy *(Hedera colchica)* is strong-growing and has the largest leaves in the genus. They are dark green and leathery, and the self-clinging aspect of ivy is a big asset.

PESTS & DISEASES

Pippa Greenwood

I just cannot help it. I have a fascination with all those things which make most other gardeners run and hide: pests and diseases. It started at a young age – I was probably about five – when I spent my hard earned pocket money on a strip of marigolds only to find that over night they had been demolished by an infestation of looper caterpillars!

I have always loved being outside and from an early age trailed around the garden with my mother. I was soon allowed to have my own small plot which I tended with a great deal of care, enjoying both the colourful and pretty side of gardening as well as the chance to observe a plentiful supply of 'bugs and beasties'.

I was later to turn my love of all things natural into the start of my career as I studied Botany at Durham University and then having graduated studied for my MSc at Reading University. Following various temporary jobs working for the Ministry of Agriculture and for a producer of biological controls, I started work at the RHS Garden, Wisley. I had great fun running the Plant Pathology Department and getting the opportunity to talk to huge numbers of gardeners about their gardening problems. After eleven years I decided it was time to move on and became a full time freelance gardening writer and broadcaster. I have now been part of the BBC *Gardeners' World* team for more than twelve years and been a regular panel member on Radio 4's *Gardeners' Question Time* since the production was taken over by Taylor Made Productions. I write regularly for the *Mirror*, *Gardeners' World Magazine*, *Amateur Gardening* and, like the other authors of this book, I have also written several books.

I garden in Hampshire, surrounded by some of the most stunning English countryside I have ever seen – it is so gorgeous that I sometimes wonder why I am creating a garden – nothing I could create will ever be as lovely as the surrounding fields and woodland. I share the garden with the family, including a cat, some geese and a plentiful supply of wildlife. For the last couple of years I have also been using the developing garden as the main location from which my items on *Gardeners' World* are filmed, but that's another story!

LEAVES

A lot of my plants are covered in a white floury substance, with the leaves often worst affected; but in some cases even the flowers seem to be covered in it. What is it, and what can I do about it?

It sounds as if powdery mildew diseases are responsible. There are a lot of different powdery mildew fungi, each of which usually attacks either a single type of plant or a closely related group of different plants. On the whole you will find that the powdery growth, which does look rather like a floury deposit, is concentrated on the upper surfaces of the leaves, but it may occasionally attack the lower surfaces and also the stems, flower heads and any other above-ground parts of the plant.

Powdery mildew fungi are generally encouraged by certain growing conditions; in particular it seems that plants that are rather dry at the roots are more prone, so it is essential that you keep the soil or compost around the bases of the affected plants adequately moist at all times. Regular watering and the use of a good bulky organic mulch around the root area should help. In addition, powdery mildews tend to thrive when air circulation is poor, so anything you can do to improve air movement around the plant will help – in some cases a bit of judicial pruning may be the answer, or perhaps opening the vents or windows of the greenhouse wider.

Many of the powdery mildews over-winter on fallen leaves, so it makes good sense to rake up and dispose of these leaves on a regular basis. If you

Powdery Mildew on Acer leaves

see any signs of powdery mildew on the stems of plants such as roses or apples, these should be pruned out when you do your routine pruning.

There are plenty of different fungicides on the market that can be used against powdery mildews and these include Nimrod T and Supercarb. Whichever product you apply, do check that it is suitable for the type of plant you want to use it on and make sure that you apply it according to the manufacturer's instructions.

There is some evidence to suggest that sodium bicarbonate solution at about 5g per litre (⅛oz per 1¾ pints) will prevent many mildew attacks. Although not cleared for use as a pesticide, this is cleared for use as a food additive, so presumably it can be used on food crops, if not flowers.

Our rhododendron has strange patches of yellow on the leaves and, when I turn these over, I find that there are pale-brown patches of what I presume to be fungus beneath the leaf. Is this a rust disease?

Your rhododendrons are affected by rhododendron powdery mildew. Unlike most other powdery mildews, the fungal growth you see here is pale brown and almost felty and can often be quite difficult to spot, but each area of fungal growth does correspond very neatly to a yellow patch of discoloration on the upper leaf surface. This is a relatively new disease and often goes unnoticed, so it has rapidly become quite common and widespread. I always suggest that before you buy a rhododendron – whether it is for yourself or as a present – you make sure that you spend a few minutes carefully checking the leaves, because this is definitely not a disease you want to have in your garden. It is particularly difficult to control because, unlike many other plants, most rhododendrons hold their leaves throughout the year, so the fungus is able to continue spreading and infecting new leaves on the plant and can even spread to other rhododendrons in the area for 12 months of the year. If there are not many leaves affected, then I suggest that you pick them off and add them to the compost heap. You could also try spraying the plant with one of the suitable proprietary fungicides, such as Nimrod T or Supercarb. These should be applied precisely according to the manufacturer's instructions.

Like other powdery mildews, this one is likely to be all the more troublesome if the plant is at all dry at the roots, so regular watering and the use of a good bulky organic mulch over the entire root system are musts. If there is anything you can do to improve the air circulation around the plant, this too will help. Perhaps you could prune back any overhanging shrubs or trees, as the rhododendron is unlikely to appreciate you attacking it with a pair of secateurs!

I have seen a strange, slightly fluffy-looking, whitish growth on the undersides of the leaves of lettuce, hebe and onion and occasionally on some of my other plants. It doesn't seem to answer the description of a powdery mildew or a grey mould and looks rather like a cross between the two. Have you any ideas?

The samples are under attack from downy mildew fungi. There are likely to be several different species of the fungus involved. They are all closely related and are all likely to be encouraged by damp conditions. Unlike powdery mildews, downy mildews are generally seen on the lower surface of leaves and are definitely somewhat fluffier, often having a faint purplish tinge to their basically white appearance. You should remove infected leaves promptly and then spray with a suitable fungicide. There is only one product currently on the market that will control this type of fungus and that is Dithane 945. If you make the mistake that many people do and try to treat it with one of the powdery mildew fungicides, this will not work, as the downy mildews belong to a completely different family.

Damp conditions encourage downy mildews, so when you water the plants always try to direct the water to the base of the plant and avoid wetting the foliage. It may also help if you space plants such as onions and lettuce slightly further apart, as this will help to lower the humidity in the air around the leaves. You should also be particularly vigilant about weeds, as weeds growing in between plants will help to reduce air circulation and so increase the risk of downy mildews developing.

As far as your lettuces are concerned, it is worth trying to seek out some resistant varieties by checking through the seed catalogues carefully before you decide which seeds to buy. Resistant varieties should be clearly marked but, for starters, I suggest you consider trying 'Avoncrisp', 'Avondefiance', 'Lakeland' or 'Saladin'.

Some of the leaves on my apple look as if someone has drawn wriggly lines on them with a brown crayon and there are some dry brown circles on the leaves as well. What is this?

Your apples have been attacked by apple leaf-mining moth. The lines may be either a silvery white or brown colour and are caused by the tiny green caterpillars of the moth *Lyonetia clerkella*. These live inside the leaf, and as they eat the leaf tissue, they cause the wriggly lines to develop. Occasionally they eat out a mine (a groove or tunnel), which creates a complete circle and so causes the leaf tissue within the circle to die, leaving the brown circles you have seen. You may also see similar symptoms on edible and ornamental forms of apple (including crab apple) and *Prunus* (including plums, cherries, nectarines and peaches). Despite the fact that the damage caused can look quite dramatic, I have never seen it have any significant effect on the overall health of a tree or its ability to produce a good crop, because the problem usually only occurs towards the end of the growing season. However, if the tree is only recently planted, then a severe attack could possibly cause damage, so you might consider spraying with a suitable insecticide such as Sybol or Malathion.

What is the brown powder developing in patches on the leaves of some of my plants and the orange powder developing on others? Lots of different things are affected, including hollyhocks, roses and leeks. When the leaves are badly damaged they shrivel up and die quite quickly.

All these leaves are under attack from rust diseases. These are caused by a wide range of fungi and what you have seen are the pustules or groups of spores on the leaves of your plants. Rusts can develop at pretty well any time of year, but are particularly common during damp periods and towards the end of summer and early autumn, when conditions are often quite warm and yet also fairly moist. In order to infect the leaves on which they land, the rust spores need a minute film of moisture to be covering the plant's surface. This does not mean to say that the leaf is so damp that you can see the moisture; it could simply be that there is very humid air around it. So anything you can do to reduce humidity and improve air circulation will obviously help to minimize the problem. In addition, when you water the plants you should always try to avoid wetting the leaf surface.

I suggest that you pick off as many of the infected leaves as you possibly can. If you do this on a regular basis, you will help to reduce the spread of the problem. If the leaves have already fallen to the ground you should rake or collect them up, as some rust fungi can over-winter on fallen leaves. In some cases, on rose leaves for instance, you may see several different types of spore developing. In the summer months you will see bright orange spores and then towards the end of summer you are likely to see dark brown spores, which are particularly resistant to more adverse weather conditions and so better able to ensure that the fungus successfully over-winters and can re-infect your plants the following year. Quite often you will also see that each spore mass or pustule corresponds to a spot or area of yellow discoloration on the upper surface of the leaf.

In some cases, it may be possible to buy plants that are resistant to rusts. With leeks, for instance, if you choose cultivars such as 'Titan', 'Poribleu', 'Splendid' or 'Walton Mammoth', these show a good degree of resistance and so are less likely to succumb in the first place; or, if they do succumb, they are less likely to be badly affected. It also makes sense to avoid excessive use of high-nitrogen fertilizers, including manure, as these encourage

Rust on Hypericum

soft growth, which is then much more likely to be infected by the rust fungi. Planting leeks slightly further apart so that the air can circulate more efficiently will also help to minimize the problem.

If you ever see rust fungi developing on your antirrhinums you could look out for resistant varieties of these, such as 'Royal Carpet Mixed', 'Monarch' and the 'Tahiti' series.

With non-edible plants you can spray against rust using various products, including Tumbleblite II, Dithane 945 and Nimrod T. On roses the product Systhane is said to be particularly effective against rose rust.

I have just noticed that my newly purchased chrysanthemum has strange raised, rough creamy-coloured, wart-like growths beneath the leaves. The top part of the leaf looks rather like a

moon crater with yellow spots on it. I am concerned because I have quite a collection of chrysanthemums and I want to know whether this is something that will spread to my other plants.

I am afraid the leaves are being attacked by the fungus *Puccinia horiana*, commonly known as the white rust fungus. Heaven knows why it is called 'white' rust, as you are quite correct in describing the raised pustules as being a cream or buff colour. As the pustules age they darken to a pale tan-brown colour and, at the same time, you are likely to see the leaves become more distorted and perhaps even die. Like other rusts, this one is encouraged by humid, moist atmospheres and is likely to thrive and spread rapidly if the plants are growing quite closely together.

White rust on chrysanthemum leaf

It is essential that you avoid putting the infected plant in with your other currently healthy ones. If you have already done this, then you should remove it as promptly as possible and then keep a very close eye on the remaining plants. Ideally, unless the plant is particularly important to your collection, I would suggest that you destroy it rather than risk the disease

spreading to the others. However, you could consider picking off all the infected leaves as soon as you can and then spraying this plant, and any others that could have become infected, with a suitable fungicide such as Tumbleblite II or Nimrod T. You will need to give at least three applications to have the desired effect.

The fungus is very persistent and it is believed that the spores can remain viable for several hours, even well away from any chrysanthemum plants, so this means that you could potentially spread the disease on, say, the cuff of your jumper, were you to touch infected plants in your garden and then visit a friend who has chrysanthemums in her garden. The fungus is able to over-winter from one year to the next on over-wintering plants and stools, and I would certainly not advise you to consider taking cuttings from any infected plants. This disease really is bad news, I'm afraid; so if you possibly can, grit your teeth and dispose of that new plant.

What is causing the dark-brown rings of powder on the lower surfaces of the leaves of my pelargoniums?

Your pelargonium is being attacked by pelargonium rust, caused by the fungus *Puccinia pelargonii-zonalis*. This typically causes circles of spores to develop and these are often seen in distinct concentric rings. The upper surface of the leaf is then usually marked by corresponding yellow blotches. You will find that the infection spreads really quickly, particularly if conditions around the plant mean that the humidity is high – so you must make sure that you remove this plant promptly and then check any other pelargoniums in your garden or greenhouse. If only a few leaves are affected, then you should be able to pick them all off and, if you combine this with spraying with a suitable fungicide, such as Dithane 945, Tumbleblite II or Nimrod T, you should see a dramatic improvement and hopefully stop the disease in its tracks. It is also worth bearing in mind that if you dramatically improve the air circulation so that the humidity is lowered, you should reduce the risk of the infection recurring.

I have noticed brown and sometimes reddish-brown spots on the leaves of a wide range of plants in my garden. Is it possible that these are caused by some sort of fallout, as we are underneath the flight-path of a sizeable airport and I am concerned that this could be responsible?

This time it is good news. I can confirm that all the leaves are showing signs of fungal leaf-spot infection of one sort or another. Fungal leaf spots are really common and rarely of any great significance as far as the plant's general health and development are concerned, but they can be quite disfiguring, particularly if it is a plant that you grow for its attractive leaves; even if the leaves are not the main emphasis of the plant, if they are badly disfigured they can detract from the attractive flowers.

On the whole, leaf spots are only likely to cause a lot of damage on plants that are stressed in some other way, perhaps because they are growing in slightly unsuitable conditions or are under attack from some other, more significant pest or disease; so one of the best ways of preventing their appearance is to try to do everything you can to improve the growing conditions of the affected plants – be that by watering, feeding or perhaps even considering moving them to a different spot.

I suggest that you pick off any really badly spotted leaves and add them to the compost heap, then hopefully you will see that later flushes of foliage remain healthy. If the problem is very severe or the plant is particularly young, then it may be worth spraying with a suitable fungicide, such as Dithane 945, as this should help to control many of the more common leaf spots. Generally I suggest that you concentrate on improving the cultural or growing conditions and have a general tidy-up of the plant.

Fungal leaf spots (hellebore leaf blotch)

Whatever I do I still find that my roses succumb to black spot. What am I doing wrong and what can you suggest that I do to get on top of the situation?

Black spot *(Diplocarpon rosae)* is undoubtedly the real bane of any rose-lover's life, and although there are varieties that seem to show a degree of resistance, this is rarely reliable and if you want to grow a wide range of plants, or any particular favourites, they will not necessarily show useful degrees of resistance. Those purplish-black patches that develop on the leaves soon cause the foliage to yellow and drop, and if the problem occurs several years in succession, or on a young or recently planted rose, it may be quite damaging.

I suggest that you start by picking off the most badly affected leaves and collecting up any that have already fallen to the ground beneath the plant. This will help to reduce the risk of the disease carrying over or spreading to other parts of that rose, or indeed to other roses that you are growing. In the spring, when you are doing any early spring pruning, you should take a really close look at the stems and if you see any that are bearing very tiny pin-prick-sized, purplish-black spots, this is likely to be the over-wintering stage of black spot, so you should try to prune out these infected stems wherever possible. If you do not do this, as soon as the leaves unfurl in the spring, the spores are likely to be released from the spots on the stems and start to infect the new leaves. You are particularly likely to find these stem spots on any species roses that you are growing.

If you really want to ensure that your roses remain as free from black spot as possible, then you do need to consider a fungicide spray programme. You should ensure that the spray is put on precisely according to the manufacturer's instructions and start as soon as you have carried out that spring pruning, or at least before the leaves start to appear. It may sound crazy to spray against a leaf disease before the plant is carrying any leaves, but by doing this you are likely to go a long way towards preventing the problem developing to any great extent later in the season. You will need to apply several doses of the fungicide at the intervals stated on the pack. There are several treatments you could consider, including Nimrod T, Tumbleblite II, Dithane 945, Supercarb or one of the treatments based on copper.

Despite the fact that a lot of people suggest spraying the soil surface with a fungicide or disinfectant over the winter months, I really don't see that there is a lot of point in doing this, as if you bear in mind the way in which fallen leaves tend to become scrumpled up and packed down quite closely, I think it is highly unlikely that any significant amount of fungicide would ever penetrate through to the fungus. I would say that you are far better off concentrating your efforts on doing some of the things I have suggested.

If you want to choose some new roses at any stage, then I suggest that you send off for several different catalogues from specialist rose growers. You will find that many of these catalogues now mark varieties that are regarded as showing a particularly good degree of resistance to black spot. Do bear in mind, however, that you are unlikely to find many – if any – that show complete resistance; it is more a case of them being notably less susceptible.

I can vouch that black spot on roses is definitely reduced by thick mulches put on after leaf fall.

Both my ornamental crab apple tree and one of the edible apples look as if they are under attack from black-spot disease. I thought this only attacked roses, but this year it seems to have spread to the leaves of these two trees as well. Am I right?

There is one good thing about black spot and that is that it only attacks roses, but the leaves from your two *Malus* trees are showing signs of attack by a different fungus, *Venturia inaequalis*, the cause of the disease known as apple scab. It is also worth looking at any pears you grow in the garden as these may possibly be showing signs of a similar infection known as pear scab. The blackish-brown or khaki-coloured spots develop in the leaves, and later in the year you may notice blackish-brown, fairly scabby-looking patches on the skin of some of the fruits. Affected leaves may fall early, often because the leaf stalk or petiole is infected, and if the fruits are badly scabbed they may become deformed and crack or split, as the fruit tries to expand but is unable to do so because of the tough coating of fungal growth that has developed on the skin.

The fungus itself is able to over-winter or remain from year to year on the fallen infected leaves and on scabby patches that develop on the young stems of the tree. If the weather early on in the year is damp, then apple scab and other closely related diseases, including pyracantha scab and pear scab, are likely to be particularly severe. Similarly, if the trees have a rather congested branch system, you will find that they are also more prone to attack. Both closely packed branches and wet weather mean that humidity is likely to be high around the leaves, or that they are covered in a film of moisture due to high rainfall. As a result the fungus spreads and infects particularly readily.

Obviously there is nothing you can do about weather conditions, but it may be worth considering thinning out the trees somewhat, so that the air circulation around the developing leaves is improved. You should also attempt to rake up regularly and dispose of affected leaves, and when you carry out any winter pruning you should take a really long, hard look at the younger stems and prune out any that are showing the characteristic scabby patches. If you wish you could spray the tree with a suitable fungicide, such as Supercarb, Dithane 945 or Nimrod T; any of these should be applied pre-

Apple
scab

cisely according to the manufacturer's instructions. If at any stage you
decide to try and grow a new variety of apple, it is worthwhile looking
through the catalogues of some of the specialist growers or asking their
advice about resistant varieties, as there are some that seem to be less readily infected, including 'Gavin', 'Lane's Prince Albert', 'Sunset' and
'Discovery'.

**Almost overnight some of the leaves on my peach tree became
thickened, swollen and covered in raised blisters. Many of the
leaves were a red or purplish colour and I have noticed that
some that developed earlier on have now become covered in a
whitish bloom. What on earth is responsible?**

This is a classic case of peach-leaf curl caused by the fungus *Taphrina defor-
mans*. Despite its common name, this fungus also attacks nectarines and
both edible and ornamental forms of almond, so if you grow any of these
trees in your garden as well, I suggest that you check these for signs of
infection too. The leaves often become infected before they appear in the
spring, because one of the places where spores over-winter is on the bud
scales of the leaves. You will find that many of the affected leaves fall
rather earlier than they should and, as a result, the tree may look rather
sorry for itself by early to mid-summer. The leaves that have got the white

bloom on them are covered in a layer of fungal spores, which will then be readily carried to other parts of the tree by rain or water splash, or in air currents. A second flush of foliage invariably develops if damage from peach-leaf curl is severe, so you need not be concerned that the plant is going to remain looking bare for long. Luckily this second flush of leaves usually remains perfectly healthy.

If the tree is small, or if the tree is larger and you are feeling particularly energetic, then you should remove all the infected leaves. You may feel that by doing this you are wrecking the tree, but they will fall naturally anyway and if you remove them promptly you should limit the spread of the disease to a good extent. It is essential that you keep the tree well watered and fed, as this will encourage it to put on new growth and will compensate to some extent for the early leaf drop. If the tree is trained against a wall or other vertical surface, you can go a long way towards controlling the disease by creating a form of temporary protection, which will prevent spores from landing on the stems, buds or leaves. What you need to make is, in essence, an open-sided, bus-shelter-type structure, made from clear polythene. The shelter needs to be placed over the tree from mid-winter until late spring if it is to be effective. You can also spray against peach-leaf curl using a copper-based fungicide such as Traditional Copper or Bordeaux Mixture. You will need to do this at least twice; usually spraying between mid- and late winter proves to be most effective in preventing the developing foliage from being attacked by the fungus. Do make sure that you have finished spraying before the flower buds start to open or else you may damage these. You also need to make a note on your calendar to spray the tree in the autumn, just before the leaves fall, with one of these fungicides.

Some of the leaves on our currant bushes look as if they have been attacked by peach-leaf curl and have got a strange, almost crumpled appearance, with a raised yellowy-green and red colour. Is this possible?

If you look underneath the affected leaves you will see that they are playing host to lots of small pale-yellow aphids. These are currant blister aphids *(Cryptomyzus ribis)*, which feed on the leaves as soon as they appear, right through until mid-summer. In the process they produce a toxin or poison, which causes the leaf to distort and discolour. After mid-summer a winged form of the aphid develops and moves on to feed on sedge woundwort plants *(Stachys sylvatica)*. The aphids then move back to the currants, where they lay their eggs, and it is in the egg form that the aphid over-winters.

Since you can still see evidence of the aphids on the leaves, you could spray them with an insecticide such as Rapid or any other product that is

recommended for use against aphids on edible plants such as currants. My personal choice would be Rapid, since it is based on pirimicarb, an insecticide that is specific to aphids and so causes little – if any – harm to other insects. This means that beneficial creatures such as lacewings and ladybirds should be left unharmed, so they will be able to continue helping you to control pests in your garden. If there are not many affected leaves on the plant or if, another year, you were only to notice the problem once the aphids had moved on, it would not be worth spraying.

I must emphasize that this pest rarely, if ever, damages the yield or the plants, and is absolutely no more than a cosmetic problem.

I have a feeling that I am responsible for the damage on these leaves. Several of the plants near where I was spraying with a weedkiller (to control some of the weeds on the path) have developed these horrible, brown scorched patches. Am I to blame or is it some disease?

I am afraid you are quite right to blame yourself. The symptoms are typical of damage by a contact weedkiller – that is to say, the sort of chemical that scorches the foliage only in the areas on which it lands. The chemicals likely to be involved include paraquat and diquat. It is quite easy for weedkiller to drift and cause fairly extensive leaf-scorching symptoms, such as those you have seen. Also, if you were growing any bulbs in the area and they were still in leaf while you were using the chemical and these too were contaminated, then you are likely to see their foliage become a bleached white or yellow colour the following season and then die back. Although only a heavy dose is likely to kill the leaves completely, you will find that it probably takes several seasons for the bulbs to recover.

Unfortunately at this stage there is nothing you can do to solve the problem, but you should certainly do everything you can to ensure that contamination does not occur in the future. This means that you need to be particularly careful that you only spray during suitable weather; that is to say, not when it is at all windy or gusty. And you should avoid spraying on particularly hot days, as this can cause warm air currents or thermals to move the weedkiller onto garden plants. In the meantime I suggest that you do everything you can to encourage good healthy growth on the plants that have been damaged. By the look of them, I think it is highly unlikely that they will die back, but it would certainly be worth your while trying to give them a bit of a boost by regular feeding throughout the growing season. You should also ensure that they are kept well watered during dry weather.

The leaves of several of my shrubs have got these strange holes taken out from around the edges; they look rather as if something has bitten them. The other evening while out on a late-night slug hunt, I noticed a few greyish-black beetles, each about 1cm (½in) long, on the leaves of the affected shrubs. Are they to blame?

I'm afraid to say there is no doubt that you did indeed catch the culprit in the act of ravaging your shrubs. The beetle you saw was the adult vine weevil *(Otiorhynchus sulcatus),* which is without any doubt the nastiest pest you are likely to come across in your garden. The sad thing is that the damage you have noticed on your shrubs, although fairly minor and unlikely to be of any significance to the shrubs themselves, does suggest that you are likely to have vine-weevil grubs in your garden as well. These can be potentially lethal to a huge range of plants, particularly those growing in containers (see p. 282).

The adult vine weevils have a few characteristics that make them particularly easy to identify: their antennae are 'elbowed', or bent at an angle, making them look rather like a pair of miniature elbows. The beetles themselves are particularly slow-moving and tend to 'play dead' if disturbed; their blackish bodies are often covered with tiny gingery-brown spots or fleck marks and, as you have noticed, you only tend to see them at night, as they spend most of the day hiding away in dark places. It is the adults that take these irregular notches from around the leaf edges and you will notice that on the whole most of the damage occurs around the base of the plant. The reason for this is simple – the beetles cannot fly, but are extremely good climbers and so tend to do most of the damage relatively close to ground level. They are capable of climbing over almost any surfaces, except those that are completely smooth. As a result you may even find them attacking plants in window boxes or laying their eggs in them. The adults are particularly prevalent between spring and autumn.

I suggest that you start a concerted effort to control the vine weevils before the problem gets any worse, and certainly before too many of the adult beetles, which are all female, get the chance to lay any more eggs. It is worth carrying out night-time hunts for these at the same time as you go and look for your local slug population. You can also attempt to trap them: one of the best methods I know is to take a piece of corrugated cardboard, roll it up loosely like a Swiss roll and then tie it up using a rubber band around the middle. If you position traps like this in among plants that are showing signs of damage, the vine-weevil adults may move into the cardboard rolls during the day, believing them to be a safe place in which to hide. You can then collect them up towards the end of the afternoon and dispose of them.

It is also worth trying to prevent the adults reaching pot plants, where

they like to lay their eggs. One of the best ways to do this is to use a ring of non-setting glue or Vaseline around the rims of plants growing in pots, and to mulch the surface with an ornamental gravel made from stone, crushed slate or any other solid and fairly impenetrable material. The mulches will mean that even if the female does make it onto the mulch, she will not be able to lay her eggs, as she cannot reach the surface of the compost.

You could also try using the biological control, which involves drenching the compost or soil around the base of plants with a liquid containing millions of minute nematodes. You cannot buy this over the counter at a garden centre, as the nematodes do not have a shelf life in the way that a chemical does, but you can buy them from one of the many biological-control suppliers, who will send them to you by mail order. The nematodes are only active against the juvenile forms of the vine weevil – that is, the larvae. There are also several different chemicals on the market that you can try using, including Provado. In addition, if you wish to plant up new containers, you could consider using one of the composts containing chemicals, which are said to keep the vine weevils at bay for a full 12 months. These

Adult Vine Wevil with damage

are sold as 'Plant Protection Composts'. Whatever you do, it is essential that you try as many methods as possible and do not give up in your attempts to keep this particularly unpleasant creature out of your garden, or at least keep its numbers at a low level.

BF These seem to be one of the pests that occurs in plagues. They were a big problem in Victorian gardens, then vanished, to recur again recently. Probably not unconnected with the habits of the plant trade, as the adults cannot fly.

What is eating these circular holes around the edges of the leaves on my plants? Several have been attacked, but the problem seems to be particularly bad on my wisteria and my roses.

The neat edges to the circular or elliptical holes is typical of damage by a leaf-cutting bee (*Megachile* sp.) and makes it easy to distinguish this from the holes that other pests, such as caterpillars, slugs or vine weevils, might make in foliage. It is the female bee who is responsible for removing the leaf sections and she does not in fact eat them, but uses them to construct little 'pods' into which she lays her eggs. I always think that these look rather like miniature cigars – they are made up of numerous leaf circles woven together. You may find them in the compost in old flowerpots or occasionally in rotten wood. A leaf-cutting bee will make lots of these structures and, when each one is finished, she fills it with a supply of pollen and nectar and then lays one egg in each, before closing it off with another circle of leaf.

You may have seen the bees around your garden and not recognized them for what they are, as they are very similar to honey bees, but have distinctly gingery-coloured hair beneath their abdomens – not the sort of thing you are going to notice easily!

Although occasionally they can cause quite disfiguring damage, it is rarely that bad and is certainly of no significance as far as the plant's health is concerned, so I would not suggest that you do anything to attempt to control them. In any case, you should bear in mind that they are also useful pollinators.

AS My mother has been looking after a colony of leaf-cutting bees for some years, becuse they make their 'tubes' down the insides of the plant pots in her greenhouse. I'm sure she wishes they would go away sometimes, but she cannot bring herself to get rid of them. They like the dry soil of pots holding cacti, succulents and dormant hippeastrum best.

I am confused, as there seem to be so many things that eat holes in the leaves of plants and I find it difficult to work out what is responsible for this damage, which consists of irregular holes. I can see no signs of slime trails, and the holes do not look like those of the leaf-cutting bee or vine weevil, so does this mean that they are due to caterpillars?

I am sure you are right; the holes are most likely to have been eaten by caterpillars and I also found one or two tiny pellets of frass, the droppings of caterpillars, so I am sure they have been responsible. It can certainly be difficult to work out who has done damage to leaves, but your thought process was perfect – you often have to work it out by a process of elimination. In some other cases when caterpillars are responsible you may also notice silken webbing, which is another common characteristic; and some caterpillars, such as those of *Tortrix* moths, actually produce webbing that sticks the leaves together in groups or folds the edge of the leaf over, so creating a safe home for the caterpillar.

Many caterpillars do much of their feeding during the evening and at night, so it may not always be easy to find the pests themselves, but looking out for the droppings is a useful clue as to who the culprit is. It is usually the younger growth that is worst affected, as it is more tender, and sadly damage to these areas tends to be more injurious to the plant as a whole. Wherever you can, you should collect up the caterpillars by hand, or if they are hiding in bound-up leaves you can try pinching the leaves so that the caterpillar inside is squashed. If the problems are bad, you could also try spraying with a suitable insecticide, such as Polysect, Sybol, Fenitrothion, Sprayday or Picket. Alternatively, if you prefer to avoid using chemicals but feel that you are unable to cope by collecting up or squashing the caterpillars, then you could try using the biological control based on *Baccilus thuringiensis*. This is usually sold under the tradename Dipel or Bactospeine and is available from normal biological-control suppliers.

My garden is plagued by slugs and snails, so can you please advise me what I can do about them? I need to know all the options, as I am getting desperate.

It seems that whatever we do, slugs and snails still continue to plague us. They do most of their feeding after it has rained or after you have watered the garden and are most active at night, rasping holes in the leaves, flowers and stems of almost every plant in the garden. Some slugs spend a very high percentage of their time below soil level and so feed on bulbs, tubers (including potatoes) and roots (including carrots). There is only one good thing about snails and that is that they tend to become much less active or completely dormant over the winter period, but sadly slugs continue to feed whatever the weather. As they move they produce a slime trail, which will help you to identify them as the culprits if you are not already sure who is to blame. When this has dried out, it appears quite silvery and is easy to detect on the above-ground parts of the plant. Slugs and snails can breed throughout the year, but the majority of eggs will be laid in the summer and autumn and you may have seen these whitish, spherical eggs, each about the size of a pinhead or slightly larger. They are often laid in groups on the soil surface or just beneath it.

Because of their ability to breed throughout the year and the fact that they are often underground, slugs are particularly difficult to control. Since it is very difficult – if not impossible – to rid your garden of either slugs or snails, I am afraid that it is more a case of making sure that you, and not they, have the upper hand! You should aim your efforts at particularly vulnerable plants during those times of year when the damage caused is most likely to weaken the plant or to be of significance to the crop. It is always worthwhile trying to keep your garden as tidy as possible, as slugs and snails are encouraged by and like to hide beneath plant debris, old flower pots, and so forth. Any cultivation of the soil will also help to disturb slugs and may bring them to the surface, where they can be eaten by predators. There are a number of natural predators of both slugs and snails, including ground beetles, hedgehogs, moles, frogs, shrews and thrushes, and anything you can do to encourage these creatures will be of great benefit.

There are several different sorts of slug pellet on the market and these can be used effectively, but you should bear in mind that many people (myself included) regard them as an unacceptable environmental risk. Those pellets based on metaldehyde poison both slugs and snails and cause them to produce excessive quantities of their slimy mucus, so that under dry conditions they will die. There are also slug pellets based on the chemical methiocarb, which have the benefit of being effective under damp conditions, whereas those pellets based on metaldehyde tend not to be. But if either sort of pellet becomes wet and starts to turn mouldy, it will not be effective. If you decide to use them you will need to apply them on a regular basis, but you should be aware that they could pose a serious threat to pets, children and wildlife.

I much prefer to use non-chemical methods, such as attempting to trap these pests under half-grapefruit skins or large cabbage leaves – provided you collect them up regularly, this will have a noticeable effect on the slug population. You can also try using traps such as 'slug pubs', which you partially fill with beer. You can make these traps quite well yourself, using plastic beakers buried in the soil with about 1cm (½ in) of their rim protruding, then filling them with beer or indeed milk. If you add a small amount of grain or porridge oats to the beer or milk, the trap becomes all the more attractive.

Other methods of control include using a self-adhesive copper strip around the circumference of the pots of patio plants – the copper contains a minute electrical charge and this deters the slug or snail and prevents it crossing the barrier. You can also create barriers on the soil surface using a wide range of materials, including soot, crushed egg shells, sharp grit, pine needles or the mulch based on cocoa shells. I find that pine needles and cocoa shells work particularly well, but do remember that they have to be replaced at regular intervals as they may be blown around by the wind or scuffed up by birds. A scientific researcher who specializes in slugs once suggested something to me that is definitely only for those with a strong stomach. He advised mowing your lawn at night, as the lawn is likely to be acting as home to huge populations of slugs. Need I say more?

If, like me, you are a keen vegetable gardener, you are also likely to be particularly infuriated by small keeled slugs, which tunnel into your carrots, potatoes and other root crops. I find that by concentrating my potato growing on the earlier-cropping varieties, it means that they are lifted before the slug population becomes too great and, as a result, I get less damage. However, you may not wish to only grow earlies and it is worth considering growing less susceptible varieties, such as 'Kestrel', 'Wilja', 'Stemster', 'Estima', 'Charlotte', 'Pentland Ivory' and 'Pentland Dell'. You should also avoid the particularly susceptible varieties 'Pentland Crown', 'Kondor', 'Golden Wonder', 'Cara' and 'Maris Piper'.

Whether slugs are a problem in the vegetable patch or in your flower garden, I would also strongly advise you to consider the biological control, which consists of millions of microscopic nematodes that are mixed up into a solution and then used as a drench on the soil around slug-susceptible plants. This needs to be applied when the soil is moist and at a temperature above 5°C (40°F). The most effective time for using it is in the spring and autumn when plants are particularly susceptible. The nematodes penetrate the slug's body and release bacteria that kill the slugs. It should have a notable effect on the slug population for a period of at least six weeks and is specially useful on root crops such as potatoes, as it acts so efficiently underground.

BF

Although some people dispute the effectiveness of slug pubs, I have found them extremely efficient, with some provisos. First, one pub is not enough – they need to be no more than 1–2m (1–2yd) apart. Second, they do not work very well with alcohol-free lager, pasteurized or tinned beer. Slugs are attracted to the yeasty smell and the best attractant is real beer mixed with some fruit juice. Third, ground beetles also drown in the pubs and need some sticks to climb out, as these beetles eat slug and snail eggs, so we want them to survive. Ground beetles can also be encouraged by creating areas of long grass not too far away. Sacrificial crops can also give the main crop time to get big enough to withstand attacks. For example, I find that sowing buffalo onions with the others saves the others, as buffalo seems to get eaten first.

What is causing these tiny, near-circular holes on the leaves of my rocket and radish plants? Something similar seems to have attacked aubretia, alyssum, wallflowers and nasturtiums, but all I have found in the area are some tiny black beetles, which jump as soon as I touch the leaves – are these really responsible?

I am sure these tiny beetles are flea beetles, a species of *Phyllotreta*. They measure 2–3mm (about ⅛in) in length and are most commonly very shiny and black, but occasionally have a bright-yellow stripe; or they can be yellowy brown or metallic blue, depending on the species. These beetles eat the tiny rounded holes in the upper surface of the leaf, and you may have noticed that sometimes they don't actually eat right the way through the leaf, but leave a brownish-white spot of dry leaf tissue. On older plants these pests may have little effect or just check the growth slightly, but they can sometimes kill seedlings, if they do a lot of damage. There are lots of different types of flea beetle and the damage is most commonly seen on brassicas, including those you described, but also swedes and turnips. There is another type of flea beetle that will also attack the foliage of potatoes and the Chilean potato vine. Flea beetles will feed between the middle of spring and the end of summer, and in bad years the injury they cause can set plants back quite a bit.

Control is difficult, but you should do everything you can to encourage seedlings to grow strongly, so that they can compensate for any damage that occurs. This includes keeping plants well watered and only sowing seeds at a time when you think germination and early growth will be rapid and vigorous. You could also consider using pesticides such as Derris, Polysect and Sybol. I have heard people suggest that you can trap flea beetles by disturbing the foliage and at the same time holding a batten of wood covered in non-setting glue just above the leaves. The idea is that the beetles jump in the air and get stuck to the adhesive surface. An interesting idea, but I suspect that it is rather too time-consuming and a bit too unreliable for me – but that's up to you!

The new leaves and shoot tips of my fuchsias and dahlias are really distorted and flecked with tiny holes and brown spots. I have looked everywhere but can't see a culprit. Is this a pest or a disease, or something that I am doing wrong?

The damage is typical of that caused by capsid bugs or plant bugs. The common species of both are about 6mm (¼in) in length when fully grown and they feed by sucking the plant's sap. As they do this they produce a toxin that kills off the plant cells in the area penetrated by the insects' mouth parts. This causes the brown spots to develop and the leaves or shoot tips to be slightly distorted. Later in the season, as the leaves try to expand, the dead areas will be unable to expand normally and so the leaf will tear, often becoming quite ragged in appearance. Capsid bugs also commonly cause quite a lot of damage on a wide range of other plants, including chrysanthemums, dahlias, forsythia, *Caryopteris*, roses and hydrangeas. They do most damage between the end of spring and the end of summer, so it is important to check plants regularly and, if you feel it is necessary, to spray with a suitable insecticide such as Fenitrothion or Sybol. If you decide to use either of these, you will need to apply it as soon as you see the first signs of feeding damage.

Damage by Capsid Bug

Some of my plants look as if they have shrunk in the wash – the leaves look quite normal on the surface, but beneath them there is a sort of baggy surface. The leaves seemed perfectly okay until the recent cold weather – could this really be responsible?

The symptoms are typical of cold-weather damage and quite often you will see a lot of distortion as well as this baggy lower surface. Although it looks rather peculiar, I would suggest that you keep all the affected leaves on the plants as they are still green and otherwise healthy, so they are providing a useful function. They are not infectious, so there is no need to remove them, but if you wish, once the plant has put on some more growth later in the spring, you could prune out the worst affected areas. There really is very little you can do to prevent this unless you are prepared to protect all the foliage on a regular basis throughout the winter months – something that I am sure is too time-consuming to be worthwhile.

The leaves of both my new rhododendron and camellia have developed a yellowing between the veins. Is this because my soil is not acid enough?

I am sure you are right: the yellowing between the veins, or interveinal chlorosis as it is otherwise known, is a typical symptom of lime-induced chlorosis and is indeed just the sort of thing you are likely to see if you are growing acid-loving (or lime-hating) plants in a soil or compost that is neutral or alkaline, rather than acidic. The symptoms are typically worst on the younger leaves and are due largely to a lack of manganese and iron. In the long term you should try to ensure that you don't put acid-loving or lime-hating plants in a similar situation in the first place; this means avoiding growing them directly in your garden soil if it is not sufficiently acid. You could either grow them in raised beds filled full of acid soil or in large containers full of ericaceous compost. It is possible to lower the pH of the soil slightly (that is, make it more acid) by applying sulphur to the soil, and you can also try feeding the plants with a fertilizer formulated especially for use on lime-hating plants.

Some of my plants have developed yellowing between the veins and I thought this was something you only saw when you grew acid-loving plants in a limey soil, but I have seen the symptoms on a lot of plants that I know do not dislike growing in my soil, which is neutral to acid. What is wrong?

These are the symptoms of magnesium deficiency and they can indeed look rather similar to those of lime-induced chlorosis, but the yellowing between the veins is generally much more severe on the older, larger leaves. This is because when magnesium is in short supply it is shunted, or moved, from the older leaves to the new growth, with the result that the new leaves are a good green colour and the older ones can be quite severely yellowed between the veins. In some cases when the green pigment disappears, you see a reddish coloration between the veins, and this is particularly common on plants such as tomatoes, but is again due simply to magnesium deficiency.

Magnesium deficiency is especially common if you garden on acid soil or any soil that is particularly free-draining, as magnesium is very easily washed or leached through the soil. It is worth trying to improve the soil's texture before planting, by incorporating plenty of organic matter, as this will make it less likely that the magnesium is leached through too rapidly. In addition, you can try applying extra magnesium to the plants and this should have a fairly rapid re-greening effect.

You will see the most rapid improvement if you apply the magnesium in the form of Epsom salts as a spray to the foliage. The Epsom salts should be used at a rate of 200g in 10 litres (8oz in 2½ gallons of water) and you should add a couple of drops of washing-up liquid to each watering can. This will act as a wetting agent and help to ensure that the solution adheres to the foliage for long enough for the magnesium to penetrate. You will need to spray or water the leaves of the affected plants once every two weeks, and after a few weeks you should see signs of improvement. Alternatively, you could use Epsom salts direct on the soil, at a rate of about 40g per square metre (1½oz per square yard), but this – although effective – will tend to produce a slower reaction.

You should also bear in mind that heavy watering or heavy rainfall will increase the rate at which the magnesium leaches out of the soil and that if you use high-potassium fertilizers, such as tomato foods, these tend to lock up the magnesium in the soil, so they make signs of magnesium deficiency all the more likely.

I have been told that some of my plants are suffering from viruses. What are the symptoms I should associate with virus diseases as opposed to fungal diseases?

The most common symptom of virus infections is yellowing – not as a general leaf yellowing, but in distinct patterns, usually flecking, mosaic patterns, ring spottings or striping. Occasionally on some plants such as orchids, the markings are a brownish-black colour. The leaves are most commonly affected, but occasionally you may see other symptoms, such as colour breaking, or streaks of unexpected colour on the petals – the classic example of this is Rembrandt tulips. Virus-infected plants are also often stunted and distorted and lack vigour, often dying within a short space of time. If you see the symptoms you should bear in mind that there are no control measures available and so it is essential that you remove and bin or burn infected plants as soon as you see them. I wouldn't even suggest composting them because, as long as the leaves are turgid (plump and full of sap), they could be fed upon by aphids, which may then spread the infection to other plants.

Aphids and other sap-feeding pests are the main means by which viruses are spread, but some are also seed-borne, so it is essential that you do not save seed of potentially infected plants. In addition, handling can spread the infection, so if you are examining or removing plants from the garden, you should make sure that you handle those that appear to be healthy before you handle those that you suspect may be infected with viruses. Once you have handled a virus-infected plant you should wash your hands very thoroughly before handling one that you believe to be still healthy. Some viruses have a very narrow host range – that is to say, they infect only one particular type of plant or a very closely related group of plants. Others, such as cucumber mosaic virus, infect not only cucumbers and related plants, but a wide variety of others. Just in case the viruses involved are transmitted by soil-living creatures such as nematodes, you should avoid growing related plants on a site from which you have removed virus-infected ones. Good weed control is also necessary, as some of the viruses may be harboured on common weeds, which can then act as a source of infection.

Because the virus particles are likely to be in every part of the plant it is essential that you avoid propagating from plants that you know are (or suspect to be) infected with viruses; instead you should use completely healthy-looking plants or, if necessary, buy in new stock. With some plants it may be possible to buy virus-resistant cultivars, so when you look through seed catalogues you should check for these. Since plants such as raspberries, strawberries and potatoes are very prone to virus infection, you should always ensure that when you buy new plants, you buy those that are certified as being virus-free. Obviously this is no guarantee that the plants will not succumb to viruses later on, but it is a very useful guarantee that the plants are perfectly healthy when you get them, and this means that you are at least in with a chance!

 **My courgette plants are strangely stunted and yellowed. Most of the plants died before they produced any fruits, but one or two produced strange knobbly fruits, which are particularly dark green and marked with yellow blotches and a pitted surface. What is causing this?**

Cucumber mosaic virus on Courgette leaf

I am afraid there is no doubt that this is due to cucumber mosaic virus, the most common reason for cucumbers, courgettes and marrows failing. You should remove the infected plants as soon as possible, together with any that you suspect may be showing signs of infection. It is essential that you bin or burn them so that there is less risk of the virus being spread to other hosts. Despite its name, cucumber mosaic virus will actually also attack a wide range of completely unrelated plants, including many ornamentals such as the passion flower, and many common weeds. The virus particles are spread by handling and by sap-feeding pests, in particular aphids (see pp. 268, 280). It is possible to obtain varieties of some of the crop plants that are potentially susceptible to cucumber mosaic virus which actually show a good degree of resistance to it: these include the courgettes 'Defender', 'Supremo' and 'Tarmino'; the aubergine 'Bonica'; the marrows 'Badger Cross' and 'Tiger Cross'; and the cucumbers 'Bush Champion', 'Petita', 'Crispy Salad' and 'Pioneer'. It may be worth your while considering growing these in future, as they are much less likely to succumb to this problem.

Some of my daffodils look basically healthy, but have got strange yellow streaks on the leaves. Is this a problem?

The most common reason for the foliage of daffodils showing yellow streaking is, I'm afraid to say, virus infection. There are numerous different viruses that can attack daffodils, either alone or in combination. Quite often the plant's vigour does not seem to be badly affected and sometimes it is only the leaves that show the symptoms, although occasionally you may get streaking on the petals or on the flower stems. I have also noticed that in some cases the symptoms only seem to appear in years when the plants have been stressed for some reason, perhaps by a particularly dry summer the previous year. However, even if the symptoms do not appear, it does not mean to say that the virus has gone, so you should still take all the precautions you can to avoid it spreading.

Ideally you should remove all the plants showing symptoms; but in practice this may mean that you have few, if any, daffodils left in your garden. I would, therefore, be inclined to suggest that rather than taking this extreme measure, you perhaps just remove those plants that are showing the most extreme symptoms, as these could be due to narcissus yellow-stripe virus, which is particularly damaging. The various viruses involved are spread by a wide range of means, including soil-living eelworms, aphids and handling, so it is difficult to tell you what other control measures you could take. It does make sense, however, to ensure that you do not transmit the viruses yourself by handling, so you should always wash your hands thoroughly after touching or digging up plants that you believe to be infected.

Shortly after treating the weeds in my lawn I noticed that some of my garden plants have developed strange distorted leaves. The leaves have become quite narrow and the leaf veins are very prominent, while the stalks are twisted. In some cases the leaves seem rather thickened and have become cupped. Is this due to weedkiller contamination?

I'm afraid there is no doubt that the symptoms you have seen are due to contamination by a broad-leaf weedkiller, typical of the sort you may have used to control many common lawn weeds. On fruiting plants such as tomatoes you may find that even quite mildly affected plants do not fruit, or produce strange plum-shaped fruits, which are hollow and do not have any seeds. If the contamination has reached any brassica plants in your vegetable plot, then these may develop rough, gall-like growths on the stem just above soil level. On the whole, infected plants will live unless they have been very severely contaminated, so you may wish to keep the plants (particularly longer-living ornamentals) and just do everything you can to

encourage healthy new growth. You can then prune out the distorted areas. With cropping plants such as tomatoes, if they are showing quite heavy symptoms, then I regret to say that I think you ought to remove them and start again, if necessary buying in some ready-grown plants from a garden centre or nursery so that you can catch up on lost time.

Contamination is particularly likely to have occurred if you have allowed the spray to drift, perhaps because you applied it on a slightly windy or gusty day, or because you applied it using a watering can or spraying equipment that you did not wash out sufficiently well before using on some of the affected plants. It is essential that in future you take great care when applying any weedkillers. You should, to a large extent, be able to avoid the problems by not spraying on a windy, gusty or hot day; if you wish, you could take extra precautions by protecting any plants near the lawn using polythene sheeting, polythene bags or cardboard boxes. I would suggest applying weedkiller using a watering can with a dribble bar attached, rather than by using a sprayer, as the dribble bar will produce larger droplets, which are then much less likely to drift. You should also keep any equipment that you use for weedkillers purely for this purpose and not use it to apply fertilizers or water.

Several plants in my greenhouse have started to shrivel up and I have now noticed some fine webbing on some of the plants. I can't see any pests, so what might be causing this?

If you look really closely on the under-surface of the damaged leaves you will see some tiny little creatures – these are red spider mites, *Tetranychus urticae*. Unless you have extremely sharp eyesight you will need to use a magnifying glass or hand lens to spot these sap-feeding mites. Despite their common name, for most of the year they are a yellowy green colour and only turn reddish-orange in the autumn and winter.

Red spider mites are particularly common on plants growing in greenhouses or conservatories or on anything that you grow as a house plant, because they thrive in hot, dry conditions. Occasionally, in hot summers, you will find them infesting outdoor plants as well. If you look closely at the upper surface of infested leaves, you will see that it is marked by numerous very tiny pinprick-sizes flecks, which mark the points where the mites have been feeding. The webbing you have seen is likely to develop only on plants that are heavily infested. The mites spin the webbing to create 'ropes' down which they escape to find new plants, once they have exhausted the food supplies on the original plant.

Control is difficult because these pests breed extremely rapidly and are often not spotted or correctly recognized, because they are so small. In addition, many strains of red spider mite have now developed resistance to the commonly used insecticides and so, however frequently and extensively

Red spider mite on *Cestrum newellii*

you spray, you may not manage to control them. I would therefore recommend that you consider using the biological control, which means that you introduce a predatory mite called *Phytoseiulus persimilis*. This rather rotund and orangish-red-coloured mite rushes around the leaves, once you have released it, and preys upon not only the adult red spider mite, but also the young stages and even the eggs. To work effectively temperatures do need to be quite warm during the day and you also need to ensure that there are no pesticide residues left in the greenhouse or conservatory, which could damage the mite that you are introducing.

I would suggest that you remove any severely infested plants, as they are not likely to recover and it would be difficult to control all the mites hiding on them. In addition, regular spraying of the foliage with plain water will help to keep numbers down, as red spider mites do hate getting wet feet! If you wish, you could also consider spraying infested plants with a suitable insecticide, such as Polysect, Sybol, Malathion or one of the insecticides based on a soap-like substance. You will find that you need to apply the chemical at regular intervals if you are to achieve useful control.

Red spider mites are reduced in number on plants that are regularly treated with seaweed extract. They can also be lured onto broad bean plants in pots put among, touching and slightly above the infected plants. Once the mites have moved across to the beans, they can then be disposed of.

What is causing the white and yellow flecks on the leaves of my primroses and some of my roses and other plants?

The symptoms suggest that the plants are under attack from leafhoppers: the roses from a specific type of aphid, the rose leafhopper *(Edwardsiana rosae)*, while the damage on other plants is most likely to have been caused by the glasshouse leafhopper *(Hauptidia maroccana)*. Despite its name, the

Damage caused by rose leafhopper

glasshouse leafhopper regularly attacks plants outside during the summer months. In both cases the pests are a pale yellowy green colour and about 3mm (⅛in) long. As their name implies, they hop and will readily jump from the plant as soon as you disturb the foliage.

If you look carefully at the leaves before touching them you may well spot them, but you are more likely to find the cast skins of the leafhoppers adhering to the lower surface of the leaf. These are shed as the insects increase in size and are the most conclusive evidence that this pest is responsible. Leafhoppers feed by sucking the plant's sap and, as they do so, they remove small quantities of the green pigment, leaving bleached spots behind. If infestations are severe, the leaves may be turned almost completely white by the end of the summer. There are no organic control measures, but if you wish you can spray affected plants with a suitable insecticide, such as Polysect, Py, Nature's Answer to Insect Pests, Bug Gun, Flydown or Sprayday or any other proprietary product that is described as being suitable for use against leafhoppers.

Every year, whatever I do, my greenhouse is full of whitefly. Can you suggest anything I can do to try and keep them at bay?

These tiny white-winged insects are definitely one of the worst greenhouse pests, and if you let the problem get out of hand you will find that the adults fly up in such great numbers that they create a real cloud. You will also notice some of the younger stages of the whitefly, which are pale green, oval scale-like growths attached to the lower surface of the leaves. As the adults and the young feed by sucking sap, they can – as I am sure you will have noticed – quite severely weaken plants, and sometimes the adults may even spread viruses in the process. So you are quite right in assuming that they need to be controlled – and sooner rather than later. As they feed you will find that an added problem is that their excreta is extremely sticky (hence the common name honeydew), and once this has landed on the foliage of plants, or indeed on any surface beneath the plants, it will attract black moulds known as sooty moulds, making the plants look particularly unattractive or unappetising. In the summer months the problem can be even worse, because the whitefly may move out onto garden plants and continue to feed out there. Luckily they will not survive most British winters unless they are given the protection of a greenhouse, but if you have plants in your greenhouse over the winter, then you may even find whitefly being active for 12 months of the year.

Control is, as you have discovered, really difficult, partly because there are now many pesticide-resistant strains of the whitefly about, and this means that however frequently and carefully you spray the plants, the whitefly will not be killed. You can try using the biological control, which involves introducing a tiny parasitic wasp, *Encarsia formosa*. This needs to

Whitefly on Gerbera leaf

be introduced as soon as the infestation is first noticed, usually in mid-spring. Several applications of the parasitic wasp may be necessary, but you should consult your mail-order supplier for details. Some gardeners like to hang sticky yellow card traps above whitefly-susceptible plants, as these will then catch some whitefly and give you an idea of the extent of the problem, so that you can ensure that you do not wait too long before introducing the parasites. If you are going to use the biological control, you also need to be careful that there are no residues from other pesticides present in the greenhouse. You therefore have to be very cautious about which pesticides you use, if you decide to try and reduce the numbers of whitefly chemically before introducing the parasite. Your best bet is to use a product based on an insecticidal soap, as this will not persist in the greenhouse.

Once you have controlled the whitefly, if you find that ornamental plants are seriously spoilt by the presence of the sooty mould growth, you can then use a sponge to gently clean the leaves.

 Glasshouse whitefly is definitely kept out by smelly French marigolds, but not by the less scented sorts.

I have got whitefly on my brassica plants. Is it possible to use the biological control, as I would prefer to avoid using chemicals?

Pretty well all brassicas may be attacked by a pest known as the cabbage whitefly and, although this may look similar to the glasshouse whitefly, it is actually a different pest and is not controlled by the parasitic wasp *Encarsia formosa*. As a pest, cabbage whitefly can be particularly trouble-some because, as you will have noticed, it can be active throughout the year, even in England's rather variable climate. Like the glasshouse white-fly, it has an immature stage that resembles a pale yellowish-green, scale-like growth on the lower surface of the leaves. Again you may find that infested plants become covered in an unappetising growth of sooty mould.

Unless the infestation is really heavy, I would suggest that you try and put up with the damage, particularly since you say that you want to avoid using chemicals. However, you could consider spraying with an insecticidal soap, which are generally acceptable to organic gardeners. Should you decide to use a different sort of chemical, however, you will find other products on the market, such as Polysect and Sprayday, that should help to control this pest.

 Brassica whitefly can be kept off if the plants are grown from the start under fine netting or fleece.

Some of my outdoor tomatoes and potatoes have these blackish patches on the leaves and now blacky-brown patches are also developing on the stems. It this potato blight?

I'm afraid so, and if you look closely at some of the necrotic or discoloured patches on the leaves or stems, you will find that during dampish periods of weather they may develop a faint, fluffy white fungal growth, which is typical of an attack of *Phytophthora infestans*, the cause of potato and tomato blight. If you happen to own a greenhouse, then it might be worth growing as many greenhouse varieties as you can next year, as these are highly unlikely to succumb to the infection.

This disease is encouraged by moist or humid air conditions, combined with warm temperatures, so it generally appears from mid-summer onwards, and it has the potential to devastate your crops completely. Now that you have seen signs of the disease, you should remove and bin or burn affected tomato plants as soon as possible. With the potatoes, I suggest that you cut off and bin or burn the haulms and then lift the tubers as soon as you can. If you remove the potato haulms promptly you should prevent the spores being washed down into the soil and infecting the tubers. If the tubers have been infected, they are unfortunately likely to rot off in store. You may also see signs of the infection on the fruits (see Fruits section).

It is possible to preventatively spray against tomato and potato blight, using a copper fungicide, such as Bordeaux Mixture or Traditional Copper; this should be applied as soon as weather conditions become suitable for the blight fungus. In the case of potatoes, this is generally about the time when the foliage meets between the rows.

Once you have had potato or tomato blight, it is essential to rotate the crops, ensuring that potatoes do not follow tomatoes, or vice versa, and that preferably you have at least a three-year gap. This is simply because one stage of the fungus can be washed into the soil from the affected above-ground parts of the plant and cause subsequent crops to be attacked the following year. With potatoes you will find that deep earthing up also helps to protect the tubers, should the infection occur, and it is worthwhile attempting to grow those cultivars that show some resistance to the disease, including 'Estima', 'Cara', 'Kondor', 'Maris Peer', 'Pentland Crown', 'Romano' and 'Record'. Unfortunately there are no resistant varieties of tomato available.

BF
Organic growers try to avoid blight by growing earlies and second earlies, which crop before blight usually arrives. Unfortunately, a new variant is coming from the Continent that strikes earlier and may affect even these. So far only the variety 'Santé' is thought to be immune.

Some of the leaves on my camellia are covered in a layer of black soot. Is this caused by pollution from the nearby motorway or is it something even more sinister?

Irritating as the nearby motorway may be, I am pleased to say that it is not responsible for the growth on the surface of the leaves of your camellia. The leaves are in fact covered with a dense layer of a fungus known as sooty mould. This is a completely harmless fungus, which is feeding on the sticky excreta known as honeydew that is being produced by the scale insects infesting the under-surface of other leaves of the plant. They suck the plant's sap and because it has such a high sugar content they are unable

Sooty mould on *Skimmia japonica*

to absorb all the sugars; as a result, their excreta has a very high sugar content and when they flick it out over the leaves, it forms a sticky layer. This then attracts the growth of sooty mould fungi.

If you examine the leaves carefully you will see tiny, pale yellowish-brown, slightly raised, waxy shell-like objects. At certain times of the year you may also see whitish powdery or slightly fluffy areas around these, which are the egg masses. There are many different species of scale insect and you may find them on other plants in your garden as well. They vary in size from about 1mm to 6mm (up to ¼in) in length, but all of them have the habit of excreting sticky honeydew. Although most scale insects are

Scale
insect

found underneath the leaves, occasionally certain types may be found clustered on the stems. Spraying them is difficult because the insect is so well
protected beneath the waxy scale. However, it may be worth trying to spray
with an insecticide such as Malathion. Since the camellia is growing outdoors, you would be best off trying to spray in mid-summer, as it is at this
time of year that it is most likely there will be a high proportion of newly
hatched, young stages of scale insect present, and this is the stage that is
most susceptible to insecticide.

Scale insects rarely manage to become a problem if the ants do not help
them. Deal with the ants first (see pp. 305-6)!

What is the best way to control greenfly and blackfly?

There seems to be a greenfly, blackfly or aphid of some sort just ready and waiting to attack pretty well every plant in the garden. With milder weather and in sheltered areas they seem to start feeding earlier and earlier in the year, sometimes causing distortion and yellowing in the process and occasionally spreading virus diseases. As an added insult, their excreta is extremely sticky and is often responsible for causing an unpleasant sticky layer on infested plants or plants growing beneath them or, in the case of aphids living on trees such as lime trees, for covering your car and drive in a sticky blanket, which is then often colonized by black sooty moulds. With all this in mind it is obvious that aphids are going to be the sort of pests that quite often do need controlling.

Occasionally it may be possible to use a strong blast of water to remove them from the stems of particularly tough plants, but quite often you may end up using a chemical to remove them. There are numerous products on the market, but my preference is to use one based on pirimicarb (Rapid), as this is aphid-specific and so poses little, if any, threat to beneficial insects such as ladybirds and lacewings, but is very effective at controlling the aphids. You could also use one of the organic insecticides, such as Derris, or an insecticidal soap, but you should bear in mind that these are less targeted or specific in their action and so can actually cause significant damage to beneficial insects and 'innocent insect bystanders'.

On some plants the aphids over-winter as eggs (for example, on fruit trees and bushes) and one method of control that you could consider is to use a tar or winter wash, which is applied while the fruit plants are dormant. These are generally quite effective, but there is now a lot of concern about their use as, in addition to controlling the aphids, they also kill off many other creatures, including natural predators and parasites of other fruit-tree pests, so you may see a surge in these different pests once you have used a tar or winter wash.

In some instances when you are looking closely at aphid infestations you may see strange buffish-coloured objects, which look rather like very plump or inflated aphids, clustered in among the living aphids. If you see these you should be careful not to destroy them as they are aphids that have been parasitized by a naturally occurring parasitic wasp *(Aphidius)* and they could, therefore, contain a new developing parasitic wasp that will help to control more aphids.

Aphids can be very effectively controlled in much of the garden if sufficient natural predators are available. Support the adult predators by giving them nectar and pollen with large numbers of flowering plants, and give them plants that get their favourite aphids, to build up their numbers – vetches and sweet cherries, for example.

It looks as if something from outer space has landed on my azalea. A few days ago it looked perfectly normal on my sitting-room windowsill, but all of a sudden these strange pale-green, shiny lumps and growths appeared on the shoot tips. What is this?

Your azalea is infected with the fungus called *Exobasidium vaccinii*, which is responsible for the disease known as azalea gall. You will find that in a short time these waxy-looking growths become covered in a white powder as a layer of spores develops on the surface. Later in the year they will wither and turn brown, but meanwhile, if you don't remove them, the spores will readily be spread to any other azaleas you might be growing. You may find that this disease is also present on outdoor azaleas. Although it looks awful, this is a classic example of a disease that worries the owner of a plant a lot more than it worries the plant itself, and I have never seen it affect an azalea's vigour or flowering in any way. However, if you want to stop the problem spreading, you should pick off the galls as soon as you see them, preferably before they turn white.

Azalea gall

ROOTS AND SOIL

I have found lots of these fat, creamy white grubs in the compost of my hanging basket and then I also noticed some in the compost around the roots of a shrub I am growing on the patio. The grubs are about 1cm (½ in) in length and are curled into a C-shape. None of the plants looks particularly healthy and, in fact, I had actually decided to dispose of the shrub. Are these grubs responsible?

Vine Weevil grub

Creamy white grubs with tan-brown heads are the larval stage of the vine weevil. Unfortunately, I am sure they will have been responsible for the poor state of health of your plants, and sadly I suspect that they may well be responsible for causing damage to a lot more. They feed on the roots and in a short space of time a fairly heavy infestation, as often occurs, can cause the plants to be so severely injured that they look very unattractive, or may kill them completely. Any plant growing in a container is particularly susceptible to attack by vine weevils and you may also find that this pest is in the compost of some of your house plants. The larvae may also be found attacking the roots of plants growing in open ground, but generally speaking they do less harm in this situation.

I would suggest that you remove any plants that you discover have the vine weevil and ensure that you put the compost in the dustbin; you should

certainly not risk using it as a mulch or incorporating it into your compost heap. You should definitely not feel tempted to reuse the compost in future years. Any existing plants should be treated, either with a biological control, which consists of pathogenic nematodes that kill off the grubs when watered onto the compost, or by drenching the compost with a suitable proprietary insecticide, such as Provado. This insecticide should keep the compost free of vine weevils for up to six months. In addition, if you are considering planting up new containers, you could consider using the range of 'Plant Protection Composts', which also contain a chemical and in this case are said to keep the plants potted into them free from vine-weevil attack for up to 12 months. You should keep a look-out for the adult vine weevils, which you are most likely to find feeding at night (see p. 258).

Various birds, in particular starlings, are attacking our lawn really ferociously, causing brown patches to develop. Why are they doing this, and what can I do about it?

The most likely reason for this is an infestation of leatherjackets, the larvae of crane fly or daddy long legs. These are an attractive food source to such birds and they are probably ripping up your lawn in search of the larvae. The larvae themselves are a grey-brown colour and up to 4.5cm (1¾in) in length. Although they will feed on the bases of various plants, they are particularly common in lawns, where they cause yellowy brown patches to develop in mid-summer.

There are several different species of daddy long legs likely to be found in gardens, but they all lay their eggs in the soil towards the end of summer and the resulting leatherjackets feed on the roots of the grasses; but generally by the time you notice the damage it is too late, as the plants are quite

Damage caused by birds digging for leatherjackets in a lawn

far gone and sadly at this stage insecticides are likely to prove ineffective. However, if you catch the problem early enough, you could try treating the area with Sybol. Alternatively, if you prefer not to use pesticides, you can catch large numbers of leatherjackets if you wait until it has rained heavily, or you water the lawn thoroughly; then towards the end of the day, when the turf is really moist, cover parts of it with black polythene. In the morning, if you lift the polythene, you will find that large numbers of the grubs have come up onto the surface of the lawn and you can then collect them up and dispose of them.

I was really distressed to find that most of the compost around the bases of the new shrubs that I have just bought is full of these eggs. Are they going to hatch into something harmful? Are they vine-weevil eggs?

These tan-brown and pale bluish-green spheres, each only a few millimetres in diameter, are – I am pleased to say – not the eggs of any harmful pest; indeed, they are not eggs at all. They are, in fact, the remains of controlled-release fertilizer granules. What you have here are the resin shells from which the fertilizer has leached. They are often mistakenly thought to be eggs and indeed, if you squeeze them, you usually find that juice squirts out, making it seem all the more likely that they are eggs! Their presence in the compost is in fact a good sign that the plants have been well looked after in the nursery and supplied with adequate food to keep them going until they arrive in your garden.

At the end of last year we were given lots of shrubs for our garden as moving-in presents. We were unable to plant them initially and now find that some of them have leafed up but do not look particularly healthy, whereas others appear to be completely dead. A neighbour has suggested that this is due to the severe winter we have just had. Could this really be true – they are all normal hardy shrubs?

Despite the fact that shrubs are hardy, you have to remember that if they are not planted, but instead stand in their pots in your garden during extremely cold weather or a very harsh winter, it is likely that they will suffer a lot of damage, in particular to the root systems. If you think about it, under normal circumstances these would be buried beneath the garden soil, which would insulate them against the worst of the weather. In a pot they are, however, exposed to the elements and it is quite possible for the

root balls of plants – even those in quite large pots – to be partially or even completely frozen. Sometimes this will obviously kill a plant outright, but occasionally it will just about manage to survive and have sufficient where-withal to produce reasonably good new foliage in the spring. However, sometimes the effort of doing this or the energy needed to maintain the new growth is too much for the plant in its weakened state and it then gets sick or sicker or even dies.

At this stage there is nothing much you can do, except encourage some new growth on those parts that still seem to be reasonably healthy. Feeding with a foliar feed applied to any healthy green leaves will be of benefit, as this should help to stimulate new root growth. In future, should you be unable to plant any container-grown trees, shrubs, climbers or indeed herbaceous plants over the winter, you should try to plunge the pots into the soil until you are ready to plant them. If this is not feasible you should group all the plants very closely together in a particularly sheltered part of the garden and then try to insulate the root balls in some way, perhaps using bubblewrap, polythene or old curtains – this will help to reduce any damage.

I have been told that there is a lot of honey fungus in the gardens of neighbouring houses. We have just moved here and I am at a loss because I do not know how to recognize this disease, but gather that it is particularly damaging.

Honey fungus is indeed the ultimate gardener's nightmare. It is unfortu-nately rather common and there are several different species and strains of the fungus *Armillaria* that may be involved, and these vary greatly in their pathogenicity or aggressiveness. This means that in some cases the fungus may be able to kill even very healthily growing plants and in others it is only likely to attack a plant that has been weakened or may only be capable of living on dead tree stumps, and so on. In the most extreme cases, honey fungus is able to attack the vast majority of woody trees, shrubs and climbers and even some of the woodier herbaceous perennials. It is not always easy to spot, as the infection starts off underground and although honey-coloured toadstools may be produced, these are only seen in the autumn and they are not always present.

If you want to see if dying plants have succumbed, you should carefully expose several of the larger roots (these need to be at least the thickness of a pencil) and remove areas of bark on them. Alternatively, you could expose the soil at the base of the trunk. If you peel back the bark in these areas and honey fungus is attacking the plant, you will see a creamy white fungal sheet, sandwiched between the woody part of the root or the trunk and the inner surface of the bark. This is the fungal mycelium of honey fungus. You

may sometimes also find the rhizomorphs or bootlaces: special toughened fungal strands, which are a greyish-black colour, sometimes branching and a millimetre or two in diameter. These are produced from infected plants or stumps and grow through the soil at a rate of about 1m (1yd) a year. Rhizomorphs are usually found growing through the soil, but may occasionally be found beneath the bark; if they are in the soil they are generally within the top 20cm (8in). Although rhizomorphs are often responsible for spreading honey fungus, infection may also occur when an infected root grows into contact with another root beneath the soil. They latch onto the

Honey
fungus
with
mycelium

roots or stem bases of susceptible plants, penetrate them and then the fungal mycelium develops. If you find white fungal strands in the soil around the plants, these do not indicate honey fungus.

When honey fungus has attacked a plant, death may appear to be quite rapid or occasionally a plant may take several years to die. It is ironic that quite often, just before it dies, a tree or shrub will produce a particularly fabulous display of flowers, or a heavy crop of fruit, in its last-ditch effort to reproduce itself before dying. When conifers are attacked, resin droplets are sometimes produced around the base of the trunk. If you do find plants infected with this in your garden, you should remove them as promptly as possible, ensuring that you dig out the entire root system or at least as much of it as you can possibly manage. Whatever you do, do not feel tempted to fell a tree and leave the stump in the ground, as this simply leaves the problem behind and the disease is likely to spread to many other plants in your garden.

Although most woody plants are susceptible, in particular many of the common hedging conifers, privet, currants, forsythia, hydrangeas, lilac, birches, cedars, wisteria, apples, rhododendrons, roses, *Prunus* trees and willows are vulnerable; there are also some woody plants that show a good degree of resistance, including yew, beech, box, cercis, catalpa, chaenomeles, clematis, cotinus, elaeagnus, pieris, kerria, photinia, pitosporum, rhus, sarcococca and tamarisk. Wherever possible you should avoid growing plants that you know to be particularly susceptible and instead concentrate on those that I have described as being fairly resistant, or those which you notice in your garden and which do not seem to succumb. Once you know you have honey fungus, it can be really depressing and you may feel as if your garden has no future; but please don't give up, and bear in mind that this disease is extremely common and, although it can do a lot of damage and can be depressing, there really is no need for you to concrete your garden over!

Can you tell me how to control or prevent carrot fly without using chemicals? The roots of my carrots, parsnips, parsley and occasionally celery have been attacked by slim, creamy yellow maggots, each nearly 1cm (½in) long, which tunnel into the flesh and sometimes leave orangey-brown marks on the outside of the roots. I trust this is carrot fly?

It certainly sounds as if the larvae of the carrot fly *(Psila rosae)* have been responsible, as they carry out damage exactly as you described and attack all the plants you mentioned. An added problem is that, once the roots have been tunnelled, they are very open to secondary infections, in particular both bacterial and fungal rots, which can mean that they will not store over the winter months. If you sow your carrot seed after late spring, you should find that you can miss the first generation of the carrot-fly larvae. Similarly, any carrots that are ready for harvesting before late summer should miss the second generation. If you want to grow carrots at a time to suit you, rather than simply to avoid the carrot root-fly problem, then I suggest that you try growing your crops under a covering of horticultural fleece. Provided this is well anchored, the female fly should not be able to gain access to the carrot or other crops to lay her eggs, so you should have no problems.

You could also construct a wooden framed 'cage' to which you attach a very fine mesh: provided this is at least 45cm (18in) tall and firmly anchored to the ground, then the carrot fly, which is a low-flying insect, will not be able to get to the seedling carrots. I find using those fleece-covered miniature tunnels very useful; although you do have to check them regularly to ensure that the fleece is still in position, they are very easy to use and, unlike the 'cage' I suggested, do not require any carpentry skills.

You could also try growing the varieties of carrot that have been shown to give a good degree of resistance, such as 'Flyaway' and 'Sytan'. I have tried these and certainly they did not succumb to carrot fly, although I do not know whether they would have done anyway. I must admit I wasn't particularly impressed with their flavour, but flavour really is a personal matter.

I have had terrible problems growing onions on my newly acquired allotment. When I grew some in our garden they grew perfectly well, but the crop on the allotment had a dense, somewhat fluffy, white fungal growth around the base of many of the bulbs. What is this?

I am afraid it sounds as if your onions have succumbed to onion white rot disease, caused by the fungus *Sclerotium cepivorum*. This is particularly common on areas where onions have been grown repeatedly, so unfortunately somewhere like an allotment – although a wonderful asset – does tend to harbour diseases like this. You may also notice some small black fungal resting bodies, known as sclerotia, which are likely to develop around the fluffy growth. These are shed into the soil and can remain viable for more than seven years, even if you do not grow onions there.

I regret there is no chemical control available and all you can do is remove and burn infected onions as soon as you find them, then avoid growing any onions or related plants on that area of the allotment for at least eight years.

I suspect that I may have got club root in my vegetable plot, as some of the roots on my brassicas are deformed. How can I be sure, and what can I do about it?

Club root is fairly easy to recognize. The first thing you normally notice is that the plants fail to thrive, often wilting as soon as the weather gets the slightest bit hot and failing to recover even when given adequate water. Cabbages fail to heart up and you are unlikely to get a decent-sized head on a cauliflower, but the real telltale symptoms are below ground, as the roots become very swollen and distorted. Members of the Cruciferae are attacked, particularly brassicas, but also certain ornamentals, such as stocks, candytuft and wallflowers. The disease will also attack some closely related weeds, including charlock, wild radish and shepherd's purse.

Club root is caused by a slime mould *(Plasmodiophora brassicae),* a soil-borne organism, which is particularly common if vegetables have been grown on the same site for many years and is therefore especially prevalent in the vegetable plots of old established gardens and on allotments. Unfortunately, the organism can remain active in the soil for more than 20 years, even if there are no host plants in that ground. It is essential that you try and do everything you can to avoid club root ever getting into your garden and this means ensuring that if you buy plants, you only ever do so from a very reputable source and that if you are in any doubt, you bin or burn affected plants. You should also be careful, because the club root organism can be introduced on tiny particles of soil, such as those that might cling to your boots, wheelbarrow or even the back of a spade.

The club-root organism is encouraged by heavily acid soils, so it is essential to do everything you can to provide the conditions it does not like. This means liming the soil and ensuring that drainage is improved. If you find any infected plants you should remove them as soon as possible. If you do not do so, the infected roots will disintegrate and release even more club-root organisms into the soil. Do not risk composting them, as the club root may well survive the composting process. There are chemicals available that are recommended for use as a root dip against club root, but generally speaking you are best off trying to get around this problem by cultural methods.

I suggest that you grow your own plants and raise them in individual pots with a minimum 5cm (2in) diameter, and preferably more. This means that when you plant susceptible plants out, they will have a head start and so will have a well-established root system, which has been raised in a healthy environment; although they may later succumb to club root, they will remain half a step ahead. As I have mentioned, you should also try and improve drainage and lime the soil. There are a few club-root-resistant varieties of potentially susceptible vegetables, such as the Chinese cabbage 'Harmony', the kale 'Tall Green Curled', the swede 'Marian' and the calabrese 'Trixy', and it is certainly worth looking through the seed catalogues

on a regular basis in attempt to track down any new resistant varieties that may be introduced.

What has happened to my daffodils? On the whole they have performed really well, but now I find that a number of them have simply failed to produce foliage and appear to have disappeared completely, and that many others have only a small amount of very pathetic-looking leaves.

The bulbs are showing signs of narcissus basal rot, caused by the fungus *Fusarium oxysporus* f. sp. *narcissi*. The fungus enters the basal plate of the narcissus bulbs (this is the slightly flattened area at the bottom end of the bulb from which the roots grow) and starts to rot it. If you cut the infected bulbs lengthwise you will see a brown discoloration spreading from the basal plate up into the main body of the bulbs, turning them a dark chocolaty brown in the process. Occasionally you may also see a pale pink, slightly fluffy fungal growth appearing on the basal plate and this is the fungus itself. The fungus is soil-borne and will remain in the soil on infected bulbs for a number of years, unless they are sufficiently badly damaged to be killed. It is interesting that this disease invariably becomes more troublesome in years that are preceded by a really hot, dry summer.

Unfortunately, there are no control measures available, but many people find that dipping the bulbs in a solution of a fungicide containing carbendazim for a minimum of half an hour, almost as soon as they have been lifted, does help to prevent the problem. In addition, if you plant any new bulbs, you should try to ensure that you plant them as early as possible in the autumn – that is, as soon as they are available – as this seems to reduce the risk of infection.

This year although many plants in my greenhouse, including some tomatoes, melons and cucumbers, have all died, the base of the stems has in each case discoloured and shrunken inwards. What is causing this and could it be coming from the border soil in which they are growing?

I am afraid that your plants are all showing signs of an infection known as foot and root rot, because it kills off the roots and the stem base or foot of the plant. Almost any soft-stemmed plant, including seedlings and cuttings, and many ornamental plants can be affected, as well as those you described. The fungi most commonly responsible are the same as those that cause damping-off disease of seedlings and are indeed likely to have built up in the border soil, if you have not changed it as frequently as you should and if

you have been growing a similar range of crops in there for a number of years.

There is no cure available and it sounds as if all your plants are quite badly affected. I'm afraid that all you can do is remove them and dispose of them. If you do this promptly you may be really lucky and find that any remaining, potentially susceptible plants manage to escape infection. I suggest that you change all the soil in the border before you try to grow any more plants in there. When watering, you should also avoid using anything other than mains water. Water in water butts has often become contaminated by just this sort of organism, which is likely to cause either this or damping-off disease, so it is best kept for established plants growing in open ground outside.

Many of my potatoes have rotted off in store and I have been told that this is due to potato-blight infection. How can I ensure that this does not happen again?

The first thing you should do is ensure that you always avoid trying to store any tubers that could have been infected by blight. Blight-infected tubers have somewhat sunken, dark patches on the skin with a reddish-brown discoloration of the flesh beneath. It is usually secondary organisms that cause the rotting and revolting smell, which are likely to occur while the potatoes are in store. It is essential that next year you do not grow potatoes or tomatoes on the same piece of ground, as it is highly likely that the soil will now be full of the motile stage of the fungus responsible,

Potato blight

Phytophthora infestans. Ideally you should practise a two-to-three-year crop rotation, which should ensure that the disease will not carry on from year to year. Infection of the tubers is likely to have taken place if the infected foliage was left on the plant, as this will have allowed spores to be washed down into the soil as soon as it rained or you irrigated the crop.

Next year, if you grow potatoes again you could consider spraying with a copper-based fungicide, such as Traditional Copper or Bordeaux Mixture, or an unrelated fungicide called Dithane 945. Ideally the chemical should be applied as soon as any weather conditions that are likely to encourage blight develop (see p. 277).

BUDS AND FLOWERS

I was really disappointed with my rhododendron; it was covered in flowers when I bought it last spring, and this year it developed buds, but these remained on the plant and turned dry. A well-established camellia showed a similar problem, but in this case the buds developed and all fell to the ground instead of opening. What is responsible?

The buds of both camellias and rhododendrons are initiated in the summer and if there is a period of dry weather, even if it is only one or two consecutive days, the buds may appear to form normally but in fact be faulty. When it comes to spring, they either remain on the plant and turn dry and brown or they simply drop, sometimes forming a carpet of buds beneath a plant that really looked as if it had such a lot of potential. It is essential that you remember this and always ensure that the plants have adequate moisture throughout the summer and early autumn. This is not the time of year when you are likely to be thinking about camellias or rhododendrons, so it is perhaps worth making a note on your calendar to water them well! A good bulky organic mulch, 5–7.5cm (2–3in) in depth, around the root area of the plants will also help to ensure that they are kept moist.

If you are growing either of these plants in a container, they are all the more likely to suffer from this problem and you should, therefore, consider trying to pot them into larger containers or insulating the sides of the pot slightly to prevent them from drying out so much in the summer. Mulching the surface of the compost around plants in containers will also help to reduce water loss by evaporation.

With camellias in particular, if the plants are either overfed or fed too late in the season, bud drop may be encouraged, so I suggest that you avoid feeding your plants any later than early June. Hopefully, if you follow this advice you should find that, even if the plants have been a bit disappointing recently, they do pick up.

In recent years more and more buds on my rhododendrons have failed to open and, instead of being a good green colour, have turned brown and dry. When I look closely I find that they are covered in tiny black bristles. What is this?

The rhododendron buds have been affected by rhododendron bud blast *(Pycnostysanus azaleae)*, a fungal problem that is spread by an insect known as a rhododendron hopper. The black bristle-like growths that you have seen are actually the spore-bearing parts of the fungus and when the leafhopper moves from plant to plant, feeding on the rhododendron sap, it brushes up against these bristles and its body may then carry the spores onto other rhododendrons or other rhododendron buds on the same plant. Although this will certainly affect the flowering and is worth controlling, I am sure you will be pleased to know that at least the general growth and vigour of the plant won't be affected.

Although some people try to control this disease by spraying against the leafhoppers, which arrive in mid- to late summer, I really see little point in this, because even if you were to successfully kill off all the leafhoppers that were on the plant (and that is highly unlikely), the chances are that the leafhoppers would simply fly in from adjacent gardens and recolonize the plant. It is a far better idea to try to pick off as many of the affected buds as you possibly can, but obviously you need to do this before the rhododendron leafhoppers arrive. It can be an incredibly boring and time-consuming job and I can only suggest that you consider employing some small child who would like some extra pocket money!

Budblast disease on Rhododendron

I am completely perplexed by my daffodils and various different narcissi. They have got a plentiful supply of healthy-looking green leaves, but very few flowers. Some produce flower stems and empty flower heads. What is responsible?

The bulbs are suffering from a conditions known as blindness. This usually occurs when the bulbs are not able to produce sufficient energy to fuel the proper development of the buds, so although they can produce healthy leaves, flowering is poor or completely absent. It is particularly common on daffodils that have been naturalized or kept in the same piece of ground for many years with little, if any, attention. The bulbs become overcrowded or receive insufficient food, and then blindness invariably results.

If you are naturalizing the bulbs, I suggest that you consider lifting them and replanting them, ensuring that they are better spaced and planted at the correct depth. If you feed the plants with a fertilizer around the roots and regularly foliar-feed them throughout the growing period, then you should find that they flower as normal within a year or two. Another thing that sometimes causes blindness is extremely dry conditions around the roots of the plants during the summer. Under these conditions, even if there is plenty of food material available and the bulbs are adequately spaced, they may not be able to take up the food because the soil is so dry. You will find that multi-headed or double varieties of narcissus are more prone than the simple, single ones, simply because they have more petals to produce.

These tiny black beetles are driving me mad; they are clustered all over many of the flowers in my garden and I find it quite impossible to pick a bunch of sweetpeas without bringing a horde of them into the house. What are they, and what can I do about them?

These are pollen beetles, a species of *Meligethes*. The majority are black, like those you have found, but some are a bronzish-green colour and all of them measure between one and two millimetres in length. You are first likely to see them on flowers in spring and then they are likely to reappear in the middle of summer. Yellow flowers are particularly likely to be heavily colonized, but pollen beetles are also very common on many other plants, including roses, runner beans, Shasta daisies and indeed sweetpeas.

Despite the definite nuisance factor, they actually pose no serious threat to the plants, although very occasionally they may damage unopened rose buds as they eat their way into them; on the whole they really are much more of an irritation to you than they are to the plant. As their name suggests, the adult beetles eat pollen, but they do not have sufficiently large appetites for this to disrupt the process of pollination. Indeed, some people

say that they actually help pollination, as they may assist it as they travel between flowers. In mid-summer you are likely to see a sudden surge in numbers and this occurs because pollen beetles often spend quite a lot of their time on oil-seed rape plants and, when these are sprayed off or harvested, they move into the surrounding areas looking for alternative flowers.

Insecticides cannot safely be used because they are likely to kill butterflies, bees and other harmless insects that visit the flowers; in any case it would be almost impossible to spray sufficiently frequently to prevent the beetles recolonizing. The only thing I can suggest is that, if you are picking flowers for indoor arrangements, you pick a bunch, shake them once or twice quite sharply but not sufficiently to damage the flowers, then put them in a jam jar of water in a dark shed or garage, which has a single light source such as a window or perhaps even an anglepoise light. Within a few hours you will find that all – or at least the vast majority – of the beetles move from the flowers to the light source and you can then safely take the flowers inside without any unwanted visitors.

FRUITS

It's really quite disgusting! I find that many of my loganberries, blackberries, raspberries and tayberries are infested with these horrible little maggots. I have also noticed that some of the fruits have dried-up patches at the stalk end of the berries. What are these maggots, and is there anything I can do to prevent them?

These are the larvae of the raspberry beetle *(Byturus tomentosus)*. This is an insignificant, small brownish-grey beetle and the female lays her eggs on the flowers during early and mid-summer. When fully grown the resultant larvae are anything up to 8mm (⅓in) in length and a creamy white colour with pale-brown markings on their backs. The grubs start by feeding at the base of the berries, but then begin to feed on the inner core.

If you want to try and control this pest, it is essential that you get your timing right, as the only stage of the lifecycle you are likely to succeed in controlling are the newly hatched grubs. If you were to succeed in controlling anything later on, they would already have done a lot of damage. On your raspberries, this means that you will need to spray when the first pink fruits are seen, and on loganberries and other hybrid berries you need to spray when about 80 per cent of the petals have fallen. On blackberries, you need to spray as soon as the first flowers open. You could use either Derris or Fenitrothion, but do make sure that if you resort to this you spray at dusk, as this minimizes the potential risk to pollinating insects such as bees.

Larvae of raspberry beetle feeding on raspberries

I have noticed that, when ripe, some of the apples from our tree have yellowy brown, slightly raised bumps that are often somewhat scabby on the skin. In addition, some of the young leaves at the shoot tips are distorted earlier in the year and riddled with tiny holes. I can see no sign of any pest. What has done this?

This is typical damage of the apple capsid *(Plesiocoris rugicollis)*, a bright-green insect measuring anything up to 7mm (⅓in) in length. This feeds on the plant sap and, as it inserts its mouthparts, it injects a poisonous substance into the apples leaves or immature fruit. Most of the feeding is done during the early summer. The poison kills off the plant cells, so as the leaves attempt to increase in size, the dead areas rip and cause the holes. When the capsid feeds on the apple fruitlets, the toxic saliva produces these raised bumps or scabby patches.

On the whole, the damage is not too serious and I would simply suggest that you eat the apples, having first cut off the damaged areas, as these do not tend to penetrate any deeper than the skin. If you find that the problem is getting worse from year to year, then you could spray at petal-fall with a suitable insecticide, such as Sybol or Fenitrothion.

Some of the fruits on my tomato developed these gingery brown areas of discoloration when the fruits were still unripe. I also noticed that some of the leaves appear scorched. What is causing this?

This is typical of tomato blight. The fungus responsible, *Phytophthora infestans*, is certainly likely to have damaged the foliage, but may also affect the fruits of outdoor tomatoes. Quite often the fruits also appear to shrink inwards and may rot, either when they are still on the plant or a few days after you have picked them. The fungus responsible is encouraged by warm, moist weather and is especially troublesome towards the end of summer. The spores are carried on water droplets or on air currents, so they are readily spread around any vegetable plot or allotment and may travel quite some distance.

Once the disease has developed there is nothing you can do to cure the affected areas, but you can attempt to prevent the problem by spraying as soon as the first tomatoes have started to set, and then at the intervals stated on the product you choose to use. You could either use Dithane 945 or a copper-based fungicide, such as Traditional Copper or Bordeaux Mixture.

Now that the disease has already occurred in your garden, you should clear up all the infected plants and bin or burn them. They should not be added to the compost heap, as this is a particularly unpleasant disease and may persist in the soil. Next year you should ensure that you grow any potato or tomato crops on a different site, just in case any of the spores are already in the soil (see p. 291).

Some of my apples have got maggots in them. What is causing this? I am surprised that the problem has occurred, because I regularly use grease bands on my fruit trees.

The creatures you have seen are actually the caterpillars of the codling moth *(Cydia pomonella)*, and many gardeners mistakenly presume that putting grease around the trunks of their fruit trees, or using grease bands, will prevent the problem, whereas in fact these devices only have any useful effect on the winter moth and are of absolutely no relevance when it comes to trying to prevent attacks by the codling moth.

Most of the damage normally occurs in mid- or late summer when the caterpillars tunnel into either apples or pears. The caterpillars are an off-white colour, with brown heads. Unfortunately, by the time you have noticed the damage, the caterpillars have generally finished feeding and are likely to have left the apples and moved to safe places to over-winter. You may often find them under loose flakes of bark on the trunk.

When it comes to control you can try using insecticides such as Polysect,

Fenitrothion or Sybol, and these can be sprayed onto the tree in early summer and then again about three weeks later. If you use pheromone traps which release natural chemicals to attract the males, these can help you work out when the adult codling moths are actively flying and so likely to be laying their eggs. This in turn will allow you to work out more precisely when the young caterpillars will be around, and it is this stage that you should aim to spray. If you only have a single apple tree, you may also find that the pheromone traps are useful in catching a sufficient number of male moths to drastically reduce the number of successful matings that occur and this will obviously reduce the number of caterpillars present.

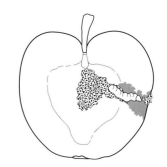

Many gardeners who do not want to use sprays, or who find that their trees are simply too large to spray, have a good degree of success by scraping off any loose flakes of bark and then wrapping the trunk of the tree in hessian. When the caterpillars then attempt to find an over-wintering site, they are fooled into thinking that the hessian would make a perfect place to spend the winter and hide away in it. You can then remove and burn it, together with the caterpillars.

Some of the fruits on my apple and pear trees have got slightly roughened greyish patches on the skin. What are these, and does it need controlling?

This is apple-scab infection, caused by the fungus *Venturia inaequalis*; on the pears it is pear scab, caused by a closely related fungus, *Venturia pirina*. These fungi are both encouraged by damp weather early in the year and cause similar symptoms on the fruits. The leaves may also be affected (see p. 254). When the damage on the skin is only slight, it is of little significance as the scabbed area rarely penetrates beneath the skin and you can simply peel off what you do not fancy eating, and the rest remains perfectly tasty. However, if the apple scab develops early in the season when the fruits are still quite small, or if it is a severe infection, then the problem can be much worse because the fungus prevents the fruit expanding normally; as a result, as it develops it becomes distorted and, worse still, may crack. As I am sure you know, once the fruit has split, it is prone to attack by the brown rot fungus, which in a matter of days will reduce it to a squidgy brown mass covered in creamy white fungal pustules – definitely not something I would suggest that anyone tries to eat!

When it comes to control, you should rake up and dispose of any affected leaves as soon as you can and on a regular basis. It is also worth pruning

out any shoots showing signs of cracking or scabbiness, as this will reduce the amount of the fungus that successfully over-winters. You can then spray with a suitable fungicide, such as Supercarb, Dithane 945 or Nimrod T, which should help to control the fungi involved. If you don't want to spray, or you feel that the trees are too big, then you may well find that with a combination of pruning to improve air circulation, pruning out infected shoots and really good garden hygiene, the problem is not recurrent, particularly if future springs are somewhat drier.

BF

Unless you are desperate to get every fruit the trees can produce, the easiest method of control is to thin the fruits heavily in several stages, removing the worst affected. This, combined with good winter hygiene, pruning out dead wood and removing affected fruits, can give very good control.

What are these strange black, leathery patches on my tomato fruits? Is it blight?

Your tomatoes are showing typical symptoms of blossom-end rot, so called because the tissues at the blossom end of the developing fruits turn black and frequently become quite tough and shrink inwards. I am pleased to say that this is not due to blight, but is due to a disorder resulting from a deficiency of calcium within the fruits. Similar problems will also potentially develop on peppers. Quite often you find that not all the fruits in a truss are affected and that some trusses bear completely normal-looking fruits.

The problem is likely to arise when the conditions around the roots of the plant are rather dry. This means that tomatoes or peppers growing in any containers – be they large pots or growing bags – are far more susceptible to blossom-end rot than those growing in a greenhouse border or in open ground in the garden. If there is an inadequate supply of moisture, however much calcium is present in the soil or the compost, the plants may not be able to take it up. Calcium is an important constituent of the cell walls and, when it is in short supply, the cells at the base of the developing fruits collapse and turn brown, causing the symptoms you have noticed.

The best way to prevent this problem is to ensure that at all times your plants are kept adequately moist at the base. This is obviously going to mean a lot of watering, particularly when they are growing rapidly, cropping heavily or when the weather is dry. It is also worth trying to grow plants in as large a container as possible and perhaps restricting yourself to two plants per growing bag, rather than three. I suggest that you pick off any similarly affected fruits – not because they are infectious, but because this will reduce the strain on the plant – and then concentrate your efforts on trying to keep the plants well watered.

I cannot overemphasize how much this problem occurs because of poor watering regimes, caused by too many tomato plants being stuffed into too-small containers with insufficient root run. The simple cure is to grow the plants in the ground.

STEMS

My forsythia has stems that look as if they are covered in stem-coloured sea urchins or little rough cauliflower heads. What is causing this?

The growths on your forsythia stems are called forsythia gall and quite often only show up on a few individual stems on the plant. The individual galls usually measure 1–1.5cm (½–⅝in) in diameter and typically have this rough surface. Occasionally you may find that several galls become fused together to create a really large mass. Although they certainly look rather peculiar, and some people find that they spoil the appearance of the stems, they do not seem to do any significant harm to the plant itself. There are no control measures available – largely because no one has ever conclusively decided precisely what causes this problem; in any case, it really is not a problem worth controlling. All I suggest that you do is to take the secateurs to the forsythia and prune out the worst-affected stems.

It looks as if grey mould has attacked the stems of some of my plants. I didn't realize it could attack stems. Can it, and is it responsible for the rotting-off of the bases of my lettuce plants?

Grey mould *(Botrytis cinerea)* can indeed attack pretty well any sufficiently soft part of a plant, including leaves, stems, flowers and buds. It is certainly likely that it has caused damage to the stems of your lettuce, as these are very prone. When infected, you usually see a gingery brown, slimy rot developing and this is capable of killing off the entire plant because it attacks on the main stem or at the base of it. Grey mould generally enters stems through points where they have been wounded, perhaps by slug attack or a frost crack, and it can even cause dieback on some fairly woody stems, such as roses. In damp conditions you may notice the typical fuzzy grey fungal growth appearing on the dead and damaged parts of the plant. This is not apparent unless the weather conditions are right.

Grey mould spores are present pretty well all over the garden and because the fungus can live in such a wide variety of places, and on such a wide range of plants, it is pretty well impossible to escape it. However, it is worth doing everything you can to have a thorough clean-up and to ensure

Grey mould on lettuce

that the 'easy prey', such as dead and dying bits of plants, fallen leaves and so forth, are cleared up on a regular basis. If you do see signs of grey mould on stems you may be able to save the remainder of the plant by promptly cutting or pruning out the infected area. If you do this, you will need to cut to a point well below the last point of damage. It should be perfectly safe to compost anything you have removed, provided it is from soft growth and will compost down quickly and readily. On remaining plants you should do everything you can to improve the air circulation, as this will tend to decrease the chances of grey mould becoming a problem.

Disaster has struck many of my seedlings this year. They are simply flopping and keeling over and dying before they reach a decent height. Germination on some of the trays is also patchy. Is this due to faulty compost?

This looks like a classic case of damping-off disease and if you catch any seedlings in the early stages of the problem, you will find that the stem bases are often discoloured or may appear water-soaked. There are several different water-borne and soil-borne fungi that are responsible for damping-off, including various species of *Phytophthora, Rhizoctonia* and *Pythium*. If the compost has been allowed to get too wet, or temperatures have been too high, damping-off is more likely to develop. In addition, if you have sown the seed rather too densely, or have left the seedlings in conditions where light levels are not as high as they should be, you are more likely to find them dying off.

It is essential that if you want to avoid this problem in future, you observe really strict hygiene, using only new sterilized compost and pots or trays that have been thoroughly scrubbed out before use. I always remind people that it is also important to use only mains water on seedlings, as water collected from a water butt may often have accumulated the damping-off fungi as it passes over the roof and down the guttering into the butt. If this has happened, you may find that if you use water from your butt, you are watering your precious seedlings with what amounts to a 'disease soup'. You should also take care to check that the seeds are sown as thinly as possible and are not kept at temperatures that are too high, and that the compost is no more moist than it needs to be. Drenching the compost with a copper-based fungicide, such as Traditional Copper, Bordeaux Mixture or Cheshunt Compound, as you sow the seeds, then again periodically as the seedlings develop and at each stage as they are pricked out, should help to prevent the disease developing in the first place.

Can you tell me a bit about winter moth and why it is that putting grease bands around a tree helps to prevent it?

It is the caterpillars of the winter moth *(Operophtera brumata)* that are the real problem. These yellowy green caterpillars eat the foliage of many fruit trees and, indeed, other deciduous shrubs and trees. They do most of the damage between bud burst and early spring. You may have noticed them on plants, as they are about 2.5cm (1in) in length and move along with a looping action. They often bind the leaves together with silken threads, and these may be the first thing that you notice. On fruit trees the caterpillars will also eat the fruit blossom and may make holes in the apple fruitlets, which means that they become strangely misshapen.

The reason why the grease banding helps is simply because when the moths emerge from the pupae that developed in the soil, the females are wingless and so have to climb up the tree trunk if they are to lay their eggs on the branches. Any sticky barrier will stop them doing this, and as a result will hugely decrease the chance of damage occurring. If you do use grease bands, they need to be in position by mid-autumn and you need to

make sure that they are kept clear of any debris that could act as bridges and allow the females to cross. If you would prefer to use chemicals, then you can attempt to spray the newly hatched caterpillars with a suitable insecticide, such as Polysect, Sybol or Fenitrothion, and you will need to do this as soon as the leaves start to appear in the spring.

What are these strange clumps of cotton wool-like stuff that I have found on some of my house plants, in particular on my cacti?

These are mealy bugs and they are indeed particularly fond of cacti and succulents, but you will potentially find that they attack not only house plants, but also many plants growing in the protected environment of a greenhouse or conservatory. If you look really closely, you will see the mealy bugs themselves – they look rather like miniature woodlice, being

Mealy bugs being tended by an ant

only about 4mm (⅛ in) in length and having a pale greyish-white body. They cover themselves in white waxy fibres, which is what makes them look rather like cotton wool. Generally they are tucked away in the leaf axils or other hard-to-reach spaces and this, combined with their waxy, fluffy coating, makes them very difficult to control. You may also find that the plants become rather sticky, because of the extremely high sugar content of the mealy bug's excreta. This is known as honeydew and gets flicked out onto surrounding parts of the plant. It soon attracts black moulds, which may make the plant look as if parts of it have been dusted with soot. To make matters worse, this honeydew also attracts ants which feed off the sweet excreta.

Mealy bugs feed by sucking sap and can weaken plants quite considerably. I have certainly known them suck cacti completely dry. They can be controlled by using an insecticide based on Malathion or an insecticidal soap; but if you use insecticides do take great care to ensure that you check the label recommendations and ensure that the plants you are spraying are not likely to be damaged by insecticides. Alternatively, you could try using the biological control, which is an Australian ladybird predator called *Cryptolaemus montrouzieri*. Both the adult and the young stage of the beetle are voracious predators of mealy bugs, but I would point out this is probably the most 'badly behaved' of all the biological controls, as the adult beetle does have a tendency to fly out of greenhouse vents or windows if given half a chance!

My apple tree, my cotoneaster and my pyracantha all look as if someone has stuck small clumps of white cotton wool on their branches. What is this, and is it harmful?

This is woolly aphid *(Eriosoma lanigerum)*, a sap-feeding insect that is usually found clustered together in groups and surrounded by a fluffy white mass of waxy threads. The woolly aphids secrete these threads, which become particularly prominent between mid- and late spring, especially on splits in the bark or on areas where the trees or shrubs have been pruned. Later in the summer you may find that the woolly aphids move onto younger branches, where they feed on the relatively soft stems and then cause these to develop lumpy swellings. These galls are quite likely to split during frosty weather in the winter.

As soon as you see signs of woolly aphid infestation, you can spray it with a suitable insecticide, such as Rapid (the one I would recommend because it is aphid-specific and so is much less likely to cause damage to beneficial or harmless insects), Sybol or any other product recommended for use against aphids on the types of plants you have. It is essential to try and get control as soon as possible, because once the infestations become heavy this is a difficult pest to combat.

BF

Growing masses of trailing nasturtiums under the trees for several years does indeed drive them away, despite being an old wives' tale.

Wooly Aphid

PESTS MORE OBVIOUS THAN THE DAMAGE

Please tell me what I can do about the ants in my garden: they seem to be becoming more and more of a problem each year. I find the heaps of fine soil on the lawn and in the flowerbeds and they drive us mad when they invade the terrace, where we try to eat lunch or the children try to play.

Although it is certainly possible to reduce the number of ants in your garden, I'm afraid to say that it is highly unlikely that you will ever succeed in eradicating them completely. I suggest that you concentrate your efforts on trying to kill off the ants in those nests that are causing real problems.

The best thing you can do is to treat the nests with any one of the many proprietary ant powders or dusts, or with one of the sprays. There are many different ones available and it is important that you try to disturb the nest before treating the inhabitants. To do this you may wish to protect yourself by wearing a pair of wellingtons and ensure that you disturb the nest using a garden fork, rather than by hand.

If the ants start to invade your house, then you can use one of the many ant-bait products or try spraying the pathways that the ants use with one of the aerosol lacquers containing an insecticide. If you do not wish to use chemicals at all, then many people find that disturbing the nests and pouring boiling water into them works quite well.

BF Ants can be a serious problem because of farming other pests, such as aphids and scale insects. Where you see ants, give them some white sugar, then watch where it goes. Once you know where the nest is, weaken it by putting clay pots on top of the ground over it. They will bring their eggs and cocoons up in the warmth of an afternoon. Remove the pots and destroy the contents – hens love them, as do fish. Once you have succeeded once or thrice, then pour a kettle or two of boiling water into the weakened nest to finish it off.

Moles, moles everywhere and they really are driving me mad. Have you any suggestions? This is the first time I have had a garden where moles have been a problem and I really don't know what to do.

Until you have had a problem with these creatures in your garden it is easy to think that people who complain about them are being rather cruel, but I can now say from personal experience that I know just how infuriating they can be, when they produce their large molehills on your lawn or tunnel beneath plants, causing the soil to subside and the plants to suffer from drought.

The first thing you should know is that it is quite likely that if your garden is fairly small, then all the damage you have seen could be the work of just one individual. Sadly, the fact that you may only be up against one mole does not mean to say that you have an easy battle ahead. There are numerous products and alleged deterrents on the market, but in my experience very few of them are effective, or at least not in a consistent way, often seeming to work better in one garden than in another. There are also many homespun remedies that people suggest, including placing children's windmills along the mole runs or in the top of the mole heap, and inserting glass bottles in them with the top end uppermost. In both these cases the idea is that, as the wind blows, the vibrations produced by the windmill or the top of the bottle deter the mole. You can buy ultrasonic deterrents, but I must admit that I have actually seen a mole making its hill around one of these on more than one occasion.

There are also mole smokes, which are rather like fireworks that you can light and place inside the tunnel. These give off toxic gases that have the potential to kill the mole, but many gardeners have told me that they find

that the gases seem to cause the mole to run away initially, but it survives and returns once the gas has dispersed. It has also been suggested that if you plant the caper spurge around the area, this acts as a mole deterrent – once again I'm afraid to say that the results I have seen have never really impressed me at all.

The most effective method seems to be setting mole traps, and although you can purchase these from some garden centres or direct from the manufacturers, they are quite difficult to set effectively and if you do not do the job properly you could end up either making the mole suffer a lot or failing to catch it at all. You can also buy humane traps, which allow the mole to enter without being killed. You can then attempt to move it to another location and release it, but I am always rather concerned that in the process of doing this it is likely that the mole will die of fright anyway.

So the long and short of it is that there is no truly reliable method. Perhaps the one means of controlling them that most people find effective is to employ a mole catcher, but finding a mole catcher may be nearly as hard as controlling the mole yourself.

BF Moles can be kept from uprooting plants with three giant pins made from old bicycle spokes or wire coathangers. These can be removed once the plant is well established. A row of seedlings can also be protected with the same pins. Beds, greenhouses and even lawns can be completely protected by embedding narrow-gauge wire chicken mesh horizontally in the soil.

Much as I love the birds in my garden, I sometimes find that I am furious with them because they have eaten newly sown seeds or done damage to my crops. Can you suggest how I can keep them away?

There are lots of things you can try, but rather as with moles, the results can be variable. Some gardeners find that using humming or buzzing lines, which you can buy from garden centres, works well. These are attached between two posts or poles, are held tight and vibrate in the wind, producing a noise that is only just audible to the human ear, but which seems to deter birds quite effectively. You can make a similar device yourself using the insides of an audio cassette tape.

Other deterrents, such as scarecrows or shapes cut to look like cats (with marbles used for eyes), tinfoil-pie cases dangling from strings, and so forth will potentially deter birds, but generally speaking the birds soon realize that they do not pose a real threat and return anyway. Your best bet is, therefore, to choose a wide range of devices and use them all in succession so that the birds don't get a chance to get too used to them.

Some crops can be successfully netted. Fruit and beans, for instance, are relatively easily covered with netting draped over canes and flowerpots over the top, or you could, of course, put your fruit into a proper fruit cage. Keeping birds off seeds can be harder. Many people recommend using twiggy pea sticks, and I find that this works quite well and they can obviously be removed as soon as the seeds germinate.

Alternatively, you could create a galvanized chicken-wire cage and place this over the seedbed until the seeds have germinated. The added advantage of this method is that you will find that it keeps cats off the area.

Can you suggest what I should do to keep worms away from my lawn? I am thoroughly fed up with the casts they leave everywhere. They seem to act as a perfect seedbed for weeds and make the lawn look unsightly.

I'm afraid there is no acceptable answer to this problem. There are, I am pleased to say, no chemicals available on the gardening market that will control worms. You may not think this is a very helpful answer, but they are such beneficial organisms in the garden, helping as they do to keep the soil structure good and to bring organic matter down into the main body of the soil, that I think it would be a real tragedy to do anything to harm them, even if you find their worm casts a nuisance. I admit the worm casts can make the surface of the lawn rather muddy and slippery and can certainly act as a seedbed for weeds, but this is a small price to pay when you consider all the benefits that worms bring. Rather than even contemplating attempting to control them, I suggest that you invest in a besom and use this to brush the worm casts at regular intervals. You will find that the worm casts are mainly a problem during spring and autumn, when the weather is warm and the soil tends to be fairly moist, so you need not spend too many hours of your life using your new purchase.

If you do not wish to buy a besom, then you can use an upturned spring-tine rake instead. You should also try to avoid walking on the lawn when it is wet, as this not only helps to compact the lawn, but also increases the chances of smearing any worm casts that are present and making them more likely to be troublesome.

My garden seems to be plagued by earwigs. Have you any suggestions as to what I can do? I would prefer not to use chemicals, but would consider resorting to them if you think this is the only answer.

Earwigs *(Forficula auricularia)* can cause some damage to plants, as they eat ragged holes in both young leaves and the flowers of many plants, particularly dahlias and clematis. During the day they tend to hide in dark places or in concealed parts of plants and emerge to feed only after sunlight. This means that if you want to confirm that earwigs are causing the damage you have seen, you may need to don your wellingtons and torch and go out after dark. One of the best methods of controlling these pests without using chemicals is to set traps for them, using the traditional method of inverting flowerpots onto bamboo canes and stuffing the pots full of straw or finely shredded paper. If you position the pots close to earwig-susceptible plants, you will find that the earwigs often use them as places to hide during the day and you can then collect them up on a daily basis.

If you find that you are still not getting on top of the problem, then you can spray the plants with a suitable insecticide, such as Fenitrothion, Polysect or Sybol, but you should do this at dusk on a mild evening for it to be most effective and for you to minimize the risk of damage to beneficial insects.

Just how much damage do woodlice cause to plants? I find them all over the place and sometimes I am not sure what exactly they have been responsible for.

Woodlice can sometimes damage seedlings or particularly soft plants, but generally established plants are not injured to any significant extent. There are several different species of woodlice that you may find in your garden and they are often found hiding away in dark places during the daytime, perhaps under logs, stones, pots or old seed trays. Quite often, because they are associated with already damaged or dead organic matter, people assume that they have caused the problem. In reality, they feed primarily on dead plant material rather than on growing plants and because they do not have very strong mouthparts, they are simply not capable of doing some of the damage that people imply they have caused. These are certainly not a creature that I would ever contemplate attempting to control and if I find that they are around in large numbers, perhaps in a greenhouse or other area where I am raising plants, then I simply attempt to have a bit of a tidy up, as this removes their hiding places.

BF

I know Pippa will argue that woodlice do little damage with their cuddly little mouthparts, but I have seen a horde of them chomping their way through my potato leaves! I find that pieces of wood or slabs of bark laid flat on the ground attract them most. Then I move it aside and suck them up with a portable mini-vacuum cleaner.

My neighbour's cat is driving me mad. It scratches up seedbeds, goes to sleep on my plants and – worse still – uses the soil in my borders as a lavatory. Please, please, what can I do?

I am afraid there is no easy answer to this and, although I am very much a cat lover and indeed a cat owner myself, I do see your point, especially when it comes to cats using the soil in your garden as a large litter tray. This can be unpleasant, to say the least, and particularly unacceptable if they use the soil in your vegetable plot or if you have young children playing in the garden. If you live in a town and happen to have several neighbours who own cats, they can become a real problem. To be honest, the best answer is to have your own cat (preferably a tom), as this generally keeps other animals out of your garden and you may have some luck in attempting to train your own to go to the lavatory in the appropriate places.

There are numerous animal-repellent sprays and powders on the market, but sadly most people report that these do not give reliable results and certainly are of little long-term protection against cats. There are also electronic devices, which produce ultrasonic sounds that are inaudible (or virtually inaudible) to humans and yet can prove highly unpleasant for cats. Generally speaking, these are the devices that most people find work best, but do be aware that they are fairly costly and do not always have the desired effect, as it seems that different cats react differently to them.

You may find that other methods, such as ensuring that the soil is kept well mulched with a moisture-retaining material such as manure, helps. Alternatively, a remedy that many readers of my newspaper column have suggested to me works well. When I first heard of it I thought that it was unlikely to work, but so many keen gardeners have said that it was just the trick for them. It is a simple remedy involving several drops of decongestant Olbas Oil sprinkled onto used teabags; the teabags are then scattered around the area that the cats like to use as a litter tray. It seems that there is something about the smell of this product that they really do not like. I have also heard of people growing catmint in an area to ensure that the local cats go to this part of the garden and tend to disregard other areas. And many people report that simply ensuring that there are few empty spaces in your garden helps to keep the problem to a minimum. If you decide to try this route, then you need to invest in a really good selection of ground-cover plants.

When it comes to cats scratching up seedbeds, then some of the suggestions made above might have an effect. Or you could try putting a simple galvanized chicken-wire cage over the area in question, and keeping this in position until the plants are of a reasonable size; or covering the newly sown area with pea sticks and removing these once the plants are quite large.

BF Cats are notoriously lazy and will invariably use a tray of soft dry litter or similar rather than wet soil. Make the effort, keep your ground wet and provide the tray, replenishing it every week, and the problem of their mess everywhere else is soon solved. Look on it as free fertility to put in shallow holes under your trees and shrubs.

These brown scorched-looking patches have appeared on my front lawn. Can you suggest what they are? I can see no signs of any obvious diseases and there are certainly no leatherjackets or other pests involved, because we have investigated these possibilities.

Judging by the rather pungent smell coming from the sample of your lawn, I'm afraid to say that I think there is no doubt that this is due to urine scorch. I wonder whether any local dogs – or, to be more accurate, bitches – have access to your front lawn, or whether you yourself own a bitch? You may also find that scorched dry patches develop towards the base of conifers or on ground-cover conifers, and this is likely to have been caused if dogs have 'lifted their leg' against these plants. If you ever manage to catch the animal 'in the act', then it is certainly worth rushing out with a bucket full of water or hosing down the areas they have urinated on with plenty of water. This will dilute the urine and prevent it scorching. Sadly, once the damage has already been done, there is little you can do except prune out the affected areas on conifers and carefully cut out the scorched patch on your lawn, then reseed or returf the area as soon as possible.

As soon as autumn arrived this year, lots of toadstools appeared on my lawn. Some were in straight lines and then one type appeared to be forming what I presume is a fairy ring. How can I control them?

I suspect that you have got two different problems here. The toadstools that are not growing in rings, but appear to be growing in lines, are most likely to be feeding on dead or dying tree roots, which are underneath the lawn itself. They could also be living on any other sort of buried organic matter. If this is the case, your best bet would be to carefully lift the turf and excavate down in an attempt to find their source of food. You should then remove this, add some extra soil to bring the level up to where it should be and then carefully replace the turf. Provided you firm it down well and keep it adequately watered, the grass should grow over rapidly. Alternatively, if you don't wish to go to this amount of trouble, then you can regularly brush off the toadstools as soon as they appear, preferably before they open out, as once they have done this they are likely to release spores, which may well increase the problem. Generally speaking, toad-stools are only prevalent during the late summer and up until the time when the first frosts arrive, so it is a fairly seasonal problem.

The fairy rings are a different matter, as they do have the potential to harm the grass. What you tend to find is that a ring develops in the lawn and, as the fungus spreads, the ring gets larger. Around the edge of the ring you tend to find one or more areas of extremely bright-green lush grass and then there is an inner ring that is also very lush, but the area between these two rings tends to be dead and brown, as the grass has been killed. If you dig into the soil you will find evidence of the fungus just beneath the soil surface and around the bases of the grass. It tends to form a really obvious, dense white mat and during the autumn you will find pale-brown toad-stools, 4–10cm (1½–4in) tall, on the outer edge of the middle zone. The dead areas are caused because the fungal growth is so extremely water-repellent that rain or irrigation cannot actually get through to the roots of the grass, so its death is simply due to lack of water. Unfortunately, there is no chemical available on the amateur gardening market that will allow you to control fairy rings, so you have only a few choices, none of which is par-ticularly attractive!

You can regularly rake up and bin or burn the toadstools, as this will help to reduce the number of spores they produce and so minimize the risk of them spreading to other areas on your lawn, or you could dig out the affected grass and the topsoil. For this to be successful you need to dig down to a depth of at least 30cm (12 in) and ensure that no soil or turf is allowed to contaminate the currently healthy areas of the lawn. You will also need to dig out the area so that it extends to 30–45cm (12–18in) beyond the edges of the ring. In most cases, this means that you will be dealing with an extremely large volume of soil and it can be back-breaking and very time-consuming work. Once you have removed all the soil and turf, you can then refill the hole you have created with fresh soil, firm it down well and returf or resow the area.

Your other option is to employ a contractor who is able to purchase and apply some of the professional products that do have an effect on fairy rings. If none of these options seems acceptable, then the only other thing you can do is simply wait until the ring grows so large that it reaches the edge of your lawn – at this stage it usually dies out.

GARDEN DESIGN SUPPLIERS

Wind break fencing:
Tenax UK Ltd
Unit 12
Ash Road
Wrexham Industrial Estate
Wrexham
LL13 9JT
Tel: 01978 664 667
Fax: 01978 664 616

Translucent tree shelters:
Acorn Planting Products Ltd
Little Money Road
Loddon
Norwich
NR14 6JD
Tel: 01508 528 763
Fax: 01508 528 775

Woodstains and paint:
Farrow & Ball
Uddens Trading Estate
Wimborne
Dorset
BH21 7NL
Tel: 01202 876 141
Fax: 01202 873 793

*For an extraordinarily wide
range of woodstains:*
Jotun Paints
Jotun-Henry Clark Ltd
Stather Road
Fixborough
Scunthorpe
Lincolnshire
DN15 8RR
Tel: 01724 400 123
Fax: 01724 400 130

Gold Leaf:
L. Cornelissen & Sons Ltd
105 Great Russell Street
London
WC1JB 3RY
Tel: 0207 636 1045
Fax: 0207 636 3655

Coppice and Hazel:
Nene Park Trust

Ham Farm house
Ham Lane
Peterborough
PE2 5UU
Tel: 01733 234193
Fax: 01733 3613420

Acrylic mirror:
SBA (Head Office)
Freemens Common Road
Leicester
LE2 7SQ
Tel: 0116 254 1262

Irrigation systems:
Tanker Irrigation
Plantasy Ltd
Birds Mill house
Broxburn
West Lothian
EH52 5PB
Tel: 01506 857411
Fax: 01506 852130

Leaky Pipe System Ltd
Frith Farm
Dean Street
East Farleigh
Maidstone
Kent
ME15 0PR
Tel: 01622 746495
Fax: 01622 745118

Sculptors:
The Crafts Council
44a Pentonville Road
London
N1 9BI
Tel: 020 72787700
Fax: 02078376891

Information on Sundials:
The British Sundial Society
4 New Wokingham Road
Crowthorne
Berks
RG45 7NR
www.sundials.co.uk./
bsshome.htm

Bound gravel:
Breedon PLC
Breedon on the Hill
Derby
Tel: 01332 862254

Bound gravel with black bitumen emulsion bonding:
Colas Ltd
Wallage Lane
Rowfront
Crawley
West Sussex
RH10 4NF
Tel: 01342 711000

Resin bonded gravel:
Fibredec
Wallage Lane
Rowfront
Crawley
West Sussex
RH10 4NF
Tel: 01342 711000

Awnings:
Timber Intent
32 Belton Road
Bristol
BS5 0JS
Tel: 0117 939 6948

Water course conservation:
The Environment Agency
Millbank Towers
25th Floor
21-24 Milbank
London
SW1P 4XL
Tel: 0207 863 8628

*Bark for play areas
(Playbark 10-50):*
Melcourt Industries
Eight Bells House
Tetbury
Gloucestershire
GL8 8JG
Tel: 01666 502 711
Fax: 01666 504 398

Trampolines:

Supertramp
Clanglands Business Park
Uffculme
Cullompton
Devon
EX215
Tel: 01884 841305

Sand:

British Play Sand Company
Longfield
Duns Tew
Oxfordshire
OX6 4JR
Tel: 01869 340224
Fax: 01869 347474

Willow:

Steve Pick Up
The Willow Bank
POBox 17
Machynlleth
Powys
SY20 8WR
Tel: 01686 430510

Terry Daunt
Nene Park Trust
Ham Farm house
Ham Lane
Peterborough
PE2 5UU
Tel: 01733 234193
Fax: 01733 3613420

Tree mats:

Acorn Planting Products Ltd
Little Money Road
Loddon
Norwich
NR14 6JD
Tel: 01508 528 763
Fax: 01508 528 775

Broadleaf P4:

Greenacres Horticultural
Supplies
P.O. Box 1228
Iver
Buckinghamshire
SL0 0EH

*Ironmongers for plasterer's
baths:*

Harrison and Dunn
Ironmongers
3 All Saints Street
Stamford
Tel: 01780 762088

Soil stabilising netting:

Tensar Mat
Tensar International
New Wellington Street
Blackburn
BB2 4PJ
Tel: 01254 262431
Fax: 01254 694302

Herb Nursery:

Jekka's Herb Farm
Rose Cottage
Shellards Lane
Alveston
Bristol
BS12 2SY
Tel: 01454 418878
Fax: 01454 411988

*Hardy olives, conservatory
plants and citrus fruits:*

Reads Nursery
Hales Hall
Loddon
Norfolk
NR14 6QW
Tel: 01508 548395
Fax: 01508 548040

Hardwood sleepers:

Atlantic
The Old Mill
Earsham
Bungay
Suffolk
NR35 2TQ
Tel: 01986 894745
Fax: 01986 892496

The 'Garden Pest Chaser':

STV International
128 Aberdeen House
22 Highbury Grove
London
N5 2DQ
Tel: 020 735 44363

INDEX